Effective schooling for the community

Education systems are currently under challenge to teach new skills and competencies to all their students, and to function under increasing financial constraints brought about by changing economic circumstances. The effectiveness of schools to meet these challenges is being questioned by politicians, business leaders and academics world-wide, with the result that school effectiveness has become one of the important themes of world education.

This book provides a new perspective on the management of schools, by bringing together the knowledge and understanding of school effectiveness and community education. Tony Townsend's research in schools in the UK, US, Canada and Australia has shown that there is a need for a review of the role of schools. He argues for the development of a 'core–plus' curriculum, which includes both the curriculum required by educational authorities (the core) and specific areas determined to be important by the school community (the plus). He also suggests that this concept can be translated to the school as a whole, where the core activity of providing a learning environment for children is supplemented by educational activities that service the needs of the community as a whole. The book offers a model for the development of the core–plus school and includes practical ideas to help school leaders both in building school programmes and encouraging greater community involvement.

Tony Townsend is Director of the South Pacific Centre for School and Community Development, and is Senior Lecturer in the Faculty of Education at Monash University.

Effective schooling for the community

Core–plus education

Tony Townsend

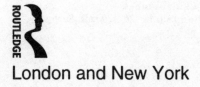

London and New York

First published 1994
by Routledge
11 New Fetter Lane, London EC4P 4EE

Simultaneously published in the USA and Canada
by Routledge
29 West 35th Street, New York, NY 10001

© 1994 Tony Townsend

Typeset in Baskerville by LaserScript, Mitcham, Surrey
Printed and bound in Great Britain by
Mackays of Chatham PLC, Chatham, Kent

British Library Cataloguing in Publication Data
A catalogue record for this book is available from the British Library.

Library of Congress Cataloging in Publication Data
Townsend, Tony.
  Effective schooling for the community: core–plus education/
  Tony Townsend.
  p. cm. – (Educational management series)
  Includes bibliographical references and index.
  1. Community and school – Cross-cultural studies.
  2. School management and organization – Cross-cultural studies.
  3. Education – Curricula – Cross-cultural studies.
  4. Educational change – Cross-cultural studies. I. Title. II. Series.
  LC215.T65   1994
  370.19'31 – dc20   93-26052

ISBN 0–415–10417–3 (hbk)
ISBN 0–415–10418–1 (pbk)

Contents

Illustrations

Foreword

In May 1981, I attended the first National Conference of the Australian Association for Community Education in Queensland. At that time, I was invited by Tony Townsend to visit Melbourne. During that visit, he introduced me to the Victorian Education Department's new building policy which was entitled 'core–plus'. The essence of the building policy was to make more efficient use of the school site by establishing a 'core' of buildings that consisted of administrative and centralised activities such as library, art room, multi-purpose room and canteen, and a 'plus' building arrangement which consisted of the needed student classrooms. These classrooms were relocatable structures which could be brought to the site or taken away as the school age population warrants. Regardless of what happened to the classrooms, the 'core' portion of the building always remained for community use.

In the next few days, Tony and I shared in a unique perceptive and innovative experience. We were caught up with the idea of what would be the result if such a building policy were used as an educational philosophy? What might happen if education were restructured on the basis of a 'core–plus' orientation? We then began to interchange thoughts regarding what might be the core and what might be the plus in such an educational philosophy.

For the next year, we continued our discussions, both personally and by means of correspondence. It was our feeling that we had a very revealing experience and that we did not want our ideas to slip away without capturing the essence of our thinking in some fashion. The core plus concept was the topic I chose when asked to give the first Frank Manley Address to the National Community Education Association Conference in Atlanta, in December 1982. Finally, we decided to at least reduce our thoughts to writing, and in 1984 we produced a document entitled *Core–Plus Education: A Model for Schools of the Future.* At the time, however, we both agreed that this was a temporary endeavour and that there was a need for a more complete and definitive work on this subject.

Now, Tony Townsend has done just that. He has refined the definition of core–plus education and related it to the concept of community education. And he has done this in a most creative way. He has analysed the effective schools research and by means of logic, research and case studies, has taken the reader through a completely different orientation for effective schools. He then uses his new perceptions of effective schools to demonstrate the need for the creation of 'core–plus education'.

Dr Townsend's book should make a substantial contribution to the field of education. Philosophically, he has offered some new directions for school managers and professional educators – directions which could lead to a much more appropriate approach to dealing with the educational needs of our current society. But Dr Townsend's book does not just philosophise. It offers practical and detailed suggestions for the implementation of the thoughts which he suggests.

From my point of view, Dr Townsend offers a challenge for those responsible for the future direction of education. For the traditional student, he argues that a wider range of educational goals will be necessary if schools of the future are to be effective and he offers a more beneficial educational opportunity for individual students through the value added approach to education. For the vast group of people whom we refer to as 'the community', his book holds promise for both the resolution of their educational needs and all of the aspects related to participatory democracy.

This book is essential reading for educators in general and for community educators in particular. For the community educators, it will reinforce much of their thinking and provide an extension of their beliefs. For all those interested in education, both professionals and others, it provides a philosophical base and concrete suggestions for moving our educational thinking into the next century.

Jack D. Minzey
Department Head Emeritus
Eastern Michigan University

Acknowledgements

I wish to acknowledge the substantial number of people who have contributed to the development, implementation and completion of this book. Firstly to staff of the School of Early Childhood and Primary Education of the Faculty of Education at Monash University, who provided support for, and time to complete, the project.

To each of the schools, and all of the people involved at those schools, who provided the base data for the study, and to the principals, staff, parents and students of the case study schools, all of whom gave generously of their time to enable me to find out the detail that the data could not provide.

To my network of community education, school effectiveness and school improvement colleagues in many parts of the world and, in particular, Professor Jack Minzey who wrote the foreword, Professors Judith Chapman, Larry Sackney and Brian Caldwell and Dr Phil Perry, and also Cyril Poster and Helen Fairlie of Routledge, who made useful suggestions along the way.

To John Lennon, who died on my birthday in 1980, who penned the words, 'Life is what happens to you while you are busy making other plans', which provided the necessary motivation to finish the project whenever I doubted that I could.

Finally, and especially, to my parents Else and Colin Townsend, who helped me to have a quality education and to my wife Juli and my children Paul, Cindy, Ben and Jenni, who enabled me to use it to the best advantage.

Chapter 1

Introduction: an international perspective on school effectiveness

> The pursuit of quality in education cannot be treated as a short-term, one-off exercise. It is a permanent priority. Education is not an assembly-line process of mechanically increasing inputs and raising productivity. How to improve its quality raises fundamental questions about societal aims, the nature of participation in decision-making at all levels, and the very purpose of the school as an institution.
>
> (OECD 1989a: 1)

BACKGROUND

For more than one hundred years since education became 'free, secular and compulsory' schools have to some extent been insulated from the economic realities confronting the rest of society. The decade of the 1980s changed, perhaps forever, the somewhat protected position of those involved in education. A deepening world-wide recession in the late 1980s and early 1990s, together with an ageing population, brought about increasing demands from other agencies within the community. Welfare, health and community service agencies all saw a lessening in the amount of money that was available to maintain these services, and schools suffered a similar fate. The global recession saw the amount of money available to public services drop dramatically. The need to compete economically on a global scale saw pressure in many western countries for schools to ensure that large numbers of students with specific skills and attitudes completed school.

The problem for schools caused by this requirement to teach new skills and competencies to all school graduates, together with the financial constraints brought about by changing economic circumstances, put education into a position where its ability to fulfil the requirements placed upon it has been brought into question. The effectiveness of schools to meet the challenge is being questioned by some politicians, some business leaders and some academics, with the result that the issue of school effectiveness has become one of the important themes of world education.

RESEARCH CONCERNS FOR SCHOOL EFFECTIVENESS

The question of school effectiveness has a long history in some countries, in particular the United Kingdom and the United States of America. Many individual studies undertaken at all levels of school decision-making, administration and implementation have contributed to a large corpus of research covering a wide range of educational concerns. Scheerens (1990) has identified four major bodies of research that addressed issues of school effectiveness; research that considers the equality of educational outcomes, that which considers educational production functions, that which came to be known as the effective schools research, and that which was called the instructional effectiveness research (Scheerens 1990: 64–8).

The first body of research considered how schools affect the equality of educational outcomes, and emerged in a number of countries in the 1960s and 1970s with reports such as those by Coleman *et al.* (1966) in the United States, Plowden (1967) in the United Kingdom and Karmel (1973) in Australia. The Coleman Report (1966), which investigated the relationship between the equality of educational outcomes and school effectiveness, has been identified as the key report in the development of school effectiveness research in the United States. The conclusion of this report can be summed up by the following paragraph:

> Schools bring little influence to bear on a child's achievement that is independent of his background and general social context . . . this very lack of an independent effect means that the inequalities imposed on children by their home, neighbourhood and peer environment are carried along to become the inequalities with which they confront adult life at the end of school. For equality of educational opportunity must imply a strong effect of schools that is independent of the child's immediate environment, and that strong independence is not present in American schools.
>
> (Coleman *et al.* 1966: 325)

Coleman found that schools accounted for only a small part of the variance in pupil achievement, a finding which was replicated by other large scale studies such as those by Jencks *et al.* (1972) and Thorndike (1973). Scheerens (1990: 65) has argued that the Coleman Report was significant to the research into school effectiveness in three main ways:

It suggested that:

– school process variables accounted for relatively little variance in educational achievement
– resources and other 'material' inputs are not very promising in explaining school outputs
– pupil background characteristics should be used to adjust raw output measures to arrive at an unbiased interpretation of the influence of process indicators on the functioning of schools.

In more recent times, however, the Coleman Report has been challenged on a number of grounds, with particular concerns being expressed about the input–output model adopted by the research and further concerns being expressed about the statistical analysis used in the study.

The second body of school effectiveness research emerged in response to the suggestion that resources and other 'material' inputs were not very significant in explaining school outputs. It considered educational production functions, that identified 'which inputs lead to more output, also considering the cost of the input' (Scheerens 1990: 65). Although similar to other school effectiveness research, this research is identified by the particular orientation of the input characteristics, all of which can be expressed in quantitative or monetary terms. A review of the results of this research led to the conclusion that, when input characteristics such as teacher salary and qualifications, teacher–pupil ratio and per pupil expenditure were considered, there was little consistent relationship between educational expenditure and pupil achievement (Hanushek 1986: 1161). The major difficulty with this group of research findings is that the specific concentration on inputs and outputs shed no light on the school processes that linked the two.

The body of research that came to be more widely known as the school effectiveness research could be directly attributed to the Coleman report, and stimulated a large body of research on both sides of the Atlantic. This research attempted to establish that schools themselves, in addition to family or social backgrounds, made a difference to the educational achievements of the students passing through them (Edmonds 1978, 1979; Austin 1979; Rutter *et al.* 1979; Mortimore *et al.* 1988). This type of research differed from earlier types in that, 'the black box of what happens in schools is opened' (Scheerens 1990: 66). It considered the variables of school culture and school organisation and educational technology. From this research school-wide characteristics were found to be consistently related to pupil achievement.

The final area of research considered issues of instructional effectiveness (Scheerens 1990: 68), which was characterised by the attention paid to the work of individual teachers or to activities at the classroom level. From this research as well, a series of characteristics have been identified which are consistently associated with pupil achievement. A review by Scheerens (1990) indicates a wide-ranging body of research that has been undertaken in the search to establish how schools affect pupil achievement. Results have clearly established that schools did make a difference, and that pupil achievement was not just a product of socio-economic background. However, many questions about school effectiveness remained unresolved. And, as Rosenholtz (1989: 1–2) points out, 'the most interesting questions in this area are not at all methodological, they are conceptual'. One of the key areas yet to be fully elaborated upon relates to how school effectiveness is defined. Many definitions have been proposed, but none have found universal acceptance. Chapman (1992) identified school effectiveness as one of what Gaillie (1964) called 'essentially contested concepts'. Since there will be a number of different perspectives of the goals of education in general, and of the role school plays in the fulfilment of those goals then, necessarily, the perspectives of what makes a school effective will vary as well.

This is a critical argument, because it provides some measure of understanding for the direction the debate has taken so far. Most of the research until now has been conducted with the researcher holding a particular view of what constitutes an effective school. This view has, in some cases, structured the parameters of the research. To many in the United States and Canada, an effective school is one whose students perform well on standardised tests. As such, the identification of more effective schools could be made by reviewing statewide or national test scores. Those in the United Kingdom were, until recently, more concerned about the rate of improvement shown by students in the school and understanding the nature of the relationship between school process variables and content variables and the individual child's performance. In this situation, effective schools could not be identified without going into the school itself. In Australia, there had been a great deal of debate and a reluctance to offer any definition of what constitutes an effective school until 1991, when the Australian Effective Schools Project (1991) defined an effective school as 'one that achieves greater student learning than might have been predicted from the context in which it [the school] works' (McGaw *et al.* 1991: 2). In each case, the definition of what an effective school is becomes critical to any other questions that might be asked.

The Organization for Economic Co-operation and Development (OECD) has been involved in supporting an international programme of research into school quality and school effectiveness for the past decade. Work has been conducted in areas such as resource deployment and management (1983, 1991), schools and quality (1989a), the relationship between school improvement and decentralisation (1989b) and the effectiveness of schooling and of educational resource management (Chapman 1991). These international perspectives have demonstrated clearly how complex the issue of school effectiveness is, and how interrelated the concept is to others such as school management, school improvement and school quality.

The OECD Directorate for Social Affairs, Manpower and Education, in a recent report (Chapman 1991), provided some insight into the broad spectrum of educational debate that school effectiveness encompasses. In the first instance, it raised some questions related to the difficulties in providing a definition of effective schools:

> The concept of 'effectiveness' is central to the management of schools and school systems; nevertheless as yet there exists no uniform definition of an 'effective school'. Definitions vary depending on the orientation or theory of those examining the issue.
>
> (Chapman 1991: 7)

The report, which considers the effectiveness of schooling and educational resource management, also comments upon the limited range of parameters that have been researched, as outlined in the following paragraph:

Given the extensive range of school objectives the difficulty of studying school effectiveness becomes clear. For the complexity of these objectives . . . will not always be capable of rational enquiry. Much research into questions of school effectiveness has tended, for this reason, to concentrate on a select number of objectives and only on those that can be stated in measurable terms.

(Chapman 1991: 8)

This statement suggests that the types of characteristics that have generally been studied in the past have tended to be chosen because of their ease of measurability from the researcher's point of view. If this is the case, then there may be some difficulty in drawing accurate conclusions about the effectiveness of schools from some of that research. The current work attempts to overcome some of these concerns.

POLICY AND ADMINISTRATIVE CONCERNS FOR SCHOOL EFFECTIVENESS

The effect that schools have on the achievement of their pupils has been not only an issue considered by researchers, but one that has been guiding educational policy-making at systemic levels and administrative practice in schools. Chapman (1991: 5) identified a series of events and situations that occurred during the past three decades which seems to have left a legacy for both educational policy-makers and the managers of schools as we move through the 1990s. A substantial and rapid growth in the size of educational systems in many parts of the world in the early 1960s was brought about by the post-war baby boom, coupled with an increasing demand by society for more schooling, and a time of economic strength. Subsequent to this period of rapid growth, a downturn in birth rates in many parts of the western world allowed those countries in the 1970s to turn their attention from expanding education towards assessing the quality of what was offered.

Concerns for school effectiveness in the United Kingdom and the United States of America were exacerbated in the 1980s by these countries having a diminished status as the economic superpowers of the world, when other countries such as Japan and Germany attracted increased economic and political status in world affairs. In the United Kingdom, works such as *The Home and the School* (Douglas 1964), *Children and Their Primary Schools* (the

Plowden Report 1967) and *Parents and Teachers: Partners or Rivals?* (Green 1968) considered the relationship between family background and success at school. When these were followed up by such documents as Boyson's (1975) *The Crisis in Education* and *The Black Paper* (Cox and Boyson 1977) the standard of students' academic performance in the United Kingdom became a critical issue. The British Government's response to these concerns was the establishment of the Assessment of Performance Unit within the Department of Education and Science in 1974.

In the USA, formal reports such as *A Nation at Risk* (National Commission on Excellence in Education 1983), *Education and Economic Progress* (Carnegie Corporation 1983), *Investing in Our Children* (Committee on Economic Development 1985) and *Who Will Teach Our Children?* (Commons 1985) indicated the level of government and public concern about the issue and created a climate in which the relationship between education and competitiveness on the international market became inextricably linked. This led to the current situation where schools are charged with turning out in the most cost effective way the maximum number of graduates with the 'right' skills and knowledge as possible. As Chapman points out, 'such pressures have forced educational authorities to reassess educational needs both qualitatively and quantitatively' (Chapman 1991: 5).

Cost became associated, as in business, with outputs in education and, given that a large proportion of government spending was directed towards education, governments were asked to account for their spending in terms similar to those used by business. The issue of the effectiveness of schools became related to the number of students who completed school successfully, and what qualities those graduates had that would enable them either to become employed or to enter higher education. Thus the twin concerns of quality and quantity merged into an issue of school effectiveness.

Changing demographics and changing social values, combined with new knowledge requirements and an economy in recession, created a climate where schools were competing for scarce community resources simultaneously with other social agencies. In the past decade, schools in various parts of the world have been asked to alter their curricula, their levels of accountability and the locus or methods of their governance. Not only are there more people attending schools now than ever before, but recent technological and other knowledge developments have made schools widen their curricula to include areas that were not even considered a generation ago. As governments try to balance the needs of rapidly ageing populations and increased demands for social and other services with increased retention rates at school and rising youth unemployment brought about by the recession, it could be argued that schools have been caught in the middle. As the absolute cost of state schooling has increased in the past decade questions have been asked about whether the amount of money being spent on education is justified by the results obtained. At a time when schools are being asked to take some responsibility for new programmes for regular students, as well as programmes aimed at special groups in the community, there is a diminution of the level of funding to enable these programmes to operate successfully.

From an internal point of view, schools are being asked to do more with less. Principals' workloads have increased as they try to undertake increased accountability and community involvement activities. This increased responsibility includes a plethora of school committee meetings, responsibility for the encouragement and management of community use of school facilities, budgetary responsibilities and the provision of academic leadership to the school staff. Teachers are being asked to prepare new curricula, to be involved in a variety of programmes outside of school or outside of school hours and, at the same time, are expected to upgrade their professional knowledge in either formal or informal ways, for the continued integrity of their programmes, for promotion, or both. Parents have been asked to increase their contributions to the school, through service on school governing bodies or other committees, by fund-raising or tutoring, or by other means, to ensure that the level of resources available to the students and the decisions being made about the school programmes are appropriate. In many schools, plant and facilities are now used on a regular basis by community groups for non-school educational pursuits.

From an external point of view, schools continue to be criticised by certain groups in the community for not providing graduates who are able either to undertake higher education programmes successfully or to be employed. There is an increasing tendency in the media to call for educational reform to increase 'standards' or to develop 'basic skills' or 'competencies'. The nature of the skills or competencies required, however, is hotly contested and is a source of debate or disagreement at the community level. Literacy and numeracy are identified as the areas causing major concern, which gives the impression that schools should be doing much the same as they were thirty years ago, before the use of computers and television, and the study of drug abuse and the environment in which we live, had become important features of any educational programme. This public discussion is mostly driven by politicians and other parties with a special interest in education, yet is reported in the media as being of 'public concern'. Although much of the information provided may have more to do with political propaganda than the reality of what is happening in schools, it nevertheless plays an important part in shaping community attitudes towards education and schooling.

From the public perspective, in some respects schools seem to be largely unchanged from when they were created nearly two hundred years ago. Teachers and students still largely work in isolated groups, where most of the information to be learned has been decided by people other than the learner. If the major differences in education over this time can be traced back to changes in class size, marginal changes in curriculum and decision-making processes, then it could be argued that much of what has emerged from the public debate level in the past seems to have had little effect on what actually happens in classrooms.

There is, however, a second level of debate which occurs at the school itself. Here teachers, and sometimes parents as well, have been actively involved in recent developments in curricula, have discussed and implemented improved communication and collaboration and have placed greater emphasis on staff development and their own further education, to improve the level of effectiveness in their own classroom or school. Many of these developments emerge from teachers' own desire to do better, rather than as a response to any 'public' calls for reform. At this level, changes in the education of children have been continuous and substantial. Parents who spend some time in the classrooms of today would see little similarity to their own days at school. Although classrooms themselves and class sizes may have changed only marginally, what happens within those classes has changed dramatically. One dilemma facing school systems of the future is how to bring the discussions occurring at these two distinct levels much closer together.

RECENT SCHOOL EFFECTIVENESS INITIATIVES: A GLOBAL VIEW

A review of recent research into school effectiveness on an international basis will provide some insight into the complexities involved in understanding school effectiveness. A consideration of the general trends emerging in various countries, with a concentration on work from four countries, the United States of America, the United Kingdom, Canada and Australia will help to establish a better understanding of the problems and dilemmas attached to the study of school effectiveness.

The United States of America

It is likely that there has been more research into issues of school effectiveness in the United States than in the rest of the world put together. In the past twenty-five years or so, a huge corpus of literature has emerged in this field. The major outcome of much of the early school effectiveness research in the United States was the implementation of many programmes of school effectiveness across the country in the late 1970s and early 1980s. These included the California State Department School Effectiveness Study (1977), the development of the National Council for Effective Schools (Mann 1984), the Santa Clara School Effectiveness Program (1984) the Michigan State Board Standards of Quality Program (1985), and the National Education Association Program (1986). All of them based their programmes on the assumption that there were characteristics of effective schools which, if adopted by other schools, would lead to a more effective school system.

The emphasis for recent change in the US has been on top-down decision-making and ensuring a close correspondence between state curricula and school activities. Many major cities, including New York, Chicago, Washington and San Diego have implemented programmes based on the school effectiveness research. However, a number of state education systems are now moving towards programmes which encourage schools 'to plan and develop innovative organization and management systems at the school building level, aimed at empowering public school professionals and improving student learning' (Freedman 1988: 1). Finn (1984) argued that schools would be more effective if they were seen as the key unit in education and were given some independence in their decision-making. Such views have helped to establish a national movement through organisations such as The National Committee for Citizens in Education, which assists schools to develop strategies that assist the belief that 'parents and citizens can and should play a more active role in the governance of their schools' (Hansen and Marburger 1988: 10). However, Tyler (1987) found that some schools could be remarkably resistant to change, with five to seven years needed for most educational innovations to show results.

Holcomb (1991) identified a series of activities that could be considered as developing an effective school improvement process. They included:

– exploring the research and process
– securing district commitment and resources
– forming improvement teams and developing team skills
– affirming the mission and belief system
– gathering and analysing data on school characteristics and student outcomes
– developing school and student status reports
– identifying data-based, mission-oriented improvement objectives
– selecting strategies and developing a plan for implementation and monitoring
– examining effective curriculum and instructional strategies related to improvement objectives
– implementing plan and monitoring results
– refining and renewing improvement efforts.

This strategy for school improvement is similar to modern approaches to school improvement in many other parts of the western world and is one that encourages high levels of input at the local level.

The United Kingdom

In contrast to the United States where research refuting the Coleman point of view began almost immediately, it took some time before researchers in the United Kingdom such as Reynolds (1976, 1982), Rutter *et al.* (1979), Galton and Simon (1980) and Galton *et al.* (1980) began to address the role of school in students' academic achievements. This hiatus is explained by Reynolds (1988) as being due to various reasons, including:

- difficulty in gaining access to schools for comparative research purposes
- the climate of opinion that individual school organizations had minimal effect upon pupils' development
- the absence of well-developed and reproducible measures of institutional climate
- the rise of a determinist sociology of education which led to a neglect of the school as an institution independent from the wider society
- the intellectual hegemony of traditional mainstream British educational research with its psychologically determined stress on the primacy of the family and community based explanations for children's 'educability'.

(Reynolds 1988: 1–2)

These early United Kingdom studies replicated much of the work being done by their American counterparts but again some of the studies attracted methodological criticisms which in turn encouraged other researchers to develop new methodologies (Aitken *et al.* 1981; Gray 1981) or strategies for analysis (Goldstein, 1980, 1984) to address these concerns in an attempt to produce valid data in the area. Such studies as the ILEA Junior School Project (Mortimore *et al.* 1988) and those by Reynolds *et al.* (1987) and Cuttance (1988a, 1988b, 1988c) have developed a wide range of data collection methods that still identified 'differences in the effects of schools, even when allowances have been made for differences in the intakes' (Reynolds 1988: 4).

With the recent changes brought about by the 1988 Education Reform Act proposals in the United Kingdom, and with a greater emphasis on nationalised testing, a great deal of effort was spent on identifying appropriate mechanisms for evaluating the effectiveness of individual schools. Goldstein (1980, 1984), Torrance (1985), Goldstein and Cuttance (1988) and Cuttance (1988a, 1988b) all identified complex formulae for the determination of school effectiveness. One of the outcomes of this type of work is that studies (Aitken and Longford 1986; Gray *et al.* 1986; McPherson and Willms 1986; Cuttance 1988a, 1988b) are now demonstrating that effective and ineffective schools are not always consistent in their results for all their pupils as was first proposed by the studies of Rutter *et al.* (1979) and Reynolds (1982). Some students perform well in ineffective schools and effective schools are not effective for all curriculum areas and for all students. The work by Sammons *et al.* (1993), which tracks the primary school students from the ILEA's Junior School Project (Mortimore *et al.* 1986) to secondary school completion, promises to provide much more information about the longitudinal effects that schools have on student performance.

Although England and Wales developed a very strong research base in school effectiveness researchers admitted some difficulty in translating the results of that research into programmes of school improvement. Researchers were prepared to admit that 'in England and Wales researchers know considerably more about the characteristics of good schools than about how to make schools good' (Reynolds and Pack 1989: 2). Yet to know the former without the attainment of the latter seems to suggest that the effective schools research may provide only empty promises. The British Government attempted to address the issues of making schools more effective and accountable through the Education Reform Act of 1988, by proposing a national curriculum and assessment procedures, but simultaneously increased substantially the devolution of managerial powers to schools. This devolution in turn created additional requirements for support and assistance from the people involved in these activities at the school level. As Pipes (1993) points out, with the privatisation by 1995 of many of the services previously undertaken by local education authorities, financial dilemmas have been created for all involved, as schools have to face the increased costs brought about by the removal of the infrastructure previously paid for by the government.

Perhaps the major contribution made by British researchers to the debate on school effectiveness has been the development of the 'value-added' distinction to the literature (Rutter *et al.* 1979; Mortimore and Sammons 1987; Mortimore *et al.* 1986, 1988). Instead of concentrating solely on school outcomes, which is a feature of the American research, it became an accepted position for British researchers to collect input data to establish the gains that students made during their time at school, rather than simply to identify where they were when they finished. This created the dilemma of which is the most appropriate method to measure school effectiveness, from the outcome point of view adopted by the Americans or from the value-added point of view adopted by the British.

Canada

In Canada, where education is a provincial responsibility, much of the early work in school effectiveness replicated the American research (Sackney 1989b). More recently, school systems have been involved in the development of either school-effectiveness or school-improvement models. Saskatchewan, British Columbia and Manitoba have been addressing school effectiveness issues for some years. Saskatchewan has undertaken the development of a core curriculum, and two local Boards of Education hosted major conferences on *Beyond School Effectiveness and Achieving Excellence* in 1988 (Sackney 1989a: 4). In addition, a number of models relevant to the development of school effectiveness have been proposed in recent times, including that of Leithwood (1987) who proposed a framework of:

- goals
- teacher and administrator inputs
- programmes and instruction
- school policies and organization
- school culture and school–community relations

as all contributing to the students' school experiences and the eventual student outcomes. A survey of two hundred and fifty larger school districts across the country indicated that more than three-quarters of them were implementing various aspects of school effectiveness research.

The British Columbia Ministry of Education has responded to a recent (1987/88) Royal Commission into education, which involved large-scale consultation with schools and local communities, by adopting a government programme entitled *Year 2000: A Framework for Learning* and providing a strategy for the development of performance indicators to support efforts in educational leadership (Dickson and Lim 1991).

Other recent research in Canada has been trying to address what Renihan and Renihan (1989) called 'second generation issues'. They argued that the first generation of school effectiveness research simply identified what is the case now, rather than what might be the case in the future. Renihan (1992) argued that:

the effective schools research has paid off, if for no other reason than that it has been the catalyst for school improvement

efforts, together with an unprecedented amount of intros-
pection among school professionals.

(Renihan 1992: 2)

The second generation issues were those features that sustained
the emergent school improvement efforts once the initial
enthusiasm had waned. One of the issues that was considered to be
important was the institutional image within the school, which was
defined as being:

the sum of subjective opinions about the quality of the prevailing
learning and social environment. It is the collective 'feeling'
developed by the various publics as a result of their observations
and experiences of the school and is accrued over the long term.

(Renihan and Renihan 1991: 5)

This 'image' is a tenuous entity, described by Sewell as 'composed
of many things; some tangible, some intangible; some measurable,
some non measurable; some significant, some insignificant; some
changeable, some unchangeable' (Sewell 1975: 4). It has, however,
become a critical feature at a time when governments of ageing
populations in most western countries are increasingly viewing
expenditure on education as being less an investment for the
future, and more an expenditure that could be redirected to
health and other welfare services.

Renihan and Renihan argued that the institutional image has two
dimensions; the cosmetic dimension, which is concerned about the
general appearance of the school, and the pastoral dimension, which
focused on the relationships of the people involved, and in particular,
the well-being of the student. They further argued that:

– effective schools are those schools which rate consistently high
  on both cosmetic and pastoral profiles
– overall external ratings of a school are more closely related to
  its cosmetic profile than to its pastoral profile
– schools with higher ratings on their pastoral profiles are more
  likely to provide more effective opportunities for parental
  participation
– elementary schools on average provide more effective opportunities for parental participation than do secondary schools
– elementary schools are more frequently rated higher on their
  pastoral profile than are secondary schools

- there is a low level of congruence between internal and external ratings of a school's pastoral profile, particularly where parental participation is low.

(Renihan and Renihan 1991: 24–5)

They have used their research to develop a series of strategies for the development of policies at systemic and local levels that would encourage the sustainability of improvement within the school. This direction seems to be a further important step in the development of the school effectiveness research.

Perhaps the most interesting longitudinal study in Canada came from the Halton Board of Education in Ontario which has been involved in a programme of improving the quality of the performance of its education system since 1986, using both American and British school effectiveness research as a basis for this development. As a result of this work the Halton school system has been reorganised to support school site decision-making (Stoll and Fink 1989, 1990, 1992; Fink and Stoll 1993). Four features were characteristics of school growth for successful and improving schools. They were:

- the development of a shared vision
- setting a climate of trust and openness
- promotion of staff collegiality
- development of a school mission.

(Fink and Stoll 1993: 3)

As with the American research the development of a team approach to school improvement seems to be a major characteristic of schools that were successful in their attempts.

Australia

In Australia, as in some other countries of the world, the term 'effective schools' is looked upon with some concern. Because of the narrow focus of the definition used by most American researchers, and because of the equally narrow, test-score-oriented nature of the bulk of the research, a politician or educational bureaucrat who identifies a scheme for improving the effectiveness of schools may well be supported by the general public, but regarded with some suspicion by school staff whose requirements for their pupils would go beyond those areas that can be easily tested. Staff feel comfortable assessing the students' performance in the subject areas in which they teach, but have concerns about how the results of that assessment might be used, both from the students' and their own point of view.

The dilemmas identified earlier are questions that have troubled Australian researchers. Sole emphasis on student performance on standardised achievement tests as the key measurement of an 'effective' school, as proposed by Edmonds (1979) has been met with various levels of scepticism. Chapman (1988) provided ample evidence that, although there was no commonly agreed upon understanding of what an effective school was, there were a number of Australian researchers such as Angus (1986a, 1986b), Ashenden (1987) and Banks (1988) who clearly indicated their concern that a concentration on effectiveness as it had been originally defined by Edmonds (1979) meant a diminution of concern about other equally relevant educational issues, such as equality, participation and social justice. In fact, they were sure of what it was not.

Angus (1986b) argued that simplistic notions of 'effectiveness' and 'school improvement' could lead to a series of activities which were 'socially conservative and educationally regressive'. Ashenden (1987) argued that performance indicators which could be used as the arbitrary determinants of school effectiveness diminished issues of social justice. The Victorian State Board of Education (1986), reflecting the political position of the incumbent government, cautioned:

> that defining outcomes as achievement on standardized tests may induce schools to begin a major re-allocation of resources into basic skill areas at the cost of other areas of curriculum.
>
> (State Board of Education 1986: 12)

Banks (1988) went as far as to suggest that, although Australia had been responsive to the effective schools literature, there were other features of Australian society and current directions in education that rendered a test-oriented concept virtually untenable.

> Policies have been developed by two education systems which were drawn from overseas effective schools movement literature, particularly that of North America, but these policies have never achieved prominence in their systems, events in the broader political arena rendering them incompatible with other policy initiatives.
>
> (Banks 1988: 1)

Because of this concern, until the 1991 national Effective Schools Project, there has been very little research in Australia that could be considered as part of the research of 'the effective schools movement'. Much of the research that was conducted in areas that might be of interest to school effectiveness researchers, including that by Caldwell and Misko (1984, 1986), Caldwell and Spinks (1986), Mellor and Chapman (1984) and Silver and Moyle (1985), all review elements that have come to be known as characteristics of effective schools. However, these studies were conducted because of concerns about facets of school improvement, school administration, school funding or the role of the principal in general, rather than identifying how any of these factors specifically affected student achievement.

The recent moves towards school restructuring in a number of states of Australia are predicated on the need to improve student learning outcomes (Dimmock 1993). Recent reports in Australia (Finn 1991; Mayer 1992; Carmichael 1992) have focused on the relationship between the school and the economy and each has stressed the need for programmes to be developed that reflect the need for Australia to be economically competitive on a global scale. Yet these reports conflict somewhat with the responses to the national Effective Schools Project questions, where school communities were asked for their opinions about what an effective school is and what makes it that way. The researchers in that project concluded:

> School effectiveness is about a great deal more than maximising academic achievement. Learning and the love of learning; personal development and self-esteem; life skills, problem solving and learning how to learn; the development of independent thinkers and well-rounded confident individuals; all rank as highly or more highly as the outcomes of effective schooling as success in a narrow range of academic disciplines.
>
> (McGaw et al. 1992: 174)

It seems that substantially more research needs to be undertaken in Australia before the apparent dichotomy will be resolved between what school communities actually require of schools and what politicians are moving towards in terms of school restructuring.

Europe

In the Netherlands, although the education system is characterised by centralised planning and policy making, the Dutch government is developing more autonomy for schools, with individual schools getting more decision-making powers over how to distribute a specific budget and over features of school policy (Creemers and Knuver 1989). Since the 1970s there have been a number of projects aimed at changing the structure of the Dutch education system, including the introduction of a basic compulsory curriculum and attention directed towards the achievement of educational outcomes. The more recent research in the Netherlands has been directed towards school characteristics and student results. The research seems to suggest that many of the factors isolated in the US studies do not exert the same importance in the Dutch situation. In particular, Scheerens and Creemers suggested that there is an absence of a strong relationship between effectiveness and leadership. In view of these results, there has been a call for the development of more context-related studies in school effectiveness to assist in understanding the differences in school effects from country to country (Scheerens and Creemers 1989).

In Hungary, the new Educational Act of 1985 aimed at decentralising the administration of schools with a subsequent increase in school autonomy. The new law laid down the principle that 'in the framework of statutory provisions and central educational programs' schools might define 'their own educational tasks, elaborate their own local educational system and work out supplementary curricula' (Halasz 1989: 3).

In Sweden, new features of government policy incorporated aspects of the effective schools research including 'increased local responsibility on the commune level', and 'the need for an instructional leader at the building level, goal setting and evaluation' (Klintestam *et al.* 1989: 3). The National Board of Education is in the process of developing a programme of nation-wide evaluation and an 'effective schools program', focusing on some of the factors identified in the US, has begun in Norrköping.

In Germany issues of school effectiveness or 'quality of schools' have emerged within a political context related to the reformation of the the country. Research that sought to compare the effectiveness of the traditional tripartite school system and the new comprehensive school system found that the effectiveness of the individual schools within each system varied more than that between systems (Einsiedler 1992: 2). The issues that have come to the fore include those where particular emphasis was placed upon pupils, their motivation, self-concept and development of learning strategies; the school and its openness to a broader range of 'life experiences'; leadership within the school and the development of teacher–parent relationships; and a re-definition of education with its subsequent effect on curriculum (Aurin and Lenz 1989: 2).

Spain has recently introduced reforms based on school effectiveness measures, although the majority of the research work there has related to school improvement. In Spain the principal of the school is elected by the teachers of the school and the new reforms encourage teachers to coordinate and implement curriculum projects at the school level (Marcelo 1992: 6).

The main issue in recent work in the Norwegian education system has been the establishment of a school system that is fair to all students regardless of differences in social class, cultural background, gender and ethnicity. As well as the international concern for pupil achievement levels, the Norwegian concern relates to designing a school system in a small but geographically spread-out country (Imsen 1992: 3). There have been two large scale projects on school evaluation conducted under the auspices of the National Council for the Primary and Lower Secondary School (Raaen 1990) and the National Council for the Upper Secondary School (Tiller 1990) which have found that school self-evaluation is a new experience for school staff and it will take some time for them to become confident and capable in this area.

The objectives of the current Finnish educational policy are twofold. On the one hand, the aim is to solve the present problems with the economy and in the world of work and, on the other, to build an educational system which will produce qualified and competent workers, not only now, but in the next decade (Kyro and Pirttiniemi 1992: 6). This has led to the development of a labour-market school, whose task is to produce manpower according to the needs of society and the demands of the labour market. Such a service-oriented school must be flexible enough to steer its activities according to demand and the development of evaluation methods for vocational education are well advanced (Kyro and Pirttiniemi 1992: 8).

Other countries

Evidence is starting to emerge that countries in all parts of the world are developing an interest in school effectiveness and school improvement. In Israel private funds have helped to establish school improvement projects on the one hand, while the Ministry of Education is making systemic decisions related to school improvement on the other. One of these decisions was 'that the school as a whole is to be regarded as the basic unit for school improvement . . . and not a particular curriculum or teaching method in a particular subject' (Bashi and Gordon 1989: 5).

Although research into school effectiveness has been limited in Hong Kong, many educational studies have focused on micro levels of school operations such as individual differences between students, teaching practices, learning processes and curriculum development, all of which contribute to an understanding of the effective school (Cheng 1992: 7). In 1986, Cheng conducted research to investigate the relationship between school effectiveness and the principal's leadership style, and recently two large-scale projects on the effectiveness of primary and secondary schools have been implemented using teams of staff from the Faculty of Education at the Chinese University of Hong Kong. It is anticipated that these two projects, which will release their findings in 1994 will contribute substantially to a better understanding of school effectiveness in the Asian context.

The Seventh-Day Adventist church has an extensive educational programme with more than 100,000 students in over 800 schools in countries in the Far East. Extensive evaluations of the effectiveness of SDA schools are carried out by Central Office personnel located in Singapore and the Philippines. Three approaches to assessment are used: a self-study conducted by the school, an on-site visit by a professional team of evaluators and the application of the Quality Schools Index for Private Schools (QSIPS) completed by two administrators and four teachers within each school. The subsequent evaluation report is then used by the school board of directors to establish priorities for areas of study, to develop implementation strategies and to outline their implementation schedule and procedures (Eager 1992: 4).

Even developing countries, including those where not all of the children attend school, are starting to become interested in improving educational systems to ensure that those children who do attend are given the best possible chance of success. The notion of school effectiveness takes on a different perspective in countries where perhaps 50 per cent of the children do not attend school at all and only 2 per cent to 4 per cent complete their secondary schooling.

In Chile, Longo (1992: 2–4) reports that in 1990 50 per cent of the more than two million children between the ages of 6 and 13 did not attend school regularly and 19 per cent did not enrol in primary school, even though it was compulsory to do so. In 1980 the Ministry of Education developed a national standardised evaluation system to measure the quality and effectiveness of schooling at the primary level. The results of carrying out this test have shown that students from government or subsidised private schools learn considerably less and have a lower self-esteem than those students who go to expensive private schools. In 1990 the Chilean government put into effect a number of programmes in an attempt to improve the quality of education. These included greater levels of government subsidy to schools in poor areas, a 20 per cent increase in the number of students receiving free meals at school and legislative reforms to improve the opportunities for lower socio-economic students. Despite the attempts to improve the quality of education, with only 2.7 per cent of the country's gross national product being used on education, much work still needs to be done.

In Zimbabwe (Nyagura 1992: 2) reports show that there has been a trebling of the enrolments in primary schools between 1980 and 1990 but that there has been a considerable degeneration in performance in national year 7 examinations over that time, where pass rates have dropped by approximately 20 per cent and high achievement levels have dropped by approximately 15 per cent in both English and mathematics. A major factor contributing to this dilemma is the high percentage of untrained teachers. Research has indicated that government schools that previously catered for the white population and private schools charging high fees were more effective than government schools which catered for the black population and private schools charging low fees and that these in turn were more effective than the rural district community schools which catered for about 70 per cent of the population. The Zimbabwean government has attempted to address these concerns by increasing the number of schools being built, by hiring more teachers and by improving the quality of the teaching force by doubling the number of teacher training positions and initiating in-service training for those teachers who were untrained. In addition, from 1992 per capita grants were increased for students in disadvantaged schools to help improve the instruction levels for these students.

Other school systems in the South African region have made concerted attempts to improve the quality of school performance. Noruwana (1988) reports that two Departments of Education, Transkei and Bophuthatswana, enabled policy-makers, practitioners and researchers to consider the theme *Effective Schools in Deprived Communities: An Agenda for Action in the Nineties* at their annual Transkei Teachers' Association Conference. A number of areas were identified for further research including investigation into the effectiveness of local schools, the development of a limited small-scale pilot study and work on the role of principals as instructional leaders.

Jordan has seen a rapid expansion of its education system over the past two decades with the result that the education system now reaches 98 per cent of children up to the age of 12 and 80 per cent of children from 12 to 18 (Ahlawat 1993: 6). Ahlawat suggests that school effectiveness in developing countries relates more to resources than to other determinants: 'schools that have a supply of textbooks and chalk and blackboard prove definitely more effective than those which are deprived of these basic learning materials' (Ahlawat 1993: 4). Cohn and Rossmiller (1987) concluded that school resources matter even more than socio-economic status for the level of effectiveness of schools in developing countries.

It can be seen by this brief overview of school effectiveness and school improvement initiatives in various parts of the world that each country differs in its school system, its methods of school governance, the availability of resources and its ability to direct additional resources to specific purposes. However, in all cases, there was an accepted need for schools to improve their performance to enhance the life of the individual student, but also to improve the country's competitiveness in the world of tomorrow.

IMPLICATIONS FOR FUTURE CONSIDERATION

In each of the countries referred to above educational authorities have used school effectiveness research to justify the decisions currently being made about the structures of education. However, there appears to be no uniformity in these decisions from country to country. There seems to be a trend towards centralised control over some areas such as the development and measurement of school goals, but with increasing responsibility at the school level for structuring learning activities to achieve those goals. Chapman pointed out that:

> some countries with a tradition of decentralised arrangements seem to have moved towards more centralised control over functions; in other countries where there has been the tradition of a more centralised approach the opposite seems to be the case.
>
> (Chapman 1991: 6)

She also pointed out that in some countries shifts in decision-making to schools seemed to be happening simultaneously with increases in centralised decision-making powers and influence. The new British educational reforms are a case in point. At the same time as a national curriculum with national testing and reporting was being prescribed, control in school budgets was being devolved to the school. Similar moves towards a national curriculum, but local control by schools, is also evident in Australia. Yet, in many respects, the use of the term school effectiveness is comparatively recent.

With the bulk of even recent American work remaining outcome-oriented, a further dilemma for the study of school effectiveness occurs. The phrase 'school effectiveness' has become value laden and has been narrowly interpreted by some as meaning 'test oriented'. The decision in England and Wales to publish the aggregated performance in national tests of a school's students at age 7, 11 and 14 has been widely criticised by teacher and parent organisations because no attempt has been made to allow for a host of sociological factors such as differences in the availability of pre-school education, the lack of quality staff in many inner-city schools, family circumstances, the situation of schools with a high percentage of students for whom English was not the mother-tongue and the like. The first full league tables, published in 1992, were not of the Standard Attainment Tests (SATs) but of attainments in the GSCE examinations taken at year 11: they were plagued by inaccuracies and misrepresented school performance particularly where able pupils took some subjects a year early. There was widespread criticism of the inadequate trialling of government tests, to the extent that in 1993 three teacher unions representing 80 per cent of the teaching force in England and Wales balloted their members to boycott some or all of the tests. There are fears that the government will replace the GSCE examinations – offered in a far wider range of subjects than those of the National Curriculum – by SATs.

Yet it would be inaccurate to judge that some countries in the world are not interested in making their schools more effective because they refuse to call their efforts 'school effectiveness'. Effectiveness in this sense may well be one element of a wider goal such as the excellent school. Much of the Australian and Canadian literature has identified more with the process orientation associated with school improvement than with the product orientation of the early school effectiveness research. There are some important differences, as Smink pointed out,

> School effectiveness is concerned with results. Researchers try to describe certain variables for school success in measurable terms. On the other hand, school improvement places the accent on the process; here one finds a broad description of all the variables that play a role in a school improvement project. Both approaches need the other to successfully modernize the system.
>
> (Smink 1991: 3)

Part of the dilemma is to clarify the relationship between school effectiveness and school improvement, and the other part is to ensure that the concepts are not used interchangeably.

There needs to be a very clear distinction made between 'the school effectiveness movement', which emanated in the United States, and the universal and long-term aim of making schools more effective. The former has been interpreted as assuming a narrow, quantitative orientation, the latter makes no such assumptions. This has created a further conceptual dilemma which relates to separating the concept of school effectiveness from the measurement of it. There appears to have been very little attempt in the past to make this distinction.

The first part of this book takes the opportunity to review the international research with a view to clarifying some of the concerns and complexities previously identified, and also describes the results of a study that was conducted in Australia. The conclusions from this study have been used to develop a broader perspective of school effectiveness, one that, to be really successful, includes the need for local communities to be mobilised for school development to be really successful. The purpose of the exercise was to establish a more complete understanding of what school effectiveness means and includes, and to use this understanding to help schools improve their attempts to become more effective.

The second part of the book provides a model for school improvement that uses the school effectiveness literature as a basis for this development, but incorporates community education principles and processes to ensure full involvement of the local community to bring this about.

Chapter 2

The effective school: towards a framework of understanding

An effective school is one that achieves greater student learning than
might have been predicted from the context in which it works.

(McGaw *et al.* 1991: 2)

Almost all education systems are currently developing policies,
programmes or research in school effectiveness, not only at the
school level, but also at the systemic, state or national levels, and it
seems that these developments are likely to be among the dominant educational themes in the 1990s. However, not everyone is
prepared to accept that the school effectiveness literature is more
than a limited attempt to describe 'what is', rather than 'what
ought to be'. Rosenholtz (1989) argued:

This is a topic with voluminous literature (and much commen-
tary), but precious little theory to guide it. Studies have been
episodic, not consciously building on each other. There has been
much independent ploughing and reploughing of the same
ground. Moreover, an air of methodological criticism hovers
about it, as though the central problem were that of merely refining output measures, of controlling for previously overlooked
variables, of quantifying what are largely case-study findings, or of
sampling still wider populations to assure generalizability.

But the most interesting questions in this area are not at all
methodological, they are conceptual. Not how to measure school
effectiveness but what to measure; the manner in which school
structure interrelates with its functioning and its productivity.
Problems plaguing this literature are not mere inconveniences to
be brushed aside until more rigorously designed studies come
along. Instead, they are fundamental to school life itself.

(Rosenholtz 1989: 1–2)

SOME CONCEPTUAL DILEMMAS

If the school effectiveness studies are plagued with conceptual problems, then it is necessary to identify, and possibly overcome, some of these before research in the area can proceed further. Two dilemmas need to be considered. The first is created by the tension between the notion of quality and the notion of equality. If quality is paramount, then standards must be identified and it must be accepted that not everyone will reach those standards. If equality is paramount, there is a danger that, in the effort to ensure that everyone succeeds to a comparable level, that no-one will reach the quality standards. The second dilemma arises from the difficulty of translating the theory of an effective school into practice. If we know what makes a school effective, then it should be easy to make the necessary changes in schools to make them that way. But, so far, this has not been the case.

Quality and equality of educational outcomes

One of the problems for the school effectiveness debate arises from the failure of researchers to define adequately the concept of effectiveness. Approaches to this task have emphasised various issues, such as the quality of educational outcomes, the equality of educational outcomes or the equality of educational opportunities. The early definition by Edmonds suggests equality of educational outcomes:

> Specifically, I require that an effective school bring the children of the poor to those minimal masteries of basic school skills that now describe minimally successful pupil performances for the children of the middle class.

>   (Edmonds 1979: 16)

The suggestion here is that all children should at least perform *minimally* well. An implication of this statement is that resources should be deployed to ensure this outcome. In schools where limited funds are available, a further implication would be that these resources would be taken from those areas which provide the extension work necessary to achieve higher standards and from those areas in which not all children can succeed, but where those with talent can fulfil their potential.

However, the idea of an equality of educational outcomes is untenable, since it is not possible to have everyone being equal first, unless first involves a dropping of the standard to one that everyone can achieve. Even if the standards are dropped to such an extent that everyone can achieve them, there will still not be an equality of outcomes since some students will merely achieve those standards and others will far exceed them. However, if the goal of effectiveness is to have equality of educational opportunity, then there may be some possibility for an acceptance of the concept. It would provide all students with the opportunity to succeed by being involved in a quality programme. Not all students would achieve to the same extent, but the opportunity to succeed, which may involve the allocation or redistribution of some resources to those who need additional help, would enable all children to fulfil their *own* potential, even though that potential would differ from student to student. In this instance, the concept is not concerned with minimal achievement of all students, but maximum personal achievement for each student.

This interpretation of equality of educational opportunity raises the difficulty of considering both quality and equality simultaneously. The two concepts may be mutually exclusive. However, Fantini argued that 'like excellence, quality is universally acceptable, but elusive in character' (Fantini 1986: 44). He argued that it is possible to consider four dimensions of quality:

- the individual student
- the curriculum
- the teacher
- the outcomes of the educational process.

The first encourages school systems to identify the best students and to give them the best education, which seems to conflict with the notion of equality. However, if the other three dimensions are considered, a combination of the quality staff and quality programmes with appropriate methods of evaluating the outcomes of the programmes, does not conflict with the idea of equality. 'When quality and equality are merged, elitism is replaced by *inclusivity*. Quality is not measured by how few students succeed, but by how many succeed' (Fantini 1986: 50). From this perspective there is no inherent contradiction in suggesting that quality and equality can exist side by side. A school that offers a quality programme, where all or most students satisfactorily complete that programme, with no variation in completion rates between students with different family backgrounds, could be seen as an effective school.

The relationship between the concept and practice of effective schools

This may be the most difficult of all the dilemmas associated with school effectiveness. Since the study of school effectiveness has generally been limited to those areas of the educational domain that lend themselves to easily understood measurement and analysis devices, then it may well be that the current understanding of what an effective school is tells only part of the story. Making schools more effective in practice is an entirely different matter. Reynolds and Pack argued that 'researchers know considerably more about the characteristics of good schools than about how to make schools good' (Reynolds and Pack 1989: 2). This seems to suggest that it may well be easier to *recognise* a school as being more or less effective than other schools than it is to *explain* why or how it came about. For this reason, much of the research has focused upon identifying characteristics associated with effective schools, in the hope that this knowledge will somehow help other schools to become more effective.

However, the research thus far has not provided a great deal of detail in terms of establishing the complex interrelationships between the identified characteristics; yet it may be here that the heart of the matter lies. If the issue of school effectiveness could be reduced to having a finite number of characteristics present within the school, then it could be argued that all schools recognised as being effective must have those characteristics operating within them. Yet the research has shown that this is clearly not the case. One characteristic, that of leadership, would seem vital to the effective school. However, not all schools that have been considered effective have had good leadership at the school site. Furthermore, some studies characterise leadership in one way, while others characterise it differently. Studies such as those by Scheerens and Creemers (1989) and Wildy and Dimmock (1992) have found that the importance placed on the leadership abilities of the principal in the United Kingdom and the United States is not duplicated to the same extent in the Netherlands or Australia.

The conclusion to be reached from this is that schools *recognised* as being effective will have present within them some or most of the critical characteristics, such as good leadership, but it is the way in which these characteristics interact that ensures that the school *is* effective. It is possible that other schools will have an identical set of characteristics, but because the interplay between them is not right, the school is seen to be less effective. To take leadership again, it is possible that in some school situations, an authoritarian principal will bring out the best in both staff and students, because those staff and students are amenable to having a single decision-maker among them. That school might be seen as effective, both by those in the school and by those outside it. However, that same principal, appointed to another school, where cooperative and collaborative decision-making was an accepted and long standing tradition, may actually create an environment that prevents the school from becoming fully effective, because he or she tries to act in a manner that succeeded in the first school. Fully to understand the complex issue of effectiveness, consideration must be given both to how effectiveness has been recognised or defined, and to the difficulties associated with those definitions, and to how an effective school operates, that is, the processes it uses to create the level of effectiveness it actually achieves.

TOWARDS A CLEARER UNDERSTANDING OF EFFECTIVENESS

It seems likely that controversy about the definition of school effectiveness arises because of the school's role as an agency for the educational development of the community. If school effectiveness is related to the achievement of educational goals at the school, school system or national levels, then conflicting views of what the goals of education are will bring similarly conflicting views of what an effective school is. The major problem that emerges for those interested in school effectiveness is how to resolve the apparent paradoxes among the goals, the priorities given to the various goals by various stakeholders, or any dissonance between the priorities accepted by a government, or a school system, and those accepted by an individual school. The different views held by school systems and schools might be considered as the macro and micro views of the role of education.

At the macro level there is an obvious current concern for school effectiveness at an international level and, within particular countries, at a national, state or systemic level. Countries around the world are considering policies and practices related to the development of more effective schools. The perspective adopted at this level is one of comparison, where schools in one system are compared with each other or with those in another system, state or country. These comparisons seem to adopt one of two competitive views, namely, either 'our schools are better than yours', or alternatively, 'our schools need to compete successfully with those in other systems if our children are to take their rightful place in the world'. Instances of the first type occur when governments release figures indicating apparent retention rates in schools or the amount *per capita* spent on education, as an indication of how 'good' their education system is. Instances of the second type occur when governments indicate that to be educationally, or economically, competitive with other countries in the world marketplace students require specific skills and that schools have a role to play in the acquisition of those skills. In both instances, the underlying rationale is that, since education is a heavy consumer of money generated by the public purse, then it needs to be accountable for that money, and that accountability is best measured in terms of the output, that is, the percentage of students who complete school and the capabilities of those students when they leave.

There is also a micro view of school effectiveness which occurs at the level of the school itself. The school is more inward looking, being concerned for the progress and welfare of the students within that school, rather than relating to concerns such as the world economy, or even to concerns that other schools might have. Individual schools have to deal with a range of individual student abilities, and some students will never be capable of attaining the types of skills demanded by those who consider the issues at the macro level. Schools have to balance the requirements of the macro view being proposed at the time with the adoption of a wider perspective which relates more to total student needs. In doing so, the school may have to accept the possibility that this might dilute the strength and focus of the educational programme for all of the students in the school.

Neither point of view is without dilemmas and critics. The major dilemma for a macro view of education is its inability to respond quickly to changes that occur in society. The introduction of computers and robotics have changed the face of industry in a very short time, but the education system was only able to respond to these changes over a substantially longer period of time, as new curricula were developed, new facilities and equipment were purchased or instituted, then tested and implemented over the course of the student's school career. Any new development that requires a major change in attitudes and skills on the part of people leaving school may take up to fifteen years to implement. And, unlike previous generations, where the speed of change was more leisurely, by the time these new attitudes and skills have been implemented and students have adopted them, society will probably have moved on again and a new set of skills may be required. The critics of the macro view of education argue that many individuals are lost to education by a rigid adherence to this perspective. Those who are unable to learn the specific skills required are relegated to an educational backwater, with all of the economic, social and personal penalties that are part of this deficiency.

The major dilemma for a school system which accepts a micro view of education, and responds to it through a devolution of decision-making and responsibility to the school level, is that it is harder to match up the wider societal goals with local community goals for students. Accepting a micro view may eliminate the consideration of macro concerns altogether. It is possible that in trying to provide a wide range of options for individuals within the system, none will have the skills required to compete at the macro level. Individuals become more important than the society in which they live. The critics of this view equate the broader view of the role of education with a drop in standards. They argue that to try and keep everybody in the system leads to a system that has no standards.

The conceptual dilemmas referred to above (p. 28) have made the study of school effectiveness more difficult. There needs to be some balance between a definition that is too specific and one that is too general, to establish what identifies the essential characteristics that describe effectiveness, rather than something else. Since all previous attempts to define school effectiveness have been considered as controversial, it may instead be better to identify some broad frameworks that aid an understanding of school effectiveness. In this way there may be a better elaboration of those complexities that are hidden by any single definition.

THE FOUR DIMENSIONS OF SCHOOL EFFECTIVENESS

There seem to be four dimensions necessary for the development of an appropriate understanding of an effective school. The first, and most critical to the understanding of school effectiveness, both conceptually and in practice, is the nature and the extent of

the educational goals considered to be central to an effective
school. The second is a consideration of the technique used to
identify schools as being effective or not and the third is the way in
which those goals will be measured. These three dimensions,
together, can be used to generate a model or framework for
understanding how effective schools might be recognised or
defined. The fourth dimension considers the school processes
used to make that school effective in practice. This dimension, in
conjunction with the goals accepted by the school, creates a
second model or framework which considers the ways in which the
accepted goals of education are actually achieved in schools.

The goals of education and the role of school

One problem for school effectiveness research is to identify some
way in which the goals of the system as a whole can be balanced
against the goals of individual schools, or individual students, so
that this balance becomes acceptable to those who adopt either
the macro view or the micro view of education. The resolution of
this problem requires a consideration of what the role of education is and how school and school systems fit into this role. In
simple terms, the role of the school is to be one of a number of
agencies, along with universities, adult education providers,
churches and community groups, involved in the attainment of
the goals of education. All schools would have similar, if not the
same, goals. An effective school is one that undertakes that role
with high levels of success. A consideration of school effectiveness
becomes a twofold issue, considering first, what are the goals of
education – that is, what schools *should* be doing, and second, how
to measure appropriately the extent to which individual schools
achieve those goals.

In Australia, a national move towards common goals and curriculum areas has helped to define the roles of individual schools. In
April 1989, a meeting identified ten national goals for schooling in
Australia (Australian Education Council 1990). These goals encompassed a number of considerations, including relevant curriculum areas, but also issues of social justice and the role education
plays in national economic development.

Some goals identified the knowledge, skills and attitudes considered to be appropriate for students in all schools and included
literacy, numeracy, information processing, analysis and problem

solving, science and technology, history and geography, languages other than English, cultural heritage, the creative arts, physical development and personal health and fitness, participating as active and informed citizens about the environment and developing a capacity to exercise judgement in matters of morality, ethics and social justice.

Other goals, which included the achievement of high standards, the development of self-confidence, optimism, high self-esteem, respect for others, and the promotion of equality of educational opportunities, reflected the social justice concerns of the Australian Education Council. Finally, the list included overtly economic goals, such as:

- the need for education to be relevant to the social, cultural and economic needs of the nation
- to provide skills which allow students maximum flexibility and adaptability in their future employment
- to provide a foundation for further education and training
- to provide appropriate career education and knowledge of the world of work.

These goals were intended to address the need for school graduates to have the skills and attitudes necessary to become competitive in the world of economics.

The listing of these goals indicates that the Australian Education Council considered that a wide range of issues needed to be addressed by every school in the country. A comparison with the goals expressed by education systems in other countries indicates that these goals would be similar, if not the same, to those held by many nations around the world. Yet some of the goals referred to can only be addressed, in practice, by school communities. Educational authorities can only list them as goals. It is possible to identify certain goals that are, or should be, accepted by all schools, and this might provide the first dimension for the two models of school effectiveness: the first that helps to recognise a school as being effective or not and the second which helps us to understand why it has become effective.

From existing data, it is possible to identify certain goals as being necessary for all schools to undertake, and the acceptance of these goals might provide the first dimension for the frameworks for school effectiveness.

1 Academic skills: incorporating all the various discipline areas that educators felt all children should know, beginning with basic literacy and numeracy.
2 Behaviour and attendance: the need for regular attendance at school and appropriate behaviour while attending school to ensure that the necessary skills have the best chance of being learned.
3 Self-concept: the non-academic skills and attitudes considered necessary to develop the student's personal feelings of worth. It might include health and human relations, and the physical, social, creative, cultural and emotional development areas.
4 Citizenship skills: the non-academic skills and attitudes considered necessary to develop a concerned and involved member of a community.
5 Employment skills: the non-academic skills and attitudes considered necessary to obtain, and remain in, employment.
6 Other educational goals: a variety of other educational goals that exist in all schools, such as the physical, social, emotional and spiritual development of students, which do not fall neatly into any of the categories already listed, but impinge upon a number of them.
7 Community goals: this area takes the role of school beyond that of teaching its students, and into the area of servicing the educational needs of the whole community. It might include such areas as after-school programmes, adult education or community development activities, or others which respond to identified community needs.

Figure 2.1 provides one possible way in which the goals of education might be characterised. It becomes the first dimension of the recognition framework for school effectiveness. It could be argued that an effective school is one that considers all of these goals, and develops strategies for ensuring that all students within the school experience success in each of them.

Identifying effective schools

A second area critical to the concept of an effective school is the problem of judging school effectiveness. The ability to recognise whether or not a school is effective is critical to an understanding of what it is that makes it that way. For a school to be recognised as

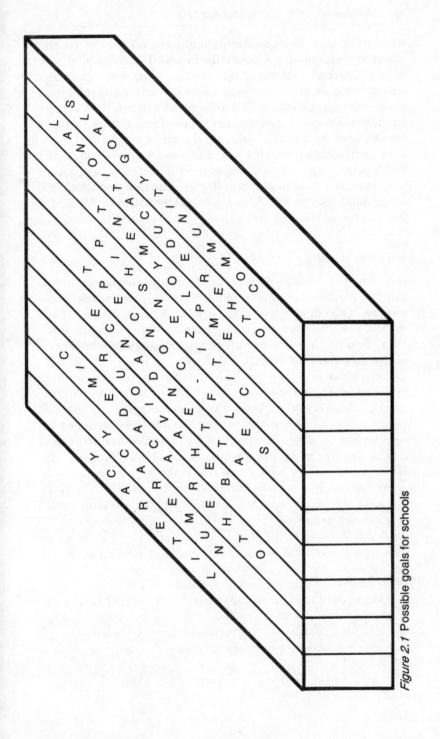

Figure 2.1 Possible goals for schools

effective, it must demonstrate its fulfilment of a set of criteria identified as promoting school effectiveness. Two that would have to be fulfilled are that the school had clearly identified goals and was achieving them. Others might include strong leadership, good home–school relations, staff development and a school climate conducive to learning. Different methods have been used to identify effective schools, including the use of standardised tests, the reputational approach and the use of school evaluation and development activities. A consideration of different approaches that have been used to identify effective schools may clarify some of the difficulties for each alternative and may also clarify some of the conceptual issues as well.

Standardised testing

One commonly accepted means of identifying effective schools is through the use of standardised testing. In this instance, students undertake a common test which is independently marked. Each student could be compared with others in a defined group, which might be a city, a region or district, an educational system, a state or a nation. Since individual students attend schools, then schools, too, can be identified as being more or less effective on the basis of the standardised data.

The results of standardised tests can be used in a number of ways as a basis for identifying effective schools. Tests might be used to compare a number of schools at a given point in time or they can be used to make judgements about schools' progress over time. The raw scores could be used to make these judgements, or adjustments might be made for family background characteristics. Schools could be judged effective if they get good raw score results at a single testing or their adjusted scores might have more credence. Schools could also be judged effective if their scores have improved over a given period. One of the difficulties is that the methods identified, as with the use of standardised testing procedures in general, are not universally accepted.

Although the use of established data bases such as test scores in academic subjects is seen as an objective way of identifying effective schools, a concern for this method of assessment is that, as it is statistically based, it automatically means that a proportion of schools will be seen to be less effective than others, regardless of what they might be doing to change the situation. If raw data, collected in a single test, is used, an individual school may have improved dramatically over a period of years, but if other schools improved as well, it may still be looked upon as being less effective or not effective at all. If adjusted data is used, the issue of quality arises. A second concern relates to the range of data collected as a basis for the judgement about how well schools are achieving their goals. It might be argued that the collection data for the easily measured academic subjects is too narrow. If a school has a wide range of goals, such as those discussed earlier, the use of standardised testing as a means of judging the effectiveness of a school, is only available to a limited number.

The reputational approach

A second means of identifying effective schools is through a reputational approach, where people who are skilled and knowledgeable about a number of schools are asked to consider the school's capabilities and progress. The reputational technique can be seen from the perspective of how a school system identifies the level of effectiveness of individual schools within that system, but also from the perspective of how a researcher might identify effective schools to be used for further study. The major concern with the reputational approach is the subjectivity of the choices made. With the 'expert' only being able to choose those schools known to him, which would be a small proportion of all schools in the system, the validity of the choice will depend on the criteria being used.

The perspective of the outsider visiting the school will not only be a snapshot view of what actually occurs in the school at a particular time, but will also depend upon the information collected or not collected, for whatever reason, from the school and may be influenced by the visitor having different educational goals to those operating in the school. Again there is a limitation to the variety of school goals that the reputational process can review. Judgements can be made on the basis of written or verbal information, which can be obtained during the visit, but in many cases this type of information does not provide the whole story about the school. The success of many of the goals relies upon the processes used to fulfil them and, in many cases, the processes cannot be viewed or ascertained within the limited time span available. The reputational approach relies on information already within the school. If much of the information that is used through the reputational approach is second-hand information collected at the school, then perhaps there is little this approach can add to an understanding of a school's effectiveness that could not be achieved through a combination of other methods, such as standardised testing and school reviews.

Process of school review, evaluation and development

A third way of identifying the effectiveness of schools could be through the use of local school records considered during the school's ongoing process of self-evaluation and development. Even though a school may not be involved in a standardised testing process, the use of school written and observational records, such as academic achievement records, attendance and discipline records, teacher styles and staff development activities, and records of curriculum review and development might help to determine the level of effectiveness of a particular school. It is likely that these would be used in conjunction with one of the two previous methods in order to build a more comprehensive picture of the school. This process would involve a regular self-evaluation activity by the school.

Since a total school review encompasses a huge range of variables, such as 'the needs of children, guidance and counselling, evaluation and testing curriculum, administration, community, and the local district' (Robinson 1984: 143), and possibly a lot more, the need for a review plan becomes obvious. Such a plan, or framework, was provided in *The Self-Managing School* (Caldwell and Spinks 1988), as a result of the Effective Resource Allocation in Schools Project (ERASP) which commenced in 1982. The framework integrated 'goal-setting, policy-making, planning, budgeting, implementing and evaluating in a manner with the often unsystematic, fragmented processes which have caused so much frustration and ineffectiveness in the past' (Caldwell and Spinks 1988: 3–4). Caldwell and Spinks identified four major issues related to the development of self-management within a school: a focus on teaching and learning, a framework for accountability, the appropriate involvement of staff, parents and students, and programmes for professional development.

Community involvement in the identification process

Since both the standardised testing and reputational approaches to identifying effective schools are limited in that each can only be used for some of the many goals that schools might have, perhaps school communities themselves might be involved in the process. Since school communities are now becoming more involved in the determination and implementation of school goals, they are in a good position to judge whether or not those goals have been fulfilled. This move seems to have been one accepted by some governments. This has caused an alteration in the direction of some school effectiveness research from one where the influence of family and community background was shown to be minimal or able to be overcome, to one where the obvious influences of a child's background on his or her academic achievement are utilised to improve what happens in schools.

In Victoria, Australia, people were asked (Aglinskas *et al.* 1988) about their perceptions of the effectiveness of schools. Of 189 school community members who responded to the survey, over 80 per cent felt their school was effective, and only 2 per cent felt that it was ineffective. This finding supports Cirone (1990):

> despite the political hay that can be made by pointing fingers at education, it seems clear that the public isn't buying. They hear how terrible schools are, how business can't find literate workers, and how we compare terribly with other nations, and they rate our national schools accordingly. However, as the overall ratings indicated, they also see first-hand the miracles that occur in their own schools with their own children, and the vast majority say they are extremely pleased with what they see. They hear reports about the demise of public education, but what they actually see for their own children, for whom they are the world's harshest critics, they rate above average or excellent.
>
> (Cirone 1990: 12)

The four different means of identifying effective schools become the second dimension of the model. It can be represented visually as in Figure 2.2.

Recent school effectiveness research has seen the attempt to provide a series of indicators to judge the effectiveness of schools. These indicators have widened the scope of the judgement being

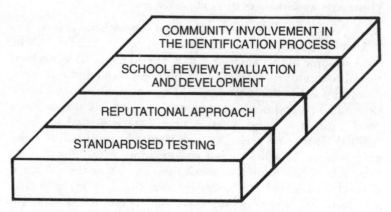

Figure 2.2 Techniques for identifying effective schools

made from purely academic performance on standardised tests to include a variety of other elements of school activity. Many of these performance indicators have been developed as a mechanism for judging the effectiveness of various goals discussed in previous paragraphs. McGaw *et al.* stressed the importance of evaluation in the school improvement process:

> Evaluation and review serve a range of purposes from helping to plan what to do next to providing an account to others about what has been happening. Because feedback is so basic to school improvement, initiatives that are designed to enhance features of the school are more likely to flourish in school environments that include evaluation and review as regular elements of the school improvement programme.
>
> In addition, evaluation and review provide another opportunity for staff, parents and students to work collaboratively. The process offers another setting in which to describe their expectations and to assess how well they have been achieved.
>
> (McGaw *et al.* 1991: 15)

This method of determination would most likely look at more than academic results, considering the many possible gains a child can make at school, since a full evaluation of a child's development involves much more than simple testing. Evaluation considers the child's development socially, emotionally, and in terms of developing independence or leadership, or in a host of other ways.

This makes the issue of standardised testing a problem since, if every possible developmental area of the child was to be tested, there would be little or no time left for learning. Somewhere in the past it has been determined that schools were designed for academic learning, and the history of education shows few attempts to broaden or alter that view. The complexities of school life and the variety of possibilities for human attainment in the 1990s does not enable a standardised testing procedure, however it is implemented, to be a totally useful measure on its own. Since the reputational approach relies on information already in existence, the use of the school review process and the involvement of the local community in the process of judging the school's effectiveness, seems to complement whatever testing procedure is used by the school. Since each of the different methods can be used for only a limited number of educational goals, then a combination of these methods would have the best chance of determining the effectiveness of the school across them all.

Techniques for measuring school effectiveness

If the techniques described in the previous section were concerned with identifying the criteria of effectiveness within particular schools, we must also consider what the acceptable standards for those criteria are. The acceptance of the legitimacy of the effective schools literature by policy-makers has created a situation which will need to be faced by local schools in the near future. It is not possible to identify a series of characteristics associated with effective schools without at least considering the issue of how to assess whether or not these characteristics are operating well in the schools. As *Schools and Quality* points out,

> There has recently emerged widespread international interest in educational indicators. The call for better and more relevant information on the functioning of schools is now audible both from within education systems and from bodies outside their traditional ambit.
>
> (OECD 1989a: 44)

The exercise of identifying qualitative information from a statistical base is fraught with danger.

The use of performance indicators that relate solely to the development of academic skills does not guarantee the successful evaluation of a particular school's overall performance. In many respects, it might be argued that these specific indicators have been chosen because they are the easiest to measure. It is easier, for instance, to measure a child's performance in reading than it is to measure the same child's relationship with, and feelings about, the classroom teacher. Yet it is possible that the level of interaction between the two and the positive or negative feelings that they have for one another, may count just as much in the child's reading score as does the time the child spends on the task of reading. The concern for the processes that are used within the school may, when it comes to helping particular children, turn out to be no less equally important than the programmes of the school. Regardless of what is being measured, there seem to be only two ways of measuring performance. Those are the 'outcome' method, which concentrates on where students are at a particular time, and the 'value-added' method, which considers how far they have progressed over time.

The outcome view of the effectiveness of schools, although it had gained wide acceptance in the United States, concerned many researchers in other parts of the world. Critics in Australia (Angus 1986a and 1986b; Ashenden 1987; Banks 1988) and Europe (Goldstein 1984; Cuttance 1987; Mortimore *et al.* 1988) were particularly concerned that the concentration on simple inputs and outputs of schools, and the subsequent recipe approach to school improvement that was adopted by US researchers and policy-makers ignored the complexities of what took place in individual schools and how those schools utilised the resources available to them. The problem with an outcome based interpretation was that it was too difficult to determine which outcomes were due to the students themselves and which were based on what the school had accomplished.

Some of the early British research was governed by an educational psychology orientation and therefore was more concerned about individual children rather than school effects. This concern was brought about by what might be considered as the 'value-added' view of school effectiveness. Schools were not to be judged simply on the results of standardised tests, since these results may have been more a factor of the children themselves rather than of anything the school had 'added', but on the basis of what development the students had made during the course of their school careers. Research, such as that by Rutter *et al.* (1979), Cuttance (1986, 1988a, 1988b, 1988c) and Mortimore *et al.* (1986, 1988) acknowledged the more complex interactions that needed to be addressed at the school level and a different view of school effectiveness emerged. The Mortimore study of fifty English junior schools, sought to 'find a way of comparing schools' effects on their pupils, while acknowledging the fact that schools do not all receive pupils of similar abilities and backgrounds' (Mortimore *et al.* 1988: 176). Factors such as the ethnic composition, language background, social class and family composition of the pupils, together with other considerations, were all used as relevant data to assist in the determination of the gains that pupils made during their time at school. The study not only considered attainment, but progress as well, in academic areas such as reading, mathematics, writing and oracy, and also the non-cognitive areas of behaviour, attendance, self-concept and attitudes towards school.

Using a value-added approach, decisions could be made, for instance, to test every student in a range of subject areas upon entry to school and before school completion to determine how much the student has learned in the time spent at school. This might in turn be judged against national or state expectations for children of similar socio-economic backgrounds. Should all or most children achieve these expectations, then the school might be considered effective. The difficulty with this approach is that it might be perceived as accepting that standards in poorer areas can be below those in more affluent areas, thus reinforcing the differences that school effectiveness was trying to eliminate. However, the value-added view of school effectiveness has gained increasing acceptability and is the accepted interpretation of an effective school by the 1991 Effective Schools Project currently underway in Australia. Despite this acceptance, McGaw *et al.* expressed the view that

> There is no definitive *how* of effective schools and so there can be no one recipe for every school to try. Schooling is too complex a business for a recipe.
>
> (McGaw *et al.* 1991: 15)

This indicates that further consideration is required of the dilemmas implicit in how we judge whether or not a school is effective.

It could be argued that neither the outcome approach nor the value-added approach is acceptable in itself, and that for a school to be effective there must be a high proportion of students who succeed on outcome measurements such as standardised tests, substantial improvement for those who do not fully succeed, and a

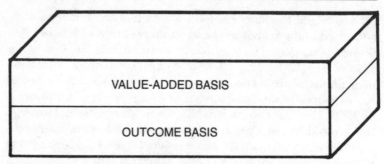

Figure 2.3 Techniques for measuring school effectiveness

value-added approach adopted for those school goals that do not easily lend themselves to statistical measuring devices. This would ensure that the final outcomes of school were seen to be important, but would also ensure that those outcomes were a product of school activity *in addition* to anything that the students themselves were able to contribute. The measurement component adds a further dimension to the conceptual model of school effectiveness, as is indicated in Figure 2.3.

THE EFFECTIVE SCHOOL: A MODEL FOR RECOGNITION

The first model is one that might assist in a better understanding of how to recognise an effective school. The three components related to a conceptual understanding of an effective school are:

– the goals adopted by effective schools
– the means used to identify effective schools
– the means used to measure the level of effectiveness of a particular school.

If these are combined, then the model contained in Figure 2.4 emerges.

Given the very real difficulty of ever achieving a universally acceptable definition of school effectiveness, the model in Figure 2.4 can be used to develop a framework that will assist in the recognition of an effective school. Some things will be non-negotiable. The school should be offering a quality programme. All students within the school, regardless of their background, should experience both success and improvement in their movement through the programme. A variety of techniques should be

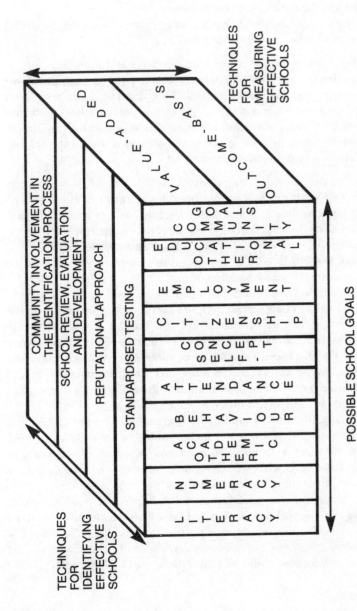

Figure 2.4 A model for recognising effective schools

used to identify whether or not the school is effective. Flexibility in programmes operating at the school level comes from the possibility that different countries, different school systems, or even different schools might have slightly different goals which could generate these different programmes.

Thus a possible definition for an effective school that might be acceptable to all parties would be:

> an effective school is one that develops and maintains a high quality educational programme designed to achieve both system-wide and locally identified goals. All students, regardless of their family or social background, experience both improvement across their school career and ultimate success in the achievement of those goals, based on appropriate external and school-based measuring techniques.

The model provides an opportunity to establish how comprehensively an individual school operates in terms of the effectiveness dimensions. A researcher can look at the range of goals undertaken by the school, can use various methods for determining the effectiveness of the school and can see whether the school is considered effective using the outcome or value-added approaches, or a combination of both.

Alternatively, the model can be used to review past research in the area. The goals researched, the method used for selecting the effective school in the study and the standards applied to the effectiveness criteria in the study can be mapped onto the framework. For instance, it would be possible to compare the dimensions of the seminal research undertaken by Edmonds (1979) and by Rutter *et al.* (1979), and to analyse the differences in the goals studied and the techniques they used.

Finally, the model could be used to establish areas of deficiency in the research as a whole. One common factor is that all of the research that has been conducted has looked at effectiveness in one of two ways, either from an outcome point of view or from a value-added point of view. If we plot the key literature onto two dimensions of the model, namely, the range of possible school goals and the techniques that can be utilised to identify whether a school is effective or not, it is possible to establish which areas of these two dimensions have been considered by the research. One possible outcome could be that represented by Figure 2.5.

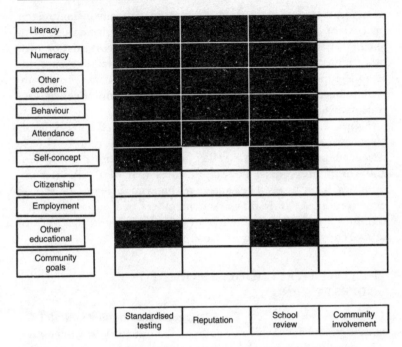

Figure 2.5 Possible areas of deficiency in the school effectiveness research

This view, which has been reconstructed using the goals researched and identification techniques used by various researchers from the USA (Weber 1971; Edmonds 1979), the UK (Rutter *et al.* 1979; Mortimore *et al.* 1988), Canada (Renihan and Renihan 1984; Stoll and Fink 1989) and Australia (Caldwell and Misko 1984; Mellor and Chapman 1984), indicates two possible gaps in the research. The first is the range of school goals that have been considered in relation to school effectiveness research. School goals relating to the skills required for employment, the skills and attitudes required for the development of citizenship and the possibility that the school needs to consider the goals of the whole school community, have been studied only minimally in the past.

Similar are the ways in which effective schools have been identified for further research. Schools have been chosen for their effectiveness on the basis of the comparative success of their students in various academic tests. That choice has been made by recognised experts in the field of education. In some instances, the process of school review and evaluation, and interviews with teachers, parents and students have been used in conjunction with other identification techniques. However, the literature does not seem to report instances where the views of the local school community have been used to *identify* schools as being effective, as a precursor to further study of those schools.

Figure 2.5 indicates that academic goals in effective schools have been well researched, but that further work is required in the non-academic areas, such as self-concept, citizenship, employment and community goals. It also indicates that local school communities have rarely been used to determine issues of school effectiveness. A study that asked members of local school communities for their views on school effectiveness and the goals of school could help to address those gaps.

THE EFFECTIVE SCHOOL: A MODEL FOR UNDERSTANDING

The argument provided above suggests that a single model for school effectiveness will not suffice. Two, at least, are necessary. Whereas the first model helps us to recognise a school as being effective or not, using certain criteria, the second model is necessary if we are to understand how that effective school came to be that way.

Processes in an effective school

A fourth dimension required for a more complete understanding of school effectiveness emerges when consideration is given to the way in which school goals are identified, resourced, implemented and evaluated, that is, the way in which the educational programme of the school is administered. In many respects, the goals of school have always been directed towards the students; but without an efficient and effective process for implementation of these goals many of them could be lost in practice. Having an efficient and effective set of processes within the school might be seen as the link between the theory of school effectiveness (recognising effective schools), discussed in previous paragraphs, and its practice (making schools effective).

The issue of school-based decision-making and management is becoming one focus of the school effectiveness literature, as political decisions in a number of countries such as the United States of America (Berman *et al.* 1988; Guthrie *et al.* 1990; Hixson 1991), Canada (La Roque 1983; Coleman 1987) the United Kingdom (Education Reform Act 1988; Holdaway 1990) and New Zealand (Caldwell *et al.* 1988; Minister of Education 1988), as well as Australia (Fordham 1983a), place more emphasis on local involvement in school management. As political decisions force those at the community level to be involved in educational management, researchers are starting to be more active in research that tests the effectiveness of school site management. Much of the school-based decision-making literature (Henderson, 1987; Henderson and Marburger, 1986; Henderson and Lezotte, 1988; Rosenholtz, 1989) suggested that if decisions relating to school people and situations were made at the school level then there was a better chance of having the right decisions made than there was if the decisions were made away from the school at a district, regional or state level. However, in many cases, the people who have to work with the new responsibilities implicit in localised control of schools are not fully consulted about what those responsibilities entail and, in other cases, the support systems that are necessary to make the new heightened level of local input work, are not provided. The political ramifications of the movement towards school effectiveness may well be just as complicated as the concept itself.

Murphy, Hallinger and Mesa argued that the central educational authority should establish what should be taught in schools through a basic core curriculum and content expectations and requirements (Murphy, Hallinger and Mesa 1985). However, Rosenholtz (1989), in her analysis of schools that were changing and schools that were not, concluded that the success of any strategy for enhancing student performance depends largely on the context in which schooling occurs, an inherent part of which involves the empowerment of the people at the school site.

A number of critical process issues emerge, each of which has an effect on the way in which the school actually operates. Each of these process issues interacts with the educational goals set for the school and with all of the other processes operating in the school to create the actual level of effectiveness experienced by that school. These internal arrangements will vary from school to school, but are in all schools to some extent, and can be general-ised into certain categories. The major school process categories that have an effect on the way the school actually operates are:

Leadership

The process of leadership will have an effect on all aspects of school performance, and can have many dimensions for con-sideration. These would include the leadership density in the school (whether one person, a few people or many different people or groups take leadership responsibility for one or more aspects of school operations) and the form of leadership being used by those in charge (authoritarian, hierarchical, democratic, task-oriented, people-oriented). Depending on each of the other processes in operation in the school, the type of leadership employed can have a positive or negative effect on the develop-ment of school effectiveness.

Decision-making

The form of decision-making and the people involved in the decision-making process will also affect achievement within the school. It is possible for decisions to be hierarchical, such as those made outside the school (by LEAs, districts, regions, educational authorities or governments) or made by a limited number within the school (principal and senior staff), or on a more democratic basis (by all staff, or by staff with some input from parents and students). No one form of decision-making can be considered as being superior to others, since all of them should be based on particular situations and circumstances. However, research indi-cates that decisions made democratically or locally have more chance of being implemented than those made hierarchically or at a distance from where they will be put into practice (Henderson 1988). The decision-making processes used will have an effect on the rest of the activities undertaken by the school, because it is this process that identifies not only the goals to be considered import-ant in the school, but also plans for development, strategies for implementation and allocation of resources to ensure that the goals are achieved.

Involvement of educational stakeholders

The involvement in the operations of the school of various stakeholders has become a recent concern for governments, education systems and researchers. Governments and educational systems in many parts of the world are encouraging local communities to be more responsible for the local school, both financially and in terms of the educational programme. Part of this process would include the types of school activity that involved the various groups, the encouragement and access given to those groups and the resources provided by the school or educational authority to enable them to become meaningfully involved.

Resource allocation

In any school, limited resources are supplied to enable school goals to be achieved. In many cases, additional resources must be found to enable the school minimally to achieve its goals. This difficulty means that decisions about the way in which school resources, both human, physical and financial, are allocated, and their actual allocation, become critical to the level of effectiveness of the school.

Curriculum implementation

The way in which the curriculum is implemented includes such issues as:

- the quality of the programme offered
- the teachers involved in teaching that programme
- the expectations held by the school community
- the motivation techniques developed and used by the school to achieve those expectations
- the amount of time allocated to various subjects or events
- the type of instruction used (whole class, groups, excursions)
- the way in which a student's progress through the programme is monitored.

It might also include issues such as the level of involvement by students in decisions about their own learning, the facilities offered by the school (such as specialist rooms and equipment) and the opportunities provided for teachers to ensure that the quality of teaching is enhanced.

School environment, climate and culture

The development of the school environment and the school culture is a complex process that relates to considerations of how various groups within the school interact with each other and other groups, how the school is seen by people within it, the physical and administrative arrangements of the school that enhance individual and collective progress, both academically and culturally, and the conditions under which each member of the school community enters the school. Students need to feel secure and positive about the school, teachers need to feel valued and be professionally enriched by their teaching, and parents and community members need to feel welcome and involved.

Communication

The way in which groups within the school communicate with each other is an important factor in how effective the school will be. Information could be open (to all, or most, people) or closed (restricted to a few people within the school). It could be one-way (from the principal to the staff or from the school to the parents) or two-way (with many people able to communicate and interact with others). This will automatically affect the way in which the school operates.

Since each of these will have an affect on each of the others simultaneously, as well as on the educational goals that are to be achieved, then the consideration of this area is far more complex than the simple recognition of whether a school is seen to be effective. The analogy that might be drawn here is the difference between knowing something and understanding it.

As such, the way in which leadership operates within the school will have an effect on the other six processes identified and on the goals that the school will have. A change in the leadership style will bring about a change (perhaps over time) in all of the others too. The same can be said for each of the other processes identified. Each will affect the operations of all the others. This means that every school must be considered as a unique combination of its processes, resources and goals. From this perspective, it makes little sense to argue that if one school tries to emulate the characteristics of another, more effective school, then it can become as

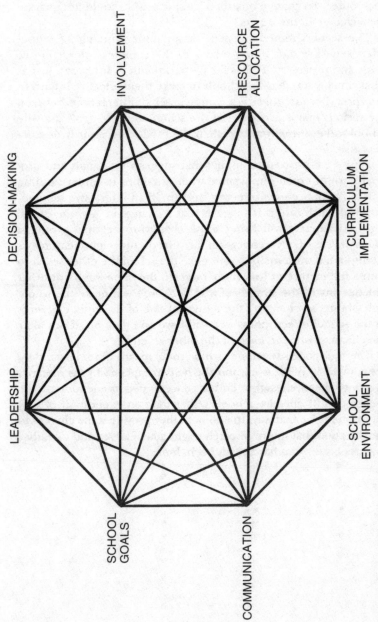

Figure 2.6 A model for understanding effective schools

effective as that school, because each school will have a different combination of resources, goals and processes that interact with each other. To change one set of characteristics could not guarantee a change in the others.

The second model needed for an understanding of school effectiveness is that which relates to the complex interaction of goals and processes. This is far more difficult to interpret, just as what actually happens in schools to make them effective is hard to interpret. Because there is a complex web of interactions between the various major processes of the school and the goals that the school will eventually adopt, then the model, necessarily, is complex also.

Figure 2.6 proposes a model that suggests that goals and processes are of equal importance when it comes to understanding how a school becomes effective, and are in an interactive relationship with each other. It suggests that a change in any one of the eight parameters will bring some change to all of the others. Alternatively, if an explication of one of the eight features is attempted, it must include reference to each of the other seven to gain a full picture of how it operates. In the same way an ant that touches any of the strands of a spider's web will make the whole web vibrate, so changing the nature of one of the eight elements in the school effectiveness web will have an effect on, if not alter the characteristics of, each of the other seven.

The two models together provide some means of understanding the complexity of the issue, and also help to explain why the research in school effectiveness thus far has concentrated its attention on the recognition of effective schools rather than an explication of how they came to be that way. In addition, they provide some clues as to the direction that future research might take if it is to add to, rather than replicate, what has already been done.

Chapter 3

Community perceptions of effective schools

An effective school can be defined as such to the extent that there is congruence between its objectives and achievements. In other words it is effective to the extent that it accomplishes what it sets out to do.

(Madaus *et al.* 1980: 22).

Many governments have emphasised their support for a variety of approaches designed to make schools more effective. Some have moved towards more localised control of school decision-making and school management, others have implemented much tighter quality control over the level of autonomy individual schools have, some have seemed to do both simultaneously. The factor that is common to all, however, is that the decisions being made about these moves will have an effect on the people working at the school site level.

The issues of where decisions about school effectiveness are made, of the levels of accountability to local communities and to the wider system, and the system support for the decisions made at the school site level have not yet been fully addressed. In many cases the people who have to work with the new responsibilities implicit in localised control of schools have not been fully consulted about what those responsibilities entailed, and in other cases the support systems that were necessary to make the new heightened level of local input work have not been provided. In other words, the people who were expected to implement the decisions being made at state or regional level, had little or no input into the outcome of those decisions and little or no support from the education authority to ensure that those new responsibilities were carried out properly.

A review of the school effectiveness literature, as described in previous chapters, established that the definition of 'school effectiveness', the concept upon which a lot of this world-wide activity is based, has been shaped, not by the people who are now being asked to implement the concept, but by researchers and bureaucrats who are at least one step, and in some cases many more, away from the situation where the concept is expected to be turned into practice. It also established that different countries, and different people within the same country, are unable to agree on any single definition of what constitutes an effective school.

THE STUDY

Since 1975, every government school in the state of Victoria has been governed by a school council. The council, made up of teachers, parents, students and co-opted community members has been responsible for many of the major decisions related to the operation of the school. Although teacher employment and teacher salaries are controlled at the state level, school councils have responsibility for many other decisions related to school operations. These include:

- proper expenditure of other money that came into the school, through government grants or fund-raising
- employment of ancillary staff, such as cleaners, secretaries and community education staff
- building and ground maintenance
- making recommendations related to changes to school buildings
- determination of the educational policies of the school, within guidelines laid down by the state.

In many respects school councils have actually managed schools from the local level.

A major study was undertaken in Australia in 1990–1 to establish an understanding of what school effectiveness meant and included from the point of view of the people involved in the implementation of this concept at the local level within the state of Victoria. It gave the people who are involved with the implementation of the effective school concepts – principals, teachers, school councillors, parents and students – an opportunity to identify their perspective of what an effective school was and what elements needed to be present before they were prepared to call a school effective.

The purpose of the study was to determine the relationship, if any, between the perceptions of principals, school councillors, teachers, parents and students in government schools in two different regions of the Victorian Ministry of Education towards issues related to the effectiveness of schools. The variables considered in the study were:

- perceptions of the respondents in relation to possible roles of an effective school
- perceptions of the respondents in relation to important elements contributing to the effectiveness of a school
- perceptions of the respondents in relation to the effectiveness of their own school.

The state of Victoria, the central focus of the research, had more than half a million students and over fifty thousand teachers in more than two thousand government schools and a little over two hundred thousand additional students in non-government schools. The state was regionalised into eight regions with student populations as low as 25,000 in the smaller country regions ranging to over 125,000 in the largest metropolitan region. The state budget for education occupied just over one quarter of the total budget for the state.

The study was conducted in eighty-one schools in two distinct metropolitan regions of the city of Melbourne. One region, the Southern Region, was characterised by a middle-class and professional population, whereas the other, the Western Region, was characterised by a more working-class and generally lesser educated population. In each region primary schools and secondary schools within the state government education system agreed to take part. For each school, the principal, three school councillors, three teachers not on the school council, three parents not on the school council and (in secondary schools only) three students were asked to respond to the survey instrument. The study sought to collect and analyse the responses of principals, school councillors, teachers, parents and students to three major questions:

- can we identify a major role for an effective school?
- are there elements of school operations that will help schools become more effective?
- do people who work at the school level perceive their school to be effective?

The survey population

Eighty-one schools were involved in the study, forty-two from the Southern Metropolitan Region and thirty-nine from the Western Metropolitan Region. A total of 583 questionnaires were returned. In all 417 people from the primary schools and 166 from secondary schools responded. The demographic characteristics of the sample population are identified in Table 3.1.

Table 3.1 The sample population

Characteristic	Sth Met. Region		West Met. Region		Total	
	No.	%	No.	%	No.	%
School type						
Primary	238	71.9	179	71.0	417	71.5
Secondary	93	28.1	73	28.9	166	28.5
School location						
Urban	279	84.8	211	83.7	490	84.3
Rural	50	15.2	41	16.3	91	15.7
Number on roll						
Under 50	14	4.2	17	6.7	31	5.3
Between 51 and 150	8	2.4	37	14.7	45	7.7
Between 151 and 400	127	38.5	126	50.0	253	43.5
Between 401 and 800	127	38.5	51	20.2	178	30.6
Over 801	54	16.3	21	8.3	75	12.9
Gender						
Male	135	41.0	87	34.5	222	38.2
Female	194	59.0	165	65.5	359	61.8
Age						
Under 20	23	7.0	28	11.1	51	8.7
Between 21 and 30	19	5.7	45	17.9	64	11.0

Between 31 and 40	136	41.1	103	40.9	239	41.0
Between 41 and 50	124	37.5	67	26.6	191	32.8
Over 51	29	8.8	9	3.6	38	6.5
Ethnic background						
Australian	288	87.3	219	86.9	507	87.1
Other English Sp.	29	8.8	18	7.1	47	8.1
Non-English (Europe)	13	3.9	13	5.2	26	4.5
Non-English (Asia)	0	0.0	1	0.4	1	0.2
Other non-English	0	0.0	1	0.4	1	0.2
Position in school						
Principal	37	11.2	31	12.3	68	11.7
School councillor	87	26.3	69	27.6	156	26.9
Teacher	87	26.3	70	27.8	157	26.9
Parent	96	29.0	53	21.2	149	25.6
Student	24	7.3	29	11.6	53	9.1

WHAT IS THE ROLE OF AN EFFECTIVE SCHOOL?

For this section of the survey, respondents were given first the opportunity to indicate their level of agreement with fourteen statements that listed various roles that might be associated with effective schools and then were asked to identify what they considered to be the major role of an effective school.

The tasks of an effective school

Respondents generally were in agreement with all fourteen of the statements listed in the questionnaire, as indicated in Table 3.2, where a score of one equalled strong agreement, two equalled agreement, three equalled an uncertain response, four disagreement and five strong disagreement.

Table 3.2 Mean scores for the roles of an effective school

School role	Sth Met. Reg.	West Met. Reg.	All
1 An effective school will provide students with a good understanding of basic academic skills.	1.294	1.401	1.343
2 An effective school will provide students with the skills necessary to become employed.	1.633	1.737	1.681
3 An effective school will provide students with the opportunity to develop leadership skills.	1.839	1.913	1.877
4 An effective school will provide students with a caring and supportive environment.	1.345	1.405	1.375
5 An effective school will provide students with the skills necessary to become a productive and useful citizen.	1.480	1.560	1.511
6 An effective school will provide students with the attitudes and skills necessary to develop a healthy understanding of themselves and others.	1.426	1.476	1.453
7 An effective school will provide students with a balanced curriculum that encourages a wide range of learning experiences.	1.263	1.321	1.292
8 An effective school will provide students with the opportunity to develop a value system that reflects the major values of our society.	1.967	1.992	1.984
9 An effective school will provide students with teachers who act as role models for the development of community values and habits.	1.970	1.996	1.984
10 An effective school will provide students with an opportunity to be involved in the decision-making processes within the school.	2.067	1.865	1.984

11	An effective school will use a range of assessment strategies to identify the student's level of achievement and also any learning difficulties that may diminish the student's learning potential.	1.408	1.478	1.442
12	An effective school will provide parents with regular communications about their child's achievements.	1.341	1.466	1.404
13	An effective school will provide parents with an opportunity to be involved in the development of school policies and processes.	1.665	1.610	1.643
14	An effective school will provide parents with the understanding that the school is responding to the needs of the local community.	1.876	1.817	1.851

An analysis of the statements on a regional basis using an analysis of the variance from the mean (ANOVA) showed that there were statistically significant differences in the responses between regions for the sample as a whole school group only for statements 1 (academic), 10 (student involvement) and 12 (communication). Respondents in the Southern Region were significantly more positive about statement 1, *an effective school will provide students with a good understanding of basic academic skills* (0.05 level of significance) and statement 12, *an effective school will provide parents with regular communications about their children's achievement* (0.01 level of significance). On the other hand, respondents in the Western Region were significantly more positive about statement 10, *an effective school will provide students with an opportunity to be involved in the decision-making processes within the school* (0.01 level of significance).

There were significant differences in the responses within the five groups for all of the statements except 11, *an effective school will use a range of assessment strategies to identify the students' level of achievement and also any learning difficulties that may diminish the students' learning potential.* Principals were most strongly in favour of eleven of the fourteen statements, with the only statements more strongly supported by other groups being statement 2, *an effective school will provide students with the skills necessary to become employed* (by all other groups), statement 8, *an effective school will provide students with the opportunity to develop a value system that reflects the major values of our society* (by parents), and statement 10, *an effective school will provide students with an opportunity to be involved in the decision-making processes within the school* (by teachers, parents and students).

On the other hand, students were least positive for twelve of the fourteen statements with the only statements less strongly supported by other groups being statement 2, *an effective school will provide students with the skills necessary to become employed* (by principals) and statement 10, *an effective school will provide students with an opportunity to be involved in the decision-making processes within the school* (by all other groups). The principal group and student group were at opposite extremes in eleven of the fourteen statements and either one or both groups were in one of the extreme positions (most positive or most negative) for all fourteen statements.

For the most part, the strong support for the majority of the statements by principals, and the weak support by students, has created a situation where the results looked more significant than they are. For the other three groups only a few differences emerged. Teachers' attitudes differed significantly from school councillors for statement 5, *an effective school will provide students with the skills necessary to become a productive and useful citizen,* from parents for statement 2, *an effective school will provide students with the skills necessary to become employed* and from both school councillors and parents for statements 12, *an effective school will provide parents with regular communications about their children's achievements* and 13, *an effective school will provide parents with an opportunity to be involved in the development of school policies and processes.* Parents and school councillors only differed significantly on statement 6, *an effective school will provide students with the attitudes and skills necessary to develop a healthy understanding of themselves and others.* The overall result has left principals and students as the two extreme groups, with school councillors, teachers and parents having fairly similar and more conservative views.

The major task of an effective school

In the second part of this survey, respondents were asked to indicate what they considered to be the major role of an effective school. They were given the opportunity to select from the following list:

- the major role of an effective school is to provide a comprehensive understanding of the basic academic skills;
- the major role of an effective school is to provide students with the skills necessary for future employment;
- the major role of an effective school is to provide society with productive citizens;
- the major role of an effective school is to provide students with a healthy self-concept;
- the major role of an effective school is to develop a value system that reflects the spiritual nature of man;
- the major role of an effective school is to respond to the educational needs of its local community.

Respondents were given the opportunity to add others if they did not agree with any of the six listed. When asked to choose which of six alternatives they considered to be the *major* role of an effective school respondents provided the result contained in Table 3.3.

Table 3.3 Percentage responses for the major role of an effective school

Role	%
Academic	22.9
Citizenship	21.3
Other	20.8
Self-concept	16.9
Employment	10.3
Community	6.9
Spiritual	0.9

'Other' consisted of a total of 121 responses. Of these, 28 indicated that all six roles were equally important, 46 indicated between two and five of the roles, and 47 indicated a role not previously mentioned. These could be categorised into *a wide range of learning experiences* (7 responses); *the development of the student's full potential* (12); *the skills necessary for the future* (18) and a *commitment to learning and relearning* (10).

This result might be considered somewhat surprising given the current climate for education. Politicians, employers and some educators have been united in their concern for standards in education, although each of the groups identifies different reasons for their concern. From the federal government we have seen statements to the effect that certain types of learning must occur if Australia is to be 'the clever country' and compete with many of the economic and industrial giants on the world stage. From employers, we have had the concern expressed over many years that standards have been dropping and that the people who are seeking employment are often neither literate nor numerate. Finally, some educators have expressed concern that recent changes to the senior curriculum in Victoria would lead to a diminution of standards and an inability to judge which candidates would be capable of continuing their studies to a higher level.

Statistically, the order of the rankings was highly correlated between school councillors in each of the regions, between teachers in each of the regions and between school councillors and parents for the whole sample. However, some interesting differences emerged when one considered the results based on primary and secondary schools in each of the regions as indicated in Table 3.4. The table indicates that the responses from primary and secondary schools from both regions are roughly the same for the citizenship, self-concept, spiritual, community and other alternatives. However, substantial differences occur for the academic and vocational dimensions. It indicates that primary school respondents of both regions are much more concerned about the academic dimension (at the expense of the vocational dimension) whereas for secondary schools the academic focus was lessened and the employment focus was increased. However, it also indicates that respondents in the Southern Region placed a much greater emphasis on the academic dimension at both primary and secondary levels than did respondents from the Western Region, whereas respondents in the Western Region placed a much greater emphasis on a balanced view (as characterised by 'other') at the primary level and on the vocational dimension at secondary level than did respondents from the Southern Region. This result indicated that there were regional differences in views of what the major roles of an effective school were. The Southern Region, with its more middle-class and professionally educated population seemed to see the role of school as preparing children for further education, whereas the Western Region, with its working-class and generally lesser educated population, seemed to see school as a preparation for the workforce.

Table 3.4 The major role of an effective school: responses from primary (K-6) and secondary (7-12) schools

		Academic	Employment	Citizenship	Self-concept	Spiritual	Community	Other
PRIMARY	SOUTH							
	Principals	23.3	0	23.3	26.7	0	6.7	20.0
	School councillors	31.9	6.9	20.8	11.1	2.8	5.6	20.8
	Teachers	18.8	2.9	23.2	29.0	0	7.2	18.8
	Parents	33.3	18.2	18.2	10.6	0	3.0	16.7
	All people	27.7	8.0	21.0	18.1	0.8	5.5	18.9
	WEST							
	Principals	8.0	0	36.0	12.0	4.0	4.0	36.6
	School councillors	23.3	6.7	18.3	20.0	0	8.3	23.3
	Teachers	18.4	2.0	30.6	20.4	2.0	8.1	18.4
	Parents	34.9	13.9	2.3	14.0	2.3	7.0	25.6
	All people	22.4	6.7	20.2	17.4	1.7	7.3	24.2
	All primary schools	25.5	7.5	20.3	17.8	1.2	6.3	21.2
SECONDARY	SOUTH							
	Principals	14.3	0	14.3	14.3	0	0	57.1
	School councillors	13.3	6.7	40.0	0	0	13.3	26.7
	Teachers	31.3	0	19.0	25.0	0	6.3	18.8
	Parents	23.3	6.7	16.7	16.7	0	13.3	23.3
	Students	16.7	37.5	12.5	8.3	0	8.3	16.7
	All people	19.4	12.9	21.5	12.9	0	9.7	23.7
	WEST							
	Principals	33.3	0	33.3	0	0	16.7	16.7
	School councillors	33.3	11.1	11.1	22.2	0	0	22.2
	Teachers	5.0	15.0	35.0	24.0	0	5.0	15.0
	Parents	0	50.0	10.0	20.0	0	0	20.0
	Students	10.7	32.0	25.0	10.7	0	10.7	10.7
	All people	12.5	23.6	25.0	16.7	0	6.9	15.3
	All secondary schools	16.4	17.6	23.0	14.6	0	8.5	20.0

The answers to two key questions related to the role of an effective school were sought: what tasks should an effective school undertake? What is the major role of an effective school? The Australian study found that people at the school level have a wide range of goals for schools, some of which are academic, and others which go far beyond the academic, all of which need to be addressed if the school is to be seen as effective. The findings of the study have confirmed that the role of the effective school is related to the success of all the children in the school, regardless of their background, but has removed what might be considered an artificial nexus between academic performance and school effectiveness. This illustrates the claim that school effectiveness is an 'essentially contested concept' (Chapman 1992) in which school effectiveness only has a direct relationship to academic performance if a particular group or agency, within a particular educational context, determines it to be so. It is likely that academic development will be one of a number of goals determined by the state or the education system, but others may be considered important by local school communities. If there are state-determined goals for all children, then the people at the school level need to work to have all children achieve these goals. If there are additional goals determined by the school community, these are equally important objectives, and all children should have equal chances to achieve these objectives as well, if the school is to be seen to be effective.

The study showed that to concentrate on the academic dimension alone, or any other single dimension of the curriculum, was not acceptable to the respondents in the sample. It is, in some way, short-changing both the individual learner and the society as a whole. If we accept that education plays the dual role of providing individuals with the skills they need to operate within the society in which they live and passing on the traditions and values of that society from one generation to the next, then the role of school and, necessarily, of school curricula, must change as the nature of society and the requirements of individuals change. A single-minded concentration on certain aspects of the curriculum would do nothing to enhance that development. A description of school effectiveness that considered the changing role of school as society itself changes would address the concerns of Kerensky (1989) and Minzey (1981) who argued that schools were unable to fully address the range of social changes that were impinging upon them because the systemic decision-makers tried to reduce new concepts into 'pre-existing forms and perceptions' (Kerensky 1989: 17). They both argued that, whereas the tendency was to put new ideas into old boxes, totally new frameworks were required to address these new concerns and social changes.

In general, the study supports the findings of previous Australian studies such as those by Dunmall (1980), Bartolotta and Finn (1980), Cotter (1981), and Aglinskas *et al.* (1988) who found that the academic, citizenship and personal development dimensions of a child's development all received a high priority from local communities. As the discussions with the case study schools indicated, all were receiving significant attention at the school level. In addition, the broad view of school goals which has resulted from this study provided a similar result to that of the recent study conducted in New South Wales (Educare News, 1991), where over one thousand parents in thirty-four Catholic schools in Sydney's eastern suburbs responded to the survey conducted by the Sydney Catholic Education Office and indicated that they would prefer their child to be 'self-confident', 'happy', 'well-balanced' and 'self-disciplined', rather than the 'smartest kid in the class', 'good at sport' or 'competitive'.

The high rating for the role which indicated the development of a healthy self-concept in the child was an indication that schools have a responsibility to the individual as well as to society. In the past, schools have been charged with passing on the information necessary for the smooth induction of the child into adult life. The academic, employment and, to a lesser extent, citizenship areas typified the traditional view of what schools ought to be doing. The comparatively high level of support for the personal development element of schooling, which had previously been seen to be largely the responsibility of the home – as was the spiritual dimension, which was still seen in this study as the responsibility of the home – meant that there has been a shift in the perception of the role of the school.

Overall, the results of the study reinforce the direction that other research into school effectiveness is taking. The original definitions of school effectiveness, which were based solely on an outcome approach to academic subjects, have gradually been extended to include a range of other school goals as well. The study suggests that school effectiveness should include all school goals within its boundaries, and may also include goals that consider the development of the local community as well. From this point of view the current study reinforces the direction of recent research and suggests that an even broader perspective be considered.

There is overwhelming evidence from the responses to the questionnaire that there is identifiably no single major role for an effective school. Questions related to the roles of an effective school provided a clear indication that the academic role of the school, although still seen as being very important, can now only be interpreted as one of a number of important roles that the school needs to undertake simultaneously. Although there were some regional differences that emerged from the data, these differences were a matter of emphasis rather than of one region negating the views of the other.

THE ELEMENTS OF AN EFFECTIVE SCHOOL

In this section of the questionnaire, respondents were asked first to indicate which of eighteen selected elements, collected from the school effectiveness literature which emanated from the United States, the United Kingdom, Canada and Australia, they considered to be important elements in the development of effective schools. Then they were asked to indicate which of the elements they had identified they considered to be most important.

What makes a school effective?

The results of the question asking respondents to identify which of the eighteen listed elements they considered important indicates four levels of support. The first group of elements (A) are those that received support from more than 90 per cent of the respondents; the second (B) received more than 80 but less than 90 per cent support; the third (C) received more than 70 but less than 80 per cent support. These are shown in Table 3.5. Only one element fell into the fourth level, receiving less than 70 per cent support from all respondents: element 14, *School council involvement in the selection of senior staff* with a mean attitude score of 0.664.

The results indicated that most people in the school community see the majority of the elements listed as being important. Almost all those in the sample indicated that they felt that dedicated and qualified staff were an important component in the development of school effectiveness, closely followed by the early identification of children's learning difficulties, positive home–school relations,

Table 3.5 Elements considered to make an important contribution to the development of an effective school

Element number	Description	Mean score
	Group A	
3	Dedicated and qualified staff	0.979
9	Early identification of learning difficulties	0.919
12	Home–school relations	0.914
17	Positive motivational strategies	0.905
10	Safe and orderly environment	0.900
	Group B	
1	Clear school purpose (policy)	0.895
8	Monitoring student progress	0.876
15	Teachers take responsibility for and are involved in planning	0.869
11	Positive school climate	0.854
5	High expectations	0.832
	Group C	
16	The support of the responsible education authority	0.773
2	Academic and administrative leadership	0.771
4	Staff development	0.766
7	Time on task	0.765
13	School-based decision-making	0.758
6	Academic focus on the curriculum	0.727
18	Opportunities for student involvement and responsibility	0.720
	Group D	
14	School council involvement in the selection of senior staff	0.664

positive motivational strategies and a safe and orderly environment. Perhaps the most surprising result for this part of the survey was the comparatively low score for academic and administrative leadership, which was only seen to be important by 77 per cent of the sample. Without adequate leadership, other elements such as staff dedication, the school environment, the school policies and the school climate, would be difficult to maintain, yet these all received more support than did leadership.

In general terms, once again, principals and students were at opposite poles, with principals being the most positive respondents to all but five of the eighteen elements, and students being the least positive respondents to all but five of the eighteen elements. Teachers were the most positive group towards element 6, *academic focus on the curriculum* and element 10, *safe and orderly environment*, parents were the most positive group towards element 7, *time on task* and element 9, *early identification of learning difficulties*, and students were the most positive group towards element 18, *opportunities for student involvement and responsibility*.

On the other hand principals were the least positive group for element 9, *early identification of learning difficulties*, school councillors were the least positive group for element 8, *monitoring student progress*, teachers were the least positive group for element 18, *opportunities for student involvement and responsibility*, and parents were the least positive group for element 3, *dedicated and qualified staff* and element 10, *safe and orderly environment*.

This result indicates that overall, principals were more certain about the importance of the eighteen elements than were school councillors, teachers and parents, who were generally grouped together, and that these three groups were all more positive about the importance of the elements than were students.

Elements critical to school effectiveness

Respondents were asked to put in order which of the eighteen were their five most important elements. These were then analysed on the basis of their perceived level of importance to give each a numerical score. The results are contained in Table 3.6. It provides a clear indication of the types of elements that the sample saw as the most important issues in school development. *Dedicated and qualified staff* scored more than the next two categories put together, so it could be argued that the school community saw this element as, by far, the most critical factor for the development of the effective school. The table has been divided into three sections which identify the top, middle and bottom thirds in terms of what people in the sample perceived to be important.

Table 3.6 Rankings of the elements of effective schools

Ranking	Element number	Description	Score
1	3	Dedicated and qualified staff	1737
2	1	Clear school purpose (policy)	965
3	2	Academic and administrative leadership	697
4	17	Positive motivational strategies	668
5	10	Safe and orderly environment	606
6	11	Positive school climate	601
7	9	Early identification of learning difficulties	547
8	5	High expectations	508
9	12	Home–school relations	408
10	8	Monitoring student progress	376
11	7	Time on task	328
12	6	Academic focus on the curriculum	247
13	4	Staff development	229
14	15	Teachers take responsibility for and are involved in planning	213
15	13	School-based decision-making	184
16	16	The support of the responsible education authority	162
17	18	Opportunities for student involvement and responsibility	154
18	14	School council involvement in the selection of senior staff	76

The elements could been categorised into four groups: school staff, total school environment, instructional procedures and organisational procedures of the school and school system, and the results indicate that the major elements in the development of an effective school relate quite closely to these groupings. The majority of the elements that are in the top third of the table are elements that are contained in either the school staff or the total school environment categories. The only exception is *positive motivational strategies*, which is the only element from the instructional procedures category that has made it into the top third. All other elements that are in the instructional procedures category are contained within the second third of the table together with *home–school relations* which is part of the total school environment. Those elements that were in the bottom third of the table contain all five of the elements that are in the organisational procedures of the school and school system category together with *staff development* from the school staff category.

This result gives a clear indication that the sample as a whole has considered that elements contained within the school staff category, together with the elements contained within the school environment category are the most critical features for the development of the effective school. Only after these have been considered do the elements contained within the instructional procedures category emerge. Finally, those elements that are contained within the organisational procedures category are seen to be the least important elements in the development of the effective school. This result seems to indicate that a school can be effective if the people involved and the environment created are working well, and can do so despite what might be considered as ineffective or unsupportive organisational processes operating either at the school or the school system level.

Statistically, there was a high level of correlation for all groups in both regions, and between groups except for principals and students and school councillors and students across the whole sample. Statistically significant results were found for principals and all other groups except students, and between school councillors and all other groups except students. Teachers and parents showed significant correlations with all other groups and the results of the analysis for students and principals and students and school councillors were positive, but not significant.

Overall, two major groups of factors emerged as being critical to the perception that a school was effective. The first group was the people factor, the leadership shown in the school, the level of dedication shown by, and the qualifications held by, the teachers and the level of interactions they had with parents and students, on the one hand, and other school staff on the other. The second group considered the processes developed by the school to ensure that it operated smoothly. These included establishing clear school policies, developing a safe learning environment and a positive climate and using strong motivation techniques to influence student learning. New elements, communication and teamwork, were identified by the sample as being important contributors to the development of effective schools. Each of these elements was seen to be critical to the development of the school and each warrants further consideration from the perspective of further research in the field, and the development of future policies and practices that will further improve effectiveness at the school level.

HOW EFFECTIVE IS YOUR SCHOOL?

Respondents were asked to make a perceived judgement about the effectiveness of their own school in comparison to what they knew about other schools. The alternatives were:

- my school would be among the most effective schools in the state
- my school would be more effective than most schools in the state
- my school would be about as effective as other schools in the state
- my school would be less effective than most other schools in the state
- my school would be among the least effective schools in the state.

The response to this question is contained in Table 3.7. The results provide a clear indication that schools were seen by their communities as being more effective rather than less effective. In all, 19.3 per cent saw their schools as being among the most effective in the state, 43.8 per cent saw their schools as being more effective than most schools in the state, 34.6 per cent saw their schools as being about as effective as other schools in the state. Only 1.8 per cent indicated their schools were less effective than most other schools in the state and 0.5 per cent indicated their schools were among the least effective schools in the state.

That 63.1 per cent of the respondents believed that their schools were more effective than other schools gives a clear indication that the respondents were happy with the way their schools were performing. It was likely that many of the student, parent or school councillor groups were not in a good position to make a

Table 3.7 Percentage analysis of responses to the question about 'the effectiveness of my school'

	Southern Region					Western Region					All schools					Total group
	Prin-cipal	S. coun.	Tchrs	Parents	Stud-ents	Prin-cipal	S. coun.	Tchrs	Parents	Stud-ents	Prin-cipal	S. coun.	Tchrs	Parents	Stud-ents	
My school would be among the most effective schools in the state.	21.6	28.2	10.7	26.3	33.3	6.7	18.5	9.2	14.3	26.9	14.9	24.0	10.1	22.2	30.0	19.3
My school would be more effective than most schools in the state.	59.5	47.1	48.8	37.9	25.0	53.3	41.5	46.2	40.8	26.9	56.7	44.7	47.7	38.9	26.0	43.8
My school would be about as effective as other schools in the state.	0	23.5	35.7	34.7	41.7	0	40.0	43.1	38.8	34.6	0	30.7	38.9	36.1	38.0	34.6
My school would be less effective than most schools in the state.	18.9	0	4.8	1.1	0	40.0	0	1.5	4.1	7.7	28.4	0	3.4	2.1	4.0	1.8
My school would be among the least effective schools in the state.	0	1.2	0	0	0	0	0	0	2.0	3.8	0	0.7	0	0.7	2.0	0.5

judgement about other schools, since their current school was either the only one, or one of a few, that they had experienced. In this situation, one would expect their response to be aligned to their perception of other schools provided by the media or from discussions with other parents. However, for this group of people, the response could be said to be, at least, a statement of support for their current school, what it does and the people who work within it.

There was a significant difference between the responses from the Southern and Western Regions. People who were involved with schools in the Southern Region saw those schools as being more effective than did the people who were involved with schools in the Western Region.

School councillors were the most positive group when it came to perceiving that their school was effective, followed in order by principals, parents and students, with teachers expressing the least positive views about their schools. It is logical that school councillors and principals would be positive about their school, as they were the ones in the best position to determine the direction and outcomes of the school. To have a substantial number thinking their school was not effective would be, in some ways, an indictment of the decisions and methodologies that they had used. However, whereas none of the school councillors felt that their school was any less effective than other schools, more than one quarter of the principals did. In the Western Region this percentage was 40 per cent. However, reasons were provided for their response. Many of the 28.4 per cent of principals who indicated that their schools were less effective than other schools also indicated that they were new to the school and had not had enough time to undo some of the ineffective practices. However, the overall attitude, even from this group, was one of optimism and the feeling that the schools would be even better in the future than they were now.

The differences between school councillors and principals on the one hand and parents and teachers on the other may be explained by the relative involvement in decision-making of the groups. With principals and school councillors heavily involved in decision-making about the school, they would be more aware of the whole school operation, and therefore be more supportive on a wide front. Parents may have specific concerns for their child and their view of the school may reflect how their child is doing; and teachers may have specific classroom and related administrative interests without understanding the wider ranging issues of the school. With both of these groups having more specific interests, it was likely that they would be more conservative about their views of the school as a whole. The result of the current study contrasted with earlier claims such as the Gallup Poll finding of 1985 where over 50 per cent of respondents thought that the teaching programmes of the day were inadequate. The discrepancy, addressed by Cirone (1990), suggested that the public perception of schools in general and of the school 'my' child attends, differs in other countries as well and identified a problem for the public perception of schools.

Whereas those in the community who are not involved with regular school activities may be under the impression that schools have not changed all that much since they went to school, and be concerned about the lack of ability of current school graduates, people who have regular interaction with schools are much less condemning. They realise that the task of schools today, and perhaps increasingly in the future, is not only thankless, but almost impossible. Parents who are actively involved at the school level, 'see first-hand the miracles that occur in their own schools with their own children' (Cirone 1990), and are grateful and supportive of the teachers and the school for what they are doing for their children.

The study found that people who are currently working at the school level believed that there is a need for a time of consolidation. Schools have had to respond to, and have responded to, immense social, cultural and political pressures which have often demanded conflicting action. The study has shown that schools have changed their orientation and their strategies for achieving their goals, and that these changes have been acceptable to the communities they serve. However, political decisions about education continue to destabilise what happens in schools. Within six months of winning the 1992 election, the Victorian government implemented massive changes. There has been a significant budget cut, with the closing of some schools and a considerable lessening of the teaching force, with more of the same promised over the next few years. The increasing internal and external pressures created by the consistent changes of the past two decades, together with an increasingly uncertain future, has created increased stress for the principals and teachers who were left. Teaching is no longer the same task as it was when the current generation of parents went to school, and teachers are now required to have different skills from those required of teachers of that generation. There is now a justification for a period of consolidation of the developments made in those two decades. Part of that justification is that staff of schools, and parents, are having difficulty with, and are struggling to cope with, managing the current pace of change.

This study found that people in schools have responded to the social changes that have occurred and are doing something about them, despite the various barriers placed in their way. Schools are achieving their goals despite budget cuts and increased demands and in doing so are fulfilling their obligations to their communities. The local communities, in turn, have supported schools and school staff for doing so.

CONCLUSIONS

Overall the survey results indicated that:

- there was perceived to be no dominant role for an effective school but rather a wide ranging set of experiences that encompassed the academic, citizenship and personal development dimensions;
- issues related to the nature of the staff and to school-wide planning and administration were seen as being more important in the development of the effective school than were the specifics of what went on in the classroom or the overall organisation of the system;
- schools were seen by the people who work in them as being effective. If quality is an issue in Victorian schools, then it was not seen as being a negative in the sample schools.

Perhaps the most significant result in the research was the support for the element called *dedicated and qualified staff* which was identified as by far the most important element to contribute to school effectiveness. This result provided an even stronger impression that it is the people within the school and the way in which they work together, that makes a school effective, rather than any specific programme or direction that occurs within it. This impression was supported further when two new elements, which had not been identified in the survey instrument, were listed by respondents as key elements in school effectiveness. The first was communication and the second was described in various ways but could be categorised as teamwork. Both of these elements reinforce the essential human characteristics of the effective school, characteristics that do not easily lend themselves to the types of evaluations that have characterised school effectiveness in the past.

Chapter 4

Effective schools: the case studies

Personally, I don't think the school could get any better. The staff's good, the principal's great. They're helpful. They tell you to come up at any time at all. I don't think you could get any better than that.

(Parent, school D, 1990)

THE PURPOSE OF THE CASE STUDIES

The purpose of the case study exercise was to develop a better understanding of the results that had been obtained by the quantitative data. Some of the results had provided a perspective that differed from that found in previous research. It was necessary to explore this perspective to establish why the results of the current study differed from those that preceded it. Interviews conducted at the case study schools gave the study a richness that the quantitative data themselves could not provide.

CASE STUDIES

In Victoria, three primary schools and two secondary schools were visited as part of the original study. Subsequently, a primary school in Birmingham, England was added to the case study list to establish whether the attitudes that emerged in Australia were comparable with those in the United Kingdom.

School A

School A was a large secondary school in the Southern Metropolitan Region. One of the largest secondary schools in the state, it had 1,313 students and 109 teaching staff. The school had two campuses located diagonally opposite each other. The senior school and administration building was located on one campus and the junior school and library facilities were located on the other. A large recreation area complete with playing fields and hall space were in close proximity to the school. The principal had been at the school for three years. The school had developed strong community support, particularly in the last three years, but had recently suffered from a number of acts of vandalism, which had had a bad effect on the range of facilities and equipment to which the school had access. The school had developed a strong community programme including an exchange programme that had operated in nine different countries and included a sister school in Japan. The success rate of the school was good, with around 90 per cent of year twelve students passing the year twelve completion certificate.

School B

School B was a secondary school in a satellite city in the Western Metropolitan Region. It had 1,117 students and eighty-seven academic staff. The school was gradually decreasing in numbers as new schools in the area had taken some of the students. At the time of the interview, the principal of the school was on exchange in the United States, and the acting principal was a person who had been in the school for many years. The school placed high emphasis on student welfare because there was an isolation brought about by being in a satellite city. Twenty five per cent of the families were British migrants, and were nuclear families. These families looked to the school for guidance in a variety of areas, including how to handle children. A majority of people commuted to work in Melbourne, and although unemployment was similar to other areas of Melbourne, the current economic downturn had led to a number of families where one or both parents had recently lost their jobs. The school had responded by keeping school fees at the previous year's level. Success at the school was judged partially by academic success, with year twelve completion certificate passes ranging from 60 per cent success rate to 80 per cent success rate, and generally around 70 per cent. In the previous year the success rate was 72 per cent. Success was also judged by the extent to which students adopted appropriate values and were able to identify what they wanted, with regard to employment, and by being successful in obtaining a job.

School C

School C was a primary school in the Southern Metropolitan Region. The school started in 1989 with 400 students, currently had 500 students and twenty-six academic staff, and was supposed to peak at about 700. Current estimates indicated that the school would have an enrolment of over 1,000 by 1995. The principal had been at the school since it started, and had been a very experienced administrator at previous schools. With modern, pleasant buildings, the school had an attractive and spacious appearance. Although the academic focus was evident in the school, together with an emphasis on the development of the child's self-concept, there was also a great deal of time spent on developing cooperative practices to ensure that the development of self did not lapse into selfishness. A great deal of effort was spent encouraging parents to participate in the school and communication between school and home was regular and effective. Success was judged by the children's literacy and numeracy, capability to work on their own and with others, and also by their acquisition of an attitude towards education that encouraged further learning.

School D

School D was a primary school in the Southern Metropolitan Region. The demographic characteristics of the school made it eligible for the Disadvantaged Schools Programme. The school had 330 children and twenty-one staff, numbers which had not changed much in the past few years. The school was in a Housing Commission area, and as little as five years previously was known by staff at the school, and at regional level, as 'the zoo'. Staff turnover was consistently high, and many considered their efforts in terms of day-to-day survival. The principal had been at the school for the previous three years and had taken a number of steps to address the problems. Children were given a simple pledge that enabled the ideas of self-concept and self-control to be addressed. 'We are standing for friends we care for and respect. The flag reminds me that Australia is my home, and we must do what we can to make it fair and peaceful for everyone.' Parents, teachers and students all knew the pledge and used it as a measure of appropriate behaviour. Success was judged by having, in addition to basic competencies, appropriate behaviour, social skills, the ability to complete tasks by themselves and with others, and by students' own personal qualities.

School E

School E was a small rural primary school in the Western Metropolitan Region. The school had no defined community as there was no township within close proximity and a number of its students had transferred from other schools in the nearest town ten kilometres away. The school tripled its population in three years from twenty in 1988 to sixty-three in 1990, but had reached what the principal felt was its upper limit. There were four staff and an integration aide at the school, and a visiting art/craft specialist once a fortnight. The principal had been in the school for the previous three years and spent some of his time visiting other schools to learn what they were doing and to implement their successful activities in his school. With a small school and with every child being brought to the school by car, there was a great deal of informal communication with parents. A great deal of effort had been spent to ensure that members of the school community felt welcome to be involved at the levels they wished. Success was judged by the child's ability to cope with academic work, with 85 or 90 per cent of children progressing to the school's satisfaction and with the other 10 or so per cent being 'at risk' in one or more of the areas. Children were also judged on their ability to work by themselves, to assist others and to demonstrate appropriate citizenship skills and study skills.

School F

School F was a primary school in a suburb of Birmingham. The enrolment was around 350 which included 60 places in the nursery department. Approximately 75 per cent of the student population were from ethnic minorities, mainly Asian and Afro-Caribbean, and the area has many indicators of being socially deprived, including high unemployment, single parent families and poor housing. The current principal was appointed in 1986 and has placed great importance on the development of a community ethos and the development of a partnership approach with parents. In recent times, a new management structure was co-operatively developed by the staff. This included the implementation of quality monitoring teams under the guidance of a quality curriculum leader and the sharing of the leadership role between the principal and other staff with the development of such positions as the personnel leader and the resource leader. In April 1993 the school became the first school in Great Britain to be awarded the British Standards Institute certificate BS 5750. The school is a leader in community development activities with the implementation of a community curriculum, family–school partnership processes and the establishment in 1987 of a community network which brings together many community agencies in an attempt to identify and resolve wider community problems and issues.

THE GOALS OF THE EFFECTIVE SCHOOL

Concern was expressed by the interviewees that schools would have a very narrow view if they concentrated solely, even mostly, on the academic. Some people saw a clear differentiation between the role of home and school.

> As a teacher I would expect an academic emphasis of school. The school is the one to provide this, the other things could be provided by parents.
>
> (Teacher, school B)

Almost all of the people interviewed considered that the academic dimension was very important, but could not be considered as the sole reason for a school's existence.

> Ten or twenty years ago I don't think either the teachers or the parents would have thought the development of self-concept was a really important thing. Since the introduction of the Disadvantaged Schools Programme the importance of self-esteem has become more central.
>
> (Principal, school C)

The academic dimension, although important, had played too dominant a role in school in the past. Respondents indicated that children in schools today needed to be prepared for a range of futures, and a specific concentration on one or two school goals was seen as being no longer of value for the development of necessary skills for the future. One principal characterised the results in this way:

> After the war the academic role was most important, then in the '50s and '60s citizenship was all the go. Now we are concerned about self-concept and self-image, and if we are to prepare kids for the future, we need to prepare them for change, for a global perspective.
>
> (Principal, school A)

This seems to indicate that people at the school level are aware of the massive technological and social changes that have taken place over the past forty years. The perception of the role of school has changed from one that simply fitted the leaving student into the workforce, to one that considers the role of the individual in the wider global society.

The identification of citizenship as a key aspect of the role of the effective school was seen as being appropriate to the future directions of our society. When asked to indicate what citizenship meant, one principal indicated that his view of the development of a good citizen consisted of:

> producing a client that operates well with his fellows in the community, to not be selfish. He thinks of others and is aware of others in society.
>
> (Principal, school C)

Citizenship was not seen as being a blind adherence to society's rules, but an interaction between individuals and those around them. Citizenship was seen on a number of levels, and each of them was considered important by the school. On the first level, the individual was expected to conform to those generally accepted behaviours expected of a member of a diverse society or, if one of those behaviours was considered wrong, to do something to change it. The second level included having a respect for others and an acceptance of the different cultures, attitudes and perceptions about the world that may co-exist within a community. The third level included an active involvement in the development of the local community, and a contribution to the welfare of other people in the community, through community service. The fourth level consisted of the development of the personal initiative needed to help to make any changes required to maintain a just and relevant society. This meant that the school's aims for its students included that they become active participants in decisions made about their community rather than passive recipients of decisions made by others. This view corresponded well with those of teachers:

> Citizenship is independence but interdependence. Seeing yourself as an individual showing a bit of initiative, having an idea of what your abilities are, but having a respect for what other people are and can do for you when you are working with them.
>
> (Teacher, school D)

Teachers in the case study schools saw the development of citizenship skills as an integral part of what the school hoped to achieve. It was also one that was accepted by school councillors. Citizenship was

> to be able to function within the social structure. Give service to the community or a contribution to society.
>
> (School councillor, school A)

Parents also saw the need for the development of their children's ability to relate positively with others, demonstrated by comments such as 'being good and caring towards other people, the school, the environment' (school E) and 'developing a sense of responsibility, making a contribution to the community, having a sense of community welfare and a sense of serving' (school D). Respondents indicated the need for the development of a positive attitude towards community service if students were to become fully functioning and responsible adults. They indicated that there was far more responsibility being placed on individual communities to resolve their own problems than there had been when the interviewees themselves had been at school.

Case study schools were happy to report on the activities that were undertaken to enable the development of citizenship to take place. They were careful to point out that it was not seen as separate from the rest of the programme, but an integral part of what the students worked at in their day-to-day learning activities. The development of citizenship was undertaken in many different ways from school to school, from the use of the school pledge (school D), the development of attitudes of loyalty (school C), and having specific aims 'to encourage the child to care for and take pride in his/her surroundings and developing as a responsible and reliable member of society' (school F). It also involved particular activities such as having community exchange programmes with other countries (school A) or having responsible jobs within the school (school E).

For many of the interviewees, the development of the self-image was the development of confidence in oneself to be positive about the world. The concern for this aspect of the school programme is also a response to the massive changes in society over the past few decades where issues such as homeless children, child abuse at home, the effect that family breakdown has on children and the increases in child alcohol and drug abuse have all created a climate where the concern for the children's perception of themselves has become a critical social issue. The development of self-confidence was also seen to require an active input by the child as well as the school. Self-confidence included:

> the development of social skills, oral skills, the ability to speak publicly, looking at the values of society, alternative ways of looking at controversial issues. The development of perception skills and developing a value system. Instead of copying the value system of someone else, they would develop their own.
>
> (Principal, school D)

The acceptance by the schools that a solid education is the best means of preventing many of the results of a poor self-image led them to create specific opportunities for students to develop a positive self-concept.

As with citizenship, the case study schools had developed a variety of ways in which the development of the child's self-image became an integral part of the regular programme. These ways have included using the school pledge as a means for providing each child with emotional support, as in

> the school pledge tells our children that they are just as good and important as anyone else, no-one is more important than anyone else.
>
> (Teacher, school D)

School F used the GRASP (Getting Results and Solving Problems) as a means of developing students' self-confidence, which gave them an understanding of a process to resolve problems that may arise.

Some schools used the development and implementation of discipline procedures as a means for focusing on individual children, their perception of themselves and their behaviour (school E). Other schools set up special structures or programmes, such as public speaking or community service activities (school A). All schools attempted to establish positive relations by making sure that issues were always dealt with positively.

> We have made the child the focus and made sure that the discipline policy was simple for both children and parents to understand. Good things are praised and negative things are dealt with as quietly and quickly as possible. Usually the child comes up with the answer himself.
>
> (Principal, school D)

Discussions at the case study schools indicated that the strong support for the citizenship and personal development components of the schools were emphasised through the development of leadership skills, positive feelings about oneself and others, and the development of teamwork and support networks within the classroom and the school, but they were always within the context of the academic programme.

However, neither academic performance, nor even the development of employment skills were, in themselves, to be seen as the major thrust of the case study schools. The consistent response was that the school endeavoured to present all of these issues in a balanced way, and that successful completion of a school career involved a wide range of criteria, with the academic achievements of the student and a successful application by the student for either employment or further education being just two of many. The case study schools demonstrated a commitment to developing students who were academically capable, but who also had a commitment to working with others for the betterment of the community, and who believed that they were capable and worthwhile people.

WHAT MAKES A SCHOOL EFFECTIVE?

Almost all of the people interviewed accepted that what went on in the school could be identified as, in essence, high levels of interaction between various people within the school community (the principal, the staff, the parents and students), with the aim of producing the best possible educational programme for the students. People agreed that, without the goodwill shown by each of the groups mentioned, together with a high level of communication and teamwork, the level of effectiveness that their school currently experienced would be diminished. Interviewees provided an indication that with good will and a joint commitment to common goals, the school itself could overcome almost any external barrier to effectiveness, including a lack of government resourcing, negative attitudes towards teachers and a climate of continual change and instability.

Three things were highlighted in terms of contributing to this ability to withstand external distractions: each school had a high positive regard for the dedication and the level of activity shown by the staff members, each school had been involved in a community-based determination of where the school was going and how it hoped to get there, and each school had a committed, positive and communicative principal.

Dedicated and qualified staff

The respondents from the case study schools confirmed the value of dedicated and qualified staff to the development of the effective school. One principal summed up the issue:

> dedicated and qualified staff goes back to the wide ranging nature of the response in the first part of the questionnaire. We do look for the person who concentrates on more than just the academic.
>
> (Principal, school C)

Respondents in the interviews, when asked how they judged whether a teacher was dedicated, had no trouble in identifying such a person, although a variety of responses was given. These staff members had a wide range of attributes, including a real concern for the academic development of children and a consistent upgrading of their own knowledge to provide the best possible chances for children to learn, as suggested by the following response:

> an ideal staff member is one who fits in with the school and its policies, cares for children, has high standards and pursues them, and is determined to bring out the best in the children; teachers who are constantly improving themselves with ELIC and EMIC [language and mathematics INSET programmes] and working out better ways to do it.
>
> (Principal, school D)

Other respondents saw dedication in terms of the extra things that teachers became involved in to provide the children with the curriculum and social balance required. Dedication is:

> the amount of time teachers are prepared to put into extra-curricular activities. Some just do nine to three and that's it. Others are helping kids during lunchtime and after school. Some were out every night for two weeks helping with the deb. ball and other things. There was no extra pay, nothing.
>
> (Welfare counsellor, school B)

Such teachers accept that their role goes beyond the academic and into areas where students need support. In many respects, the provision of activities that relate to the development of citizenship skills, the development of self-image, the provision of work experience and other employment-related activities, are all conducted as extra activities above the teachers' regular commitments to classes. Such activities were appreciated by the respondents, particularly parents, as demonstrating a real concern for the welfare and future of their children.

A third feature of the dedicated teacher is the development of a very individualised programme for each and every student. Such teachers get to know the background of each of the children in their class, might spend additional time visiting parents or working out individual programmes of work for the children, and take special care that any activities take into account the various backgrounds of the children in their care.

Dedicated teachers can usually be identified by their demeanour and their attitude to their work. Some teachers are always available to help out, to do extra, to get involved with a new project. These teachers are noted for their enthusiasm, their continual stream of new possibilities, for their delight at being involved with the children and other people.

> Parents who want to go beyond the academic rely on the good nature and dedication of staff.
>
> (Teacher, school D)

These comments provide an indication of the nature and the extent of the changes in the teacher's role over the past two decades. If the range of requirements held by the school community for the children of that community has changed as has been previously suggested, then the role of teachers in servicing that change also needs to be addressed. In the past twenty years, the teaching role has changed dramatically from one where the major mission was to impart knowledge to children to one that includes developing teaching skills for a new range of curricular and other activities for children, developing their own decision-making skills, being involved in curriculum development and review, and dealing with adults as well as children.

Visits to the case study schools left no doubt that the dedication shown by teachers, in the ways described above, was well respected at the school level.

> The most important resources for people coming into this place are the gifted and dedicated staff who contribute way beyond what is required.
>
> (School councillor, school B)

> A dedicated teacher is a person who arrives early, departs later and is seen in outside school events, has obvious interests outside of the classroom, frequently discusses individual problems and does something about them. There is a little bit of magic in the classroom, it reflects in the way the person talks, the way they interact with you. They will be very visible in the school.
>
> (Teacher, school D)

Comments such as these indicate that not only are dedicated staff easy to observe in the school, but that in the case study schools at least, there were plenty of actual sightings going on. School principals, in particular, were supportive of and grateful for the work being done by their staff.

> If you don't have a vast majority of teachers who have a real conviction for teaching, some sort of zeal, it doesn't matter how good your leadership is, the school policy is, doesn't matter how good your motivation strategies are, if you haven't got the human things, it won't work.
>
> (Principal, school C)

Much of the increased school-based development that has occurred relied upon the principal and staff of a school working closely together to provide for school improvement. The responses indicated that the only way in which the range of requirements that school communities now demanded for their children could be met, would be by the school providing a number of highly skilled and highly committed professionals who saw teaching not as a job, but as a mission, and who were prepared to contribute to the programme of the school with the same amount of zeal as that which has been attributed to other types of missionaries. In all instances of discussions about dedicated teachers, one criterion kept emerging: 'a dedicated teacher is not just doing it because it is their job, they really want to teach' (Parent, school D).

School policy

One of the major concerns for many of the case study schools was the development of a set of policies to guide the school into the future. In these schools, the development of school level policies has been a recent, and as yet, unfinished activity.

> When I arrived, there was one policy in the school. The first new policy was communication. When you have two campuses, one hundred and nine teachers and people coming and going all the time, communication is critical.
>
> (Principal, school A)

At school C, the newest school:

> We have moved quickly in about six of the nine frameworks [academic disciplines] areas. We can only properly develop three per year. It all ties in with a clear school policy, we have written policies and most people know where we are going.
>
> (Principal, school C)

The first policy of the principal of school F was to overturn the previous headteacher's policy of parents leaving their children at the school gate.

The major impetus for the new policies seemed to be the devolving of responsibility for making policy and curriculum decisions to the school level, coupled by the concern of the local community to ensure that the children had the best education possible. As in school E, the reviewing of school policy provided the opportunity for administrators, staff and parents to work together as a team, and a real commitment to school improvement and school spirit was the result.

> I suppose three years ago we decided to review the school's policy. There was a commitment on the staff's behalf to make

sure that following this direction would work and the parents fully supported us . . . I think generally that the community of the school felt that change was needed otherwise the school was going to fall away and possibly self-destruct. So everyone supported change and as a result there was a lot of work put in by everybody in the area of policy direction and resources.

(Principal, school E)

Specific changes to policy have brought immediate benefits:

The change in discipline policy, the time-out room. This has been positive to the morale of the staff. Curriculum is becoming more and more academic, and that is very important from the community's point of view. The results have improved over the last six years.

(Teacher, school D)

School F made a conscious move towards becoming a community school, with policies that encouraged community members to partici- pate not only in their children's education, but in their own as well.

The development of new policies within each of the case study schools has generated a positive feeling towards the school and its work. All schools have experienced change in the past three years, and everyone interviewed agreed that their school was a better and more productive place than it had been previously. The five case study schools each provided a different but comparable model for the development of dynamic processes and people to manage this change.

Academic and administrative leadership

The principal, as the chief executive officer of the school, is respon- sible for the processes that will bring about the development of an appropriate school policy, utilising the best information and the best methods of development at the school's disposal, and the staff are responsible for ensuring that the policies are implemented in such a way as to facilitate their best possible chance of success.

The task of administration within the school, and the prin- cipal's role as the head of that administration, were seen in differ- ent ways by different groups at the case study schools. From the principal's viewpoint, the role was one that involved inspiring the staff of the school:

The administrator's job is to stimulate the dedication. Pattern-
ing is important. Teachers look to their educational leaders to
set an example. If teachers sense there is a dedication in the
administrator then they tend to model themselves on it.

(Principal, school B)

The administrator's role is to get twenty different personalities to
go towards the same goal. Much the same as the teacher's, really.

(Principal, school D)

On the other hand the teachers at the schools saw the need for the
principal to be the leader of a team and responsible to the staff for
developing a cooperative approach.

There is a feeling that the administration is more supportive
now. In the past there was the difficulty of the administration
putting together the policies and the staff had to put them into
practice even though they might have disagreed with them.

(Teacher, school D)

This role is one that some of the principals interviewed referred to
as well:

Teamwork is extremely important. When you are an administrator, you see the broad picture and you get a kick along when
the school is doing well.

(Principal, school A)

There was an understanding held by all staff interviewed, both in the
administrative and teaching areas, that unless they worked together
nothing would be accomplished. At times when industrial action was
being undertaken by teaching unions, this reliance on teamwork
created stress on both sides as the conflicting demands met head on.

The parent viewpoint on the role of the principal identified
ultimately where 'the buck stopped'. The overall development of
the school was traced back to the principal. In school D, where all
the people interviewed indicated that there had been substantial
improvement in the previous three years, the parent perception
was summed up by:

The improvement can be traced to the new headmaster. He was
strong and determined to give the school a good name. He brought
self-esteem to the children and that was important to the school.

(Parent, school D)

However, the principal would have been unable to bring about these changes by himself, and once again, the importance of teamwork and a common goal by both administrative and academic staff in the school become obvious.

In addition to playing a major role in the development of the tone and teamwork within the school, the principals in the case study schools were seen as taking a leadership role in the development of specific curriculum areas.

> The principal has an active role in curriculum. He leads by example, his enthusiasm is catching. He is not a passive person. At the same time while he is a leader, he doesn't come across as being an oracle. We all take part in the development.
>
> (Teacher, school E)

The discussions at the case study schools indicated that the elements of dedicated staff, having clear school policies and a principal who was an academic as well as an administrative leader, were the critical issues in their judgements about the level of effectiveness of their school. All other items that may have been slightly deficient could be overcome by reference back to one of the three issues mentioned. Any problems with classroom techniques could be overcome by new policies and a commitment by staff to improve their performance. Any deficiencies caused by lack of support from the parents or the education authority could likewise be overcome by additional efforts from those who were involved at the school level. However, a school with a principal who would not listen to teachers or parents, a staff who contributed only as much as they had to, or a school policy that was non-existent, out of date, or did not provide a clear direction, was seen as a school with a lot of problems.

Communication and teamwork

The visits to the case study schools provided further insight into the role that communication, and the development of a team approach, had for the work of the school. The interviewees at the case study schools were asked whether they felt that communication and teamwork were important features and how they operated within their school.

Communication was seen as being a critical factor for the development of the ethos of the school. Dedicated teachers and good leadership are brought together by the channels of communication utilised in the school.

> There is pretty good communication in this school, at staff meetings, and good communication at other levels as well. If you are to have a relatively happy school you must have good communication.
>
> (Principal, school D)

Without adequate communication between the principal and staff, neither group is in a position to work with the other for the future development of the school.

To ensure that all members of the school community are advised of what the school is doing there is a need for consistent and two-way communication between the school and the home. This can be achieved by the use of newsletters or other regular forms of communication. However, the communication also needs to move from the home to the school to enable parents to contribute to the development of the school in various ways.

> Everybody is kept fully informed of what's going on. Suggestion sheets are sent out and everyone is encouraged to make suggestions.
>
> (Teacher, school E)

School F has developed a contract arrangement to enhance the Family School Partnership. Goals, for families as well as children, are made and achievements are recorded and celebrated. This process involves regular communication between home and school.

Communication can be seen as the thread that holds all of the other operations of the school together. Without adequate communication, people would see themselves as operating more or less on their own, and be less likely to contribute to the development of the school as a whole; but if communication was open, two-way and consistent, then the people interviewed within the case study schools indicated that they felt that they were part of, and contributed to, a wider development than just their own specific role suggested. This was felt to be the case by administrators, teachers and parents alike.

Communication was also used as the linking mechanism to demonstrate to those involved in school operations how their contribution helped to create a much larger undertaking than could have been the case had people worked as individuals. This synergistic approach to school development ensured that everyone felt a valued member of the team. This is particularly necessary in smaller schools.

> If you have a staff member that won't communicate, won't join the team, then that makes it hard for all of the school. So I think you have to work harder to develop communication in a smaller school.
>
> (Principal, school E)

In this school, all of the staff, all of the parents and all of the children were known to everyone else in the school community, and this enabled the development of a team approach to decision-making.

> The school prides itself on its team approach. The staff is a team and we try to indicate to the children, as well as the parents, that we are together and that is a good model for cooperation. If children are going to get a job in an office or a factory, where there are a lot of people, you have to work together, otherwise the job won't get done. We try to provide lots and lots of opportunities for kids to have the responsibility of working in a team, working with a group.
>
> (Principal, school E)

In the larger schools, it is necessary to be more structured in the approach to developing teamwork. The establishment of an active and participatory committee system was seen as one of the best ways of providing the communication necessary for good teamwork.

> There is a need for good leaders, like the curriculum committee, the faculty coordinators. Dedicated teachers will mesh together all the loose bits around the school. Committees bring teamwork. . . . You need a structure where information is coming from all sorts of groups.
>
> (Principal, school B)

School F also developed both leadership and teamwork by collaboratively developing a management structure that emphasised quality. Parents, too, felt that the desire to be involved at the school level was directly attributable to the welcome that they received when they attempted such involvement. Statements such as these indicate how parents and teachers, working together, are able to resolve many of the issues that just a few years earlier might have led to a breakdown in communication.

I used to find teachers really intimidating and you were too scared to say something. You felt self-conscious that they were sort of better than what you were. Alone a person can feel like that. But here it is just so easy to talk to the teachers.

(Parent, school D)

Four or five years ago you were told by teachers what you should do for your child, whereas now the bond is more important, and the children are seen as the main focus.

(School councillor, school D)

The parental presence in schools also provides inspiration for their children to do better:

Parents have a far bigger input these days than three or four years ago. Parents are aware that they can help their children, not only help them directly in terms of their work, but help them cope with school and show them that school is part of their life. Children are seeing their mums and dads in school and they think therefore that it must be all right.

(Teacher, school B)

THE EFFECTIVENESS OF THE CASE STUDY SCHOOLS

Parents, teachers and students all felt that their school was doing as well as it could, given the constraints imposed on it from outside. Comments such as these provided some insight into the types of attitudes held by the school community:

We know we have the best school in the State. It's great to think that teachers and parents think that way.

(Principal, school C)

If you ask people in the street about their child's school, they think that their school is fantastic . . . Everyone thinks that every other school is not good because they read the papers, but their own school is pretty good.

(Teacher, school D)

Parents were also prepared to identify reasons for their perception that their schools were operating effectively:

I would prefer to be in a school today. They way you are taught is better. When I went to school, you had to learn and if you didn't you were considered stupid. You were put with the other idiots where no-one was taught anything. They didn't look into what your problem was, they would just smack you and tell you to be quiet.

(Parent, school C)

For many the issue of involvement was a critical factor. The more involved people became with their local school, the more supportive they became:

School communities are taking a pride in their school. They feel that they are doing their best. We're happy with our school, and we are doing a good job.

(School councillor, school E)

The people interviewed were happy to be involved with their school, they felt that it was an improving school, and considered that people within the school were doing everything possible to ensure that the children had the best possible education.

THE IDEAL SCHOOL

Those interviewed were given the opportunity to comment on what they felt might be the effective school of the future. They were asked to identify what facilities, policies and processes they felt would give the children of the year 2000 the best chance of succeeding. This was an opportunity for interviewees to reflect on what they had said already, and to provide their own views of what they saw as being the critical features of the effective school of the future.

The question prompted a wide range of responses that covered almost all possibilities that might be conceived for future development. The responses included further development of the academic programme and other aspects of the curriculum, comments about the specific roles of teachers and parents, strategies for increasing the involvement of parents and the community in school activities, the development of a wide range of facilities for the use both of the children and the community and the possibility of having adult programmes offered at the school. However, these comments confirmed the earlier views of what made an effective school. The conclusion that could be drawn was that the effective school of the future, like the effective school of today, would concentrate on a broad curriculum, be one that considered students as people as well as learners, and would have high levels of involvement of staff and parents in decisions about the direction the school would take.

Some of those interviewed perceived the school of the future to be very similar to what it is now, and felt that if schools were currently seen to be effective then they should be allowed to continue as they are. This indicated a level of satisfaction with what their school was currently achieving.

> The effective school of the future won't be very much different to what we have now, because people think we are an effective school now. But it would have a very stimulating environment with a wide range of activities that add to the quality of education.
>
> (Principal, school C)

However, another viewpoint was that schools are currently effective because they have changed, and will only remain so if the changes that will occur in our society are continually addressed. The technological advance, the rapidly changing mix of cultures in so many communities, the demands of the environmentalists, of the business community, of universities and of various groups within the community, will continue to need to be serviced. The climate affecting the credibility of schools will continue to change as the population ages, and fewer people have any direct involvement with the school system. These challenges must be met, and can only be met by a continuous reassessment of the role and operations of schools.

> I don't think the curriculum that we have now is all that bad, but we need to keep thinking about further developments.
>
> (Parent, school A)

> There needs to be a basic curriculum. I would like to see a value system being part of this basic curriculum. Technology with a computer on every child's desk will probably be in in about ten years time with a writing function and a numeracy function. It has already started.
>
> (School councillor, school A)

For many of the interviewees, the heart of the matter was still the development of the child. Some recognised that employment opportunities needed to be considered and, since there would be a wide range of options available to the adults of the future, that education needed to prepare children for this future of options. Others were more concerned about the happiness of children than the specific skills that they had. They saw an effective school as one that supported the children as well as providing them with an education.

> Kids that are well settled, loved, secure, well disciplined, mature, well looked after in the home and in the school place. No welfare problems at all.
>
> (Parent, school A)

The comments suggest that the effective school of the future should identify strategies for considering the welfare of its students in the same way that effective schools today are characterised by caring teachers who contribute more than is required of them for the benefit of the students. The concern for the current level of unemployment, particularly youth unemployment, and the devastating effect that being unemployed can have on the individual's self-respect, make these activities particularly important. The comments might also indicate the need for an expansion of the current activities of schools where consideration of ways in which the social problems that affect student performance might be addressed through school-based activities.

Some of the interviewees had definite views on the roles of various groups within the school. Some felt that the role of teachers was to teach, and that parents should have little part to play in this activity. Even within very effective schools, such as the case study schools, some parents still saw the 'professional' and 'non-professional' issue as important.

> The teaching role should be done by teachers. They are qualified and trained for these activities.
>
> (Parent, school B)

This parental view of the role of the teacher as a professional, however, was offset by the teacher's view of the possible role of the parent in the classroom. Many teachers, who had used parental knowledge and skills for the benefits of the children in the past, had no such concerns about having parents active in the classroom. Teachers saw that parents' skills could be utilised in many ways, and that the concern about future levels of funding may increase this development even more, as teachers try to reduce the adult–child ratio for areas of learning that require high levels of individual attention.

I can see parents spending more time in the grade as supporters of the teaching programme. This will depend on the level of funding that can be maintained. Parents will be a resource within the school.

(Teacher, school E)

Some respondents saw the school as having a range of additional facilities that would be available to the children and perhaps the wider community. Others went even further, to suggest that the school could become a learning centre for the whole community, with a range of facilities that assisted both children and adults to achieve their educational objectives. Such a development saw the need for clearly established policies of use by adults, but with the clear understanding that adult activities were supplementary to the major role of the school, namely, the education of the children of the community.

We will probably see further down the track, where schools will be utilised for community education centres, for adult classes after hours. If the government rules that they should fully utilise government resources then this will happen.

(Teacher, school E)

The school of the future has got to be people centred, the human element has to be retained. The environment has to be fantastic. Our policies are preparing people for the twenty-first century, the adaptable human being. We need to have schools that can continue that process when they are adults.

(Principal, school D)

These comments provide a new acceptance of the role of the school, but one that is a logical extension of where effective schools are now. The school becomes a community facility rather than one just for children, although the education of children will still be its core responsibility. The most important element of effectiveness relates to the provision of services to people. These services might include both a broader curriculum for the students than they have access to now, and the development of the school into something that could be used by the community as a whole. But the essential characteristics of an effective school would remain the same: happy and interested children, a dedicated staff who know what is expected of them and can contribute to the development of school plans and activities, and an administration that provides the resources necessary for the satisfaction of the school's goals.

Chapter 5

The core–plus school

> In schools in which collegial relations prevail . . . ordinary
> people, relying on ordinary budgets and confronted with the
> ordinary ebb and flow of energy, goodwill, and creativity,
> accomplish extraordinary things.
>
> (Little 1987: 492)

If the underlying premise of any definition for school effectiveness
is a search for those school factors that improve academic outcomes, as was typified by much of the research in the United
States, then the Australian study found that the American viewpoint was not wholly acceptable to school communities. The
concern expressed by Kirner (1989) about the inadequacies of
standardised testing has meant that the education system is moving further away from external and standardised views of academic
competence as time goes on, although not with the full support of
all sections of the community.

IMPLICATIONS OF THE AUSTRALIAN STUDY

In many respects, the results of the Australian study contradicted
much of the early research on school effectiveness, which was
based on the premise that an effective school was identified almost
solely by its academic performance. As has been discussed earlier,
perhaps a more appropriate framework for developing effectiveness would consider the notion that all students, regardless of
their background, had the opportunity to achieve the school's
goals, but that the range of goals themselves could be broader than
the strictly academic perspective held by some previous
researchers. The framework for recognising effective schools,

proposed in Chapter 2, put forward the possibility that a range of goals covering the entire spectrum of human needs and endeavours should be considered if the school was to be truly effective. It also suggested that there were some goals that all schools should have for all students, and that these goals would be determined by educational systems or governments. Further, local goals which relate to the specific needs of children who live in distinct communities might vary from school to school. This framework might be labelled *core–plus*, where the core might be the state mandated obligations of the school, including some similar to those that relate to success in literacy and numeracy, but the plus would be determined by the school community itself.

If the core–plus framework of effectiveness was accepted, then schools in the Australian study may well be viewed as effective. If the schools hoped to achieve a series of goals that matched their broad view of what schools should be offering to students, and if what the majority of students, regardless of their background, achieved at the end of their time at the school was in congruence with those original goals, even though those goals might not have been strictly academic in nature, then the school can be identified as effective.

This difference in emphasis has implications for future decisions about educational management, as it involves the empowerment of the people at the school site. It is much more difficult to judge when a person becomes empowered, or when a school community is fully involved, than it is to judge the number of students who have passed a mathematics examination. The measuring devices required need to be far more sensitive to human interaction than those that currently exist. It also means that school effectiveness is a concept that can change over time, and is dependent upon the situation in which the determination is made, rather than being static.

The common factor is not curricular in the academic sense, but based on social justice. If all students have equal opportunities to achieve the school's goals, and do so, then the school is effective, regardless of whether those goals are academic, social or personal. As Reynolds indicated

Effective and ineffective schools are likely to be characterised by differing levels of personal relationships, self perceptions, self/ other relations, teacher/teacher and teacher/headteacher relations, yet the effective schools literature does not delve into these crucial 'third dimensional' areas of school functioning.

(Reynolds 1990: 9)

This provides support for what can be considered as the core–plus framework of an effective school, where the academic, citizenship and employment roles that have always been a central component of the school's focus are complemented by a more broadly based curriculum that incorporates the development of personal skills, leadership skills and involvement activities for a range of people at all levels of school operation. Discussions of the ideal school of the future with people from the case study schools indicated the possibility for schools to consider a wider clientele than that which they already have, and to consider ways in which the school becomes a community centre or a community school. What the Australian study has found is that far more work needs to be done in the area of defining the effective school.

It seems that there is now the choice of maintaining the current definitions of school effectiveness, and continuing to have disputes about what should be measured within the framework of the definition, based upon the educational philosophy that various groups hold, or to simplify the definition to one that identifies the concern that all students, regardless of their backgrounds, have similar chances to achieve the specified goals, without necessarily specifying what those goals should be. There would be a recognition that some goals would be mandatory for all students and some would relate to the geographical and social area in which they live. For a school to be effective, all goals, both mandatory and local, would need to be achieved by all or most students. A school that concentrated only on the mandatory goals would be effective if that is what the local community chose, but a school that chose a range of other goals would only be seen to be effective if both those goals and the mandatory ones were achieved.

Future possibilities for schools

It is possible that school is seen by a proportion of the community, and perhaps a large proportion at that, as being the end point of one's education. This attitude, combined with the fact that significant numbers of students in many western communities do not complete the final year of school, or if they do, go no further in education, leads to the possibility that many in the community have a negative feeling about their time at school. These attitudes make it easy for people to accept negative reports about schools, because it matches their own memory of their time at school. Schools have to work doubly hard to undo these negative attitudes because, as the population ages, the potential increases for greater proportions of the educational budget to be diverted from education to health and welfare services. If the community as a whole has a negative view of school, these diversions of resources will go virtually unchallenged. In Victoria, for example, the proportion of the state budget allocated to education dropped from 35 per cent to 26 per cent from 1981 to 1991, and it is likely that other western countries would show similar trends.

Schools need to communicate with their local communities and school systems need to communicate with society as a whole, about the value of school activities for the community, if this trend is to be stopped. There is a responsibility for school systems to be proactive in this matter, not only by providing public relations training to principals or teachers who may be interested in undertaking such a communications role locally, and by collecting appropriate information from schools to rebut various media reports that schools are failing in their tasks, but also by expanding the role of the school to include meaningful activities for those who have already left school. This is the heart of the core–plus school concept.

The core–plus framework

An acceptance of the core–plus framework for school effectiveness, as discussed earlier, suggests the need for educational systems to reconsider the design, orientation and staffing of schools. Associated with the possibility of building different types of school facilities is the possibility of providing staff with special teaching or counselling skills for all schools, in order to provide special services to particular groups such as the disabled or people with English as a second language (ESL), and with particular consideration at the primary level, to ensure that early intervention and remediation for those who most need it takes place.

Research into early intervention strategies has indicated that the sooner an individual problem is identified and responded to, the more likely it is that there will be few longer-term problems generated. Hodgkinson argued that in the United States, 'we spend in general 15 per cent of our money on prevention programs and 85 per cent on rather ineffectual "cures" in all social service areas' (Hodgkinson 1990: 27). There was a link between a person's educational background and their later situation with regard to health, family stability, crime, transport and housing. He holds that it is cheaper, easier and more effective to:

- keep people from falling into poverty in the first place rather than to get them out later;
- keep all kinds of families intact rather than arrange adoption and foster care facilities later;
- keep students performing at grade level by 'front loading' resources toward those most at risk, rather than telling them at the end of the third grade that they failed when no effort was made to provide the resources that could have meant success;
- keep people out of prisons rather than trying to rehabilitate them later;
- keep low income people in an expanding supply of affordable housing rather than increasing the number of homeless families, often with children and one or more full-time workers;
- keep mass transit so that low income workers can continue to have jobs, housing and some freedom;
- keep kids from getting sick (or hungry) rather than providing massive programs for curing (or feeding) them after the damage has been done.

(Hodgkinson 1990: 27)

If we are to diagnose and intervene in children's problems and concerns, then there is an argument for having appropriately trained professionals based at the school, both to identify the problem and to be able to take the time necessary to alleviate the problem without taking the child away from school. The Australian study has shown that there has been a shift in the attitude of school communities over the last decade. People have become more aware of the pressures on children brought about by the changes that have have occurred within society as a whole. If these pressures continue to build, then the number of homeless children, the number of children from single parent families and the number of abused children will continue to grow. If Hodgkinson's projections are correct, then there are needs of the following types:

- adequate funding should be arranged to enable schools to deal with a far wider range of issues than they currently are able to do;
- government agencies but work together to establish strategies for the use of educational programmes at the school level to assist the destruction of the cycle of regression;
- trained professionals, recruited either by retraining teachers or from other service agencies, should be allocated to every school to ensure that issues relating to the development of many of the non-academic facets of the child, which teaching staff are not trained to undertake, or do not have the time to undertake, become part of the school's responsibility to the child and its local community;
- the design of the school facilities must be such that the above activities can take place.

It is also likely that these types of needs will continue to grow until they are, in fact, addressed by the community as a whole. This will create the need for parents to have ready access to services currently being provided by a host of different agencies, and an appropriate gateway to these services could well be the local school. The acceptance of a core–plus curriculum brings with it the possibility of the core–plus school. Consideration needs to be given to widening the brief of schools to assist in the resolution of the educational needs of all the people in the community that it serves, not just the community's children.

The study has shown that some Australian schools have changed to meet the new demands placed on them by a changing society, and it has also shown that local communities have responded positively to those changes. The considerations identified in the preceding pages indicate an acceptance that schools need to continue to change if they are to remain relevant and useful within the community. Schools can no longer afford to be static institutions because society no longer changes gradually. To respond to the rapidly changing world, schools must teach new knowledge, new skills and new attitudes. This study has shown that schools are doing this, and are doing it to the local community's satisfaction. The development of the core–plus school provides the opportunity for schools to be both architects and supporters of community development and change.

THE CORE–PLUS SCHOOL: THE THIRD GENERATION OF SCHOOL EFFECTIVENESS

It is possible to identify a number of distinct stages in the school effectiveness debate. The first generation of school effectiveness consisted of the early research which was concerned with initiating the process of school improvement by identifying the characteristics associated with effective schools. It was hoped that if schools had this information they would commence an improvement process. Renihan and Renihan later described second generation school improvement issues, which related to 'sustaining the [school improvement] process by whatever effective means can be employed' (Renihan and Renihan 1989: 5).

It could be considered that the core–plus notion might be the start of the third generation of school effectiveness and school improvement efforts. The first and second generations concentrated on a limited though expanding view of the role of the school. The third generation of school effectiveness takes the debate to a much wider plane. If the concept of an effective school was expanded to include the whole community, instead of just students, as the client group for the school, then the core–plus school might emerge.

Chapman refers to the Wittgensteinian (1958) notion of 'the rope' as a better means to explain 'the qualitative and quantitative aspects inherent in the concept of school effectiveness' (Chapman 1992: 3). The same notion could also be used to describe the need to consider a multi-faceted approach to the role of schools. If the framework for an effective school, as contained in previous paragraphs, is one that is acceptable to the various educational interest groups, then the possibility of a new type of school emerges. This proposal, which could be called a core–plus view of school effectiveness, identifies a school where the core programme of academic and other required studies is complemented by additional school-determined activities. It permits a wider focus: one that includes a core of academic goals and other requirements mandated by the state or educational authority, together with additional goals identified by the school itself as being appropriate features for that school.

Just as a rope neither has a single fibre running from one end of its length to the other, nor two distinct fibres running from either end and meeting in the middle, so, too, the core–plus definition of school effectiveness would not rely upon just one or two key features, such as the mandated curriculum or the principal of the school, for its success. The core–plus school relies upon the individual concerns and judgements of the people involved at the school level to build the strength of the overall rope. The Australian study showed that the spread of opinion about what the major role of an effective school was, not only existed in the sample as a whole, but was also present in those individual schools that were perceived to be particularly effective. Individual respondents within the case studies also varied in their view as to the major role of the school. Such variation in the individual strands, when woven together by teamwork and communication, created the essential thread of the school that ensured that all the individual needs received a response.

If the analogy of the rope were taken one step further, it would be possible to generate the analogy of the fabric of society. If all the ropes, or the threads of a fabric, are identical in colour and thickness, then the fabric itself is usually designed for a single purpose. On the other hand, if the individual threads are different colours, different thicknesses, are composed of slightly different materials, and so on, the fabric becomes a tapestry, rich, full of colour, and capable of many different interpretations. In a society that is dominated by the economic rationalist ideology, or any other single ideology, the school system that uses the original definitions of school effectiveness, with its concentration on like curricula and standardisation, will most likely produce a uniform and possibly colourless society.

Alternatively, a core–plus approach to schooling would create a school system where all the individual threads (schools) would differ, based on their own local characteristics, although they would have a similar underlying composition, brought about by the common areas of the curriculum. A tapestry woven from the ten thousand or so threads of any school system would become interesting and colourful. Many of those individual threads would provide the direction in which the economic rationalists would have us go, and all of the threads would have some common element that would enable this to occur; but others would enable the diversity and richness of a community to show through even while we were moving in that direction. The richness of heritage, the diversity of cultures, the strength of sporting prowess and the community spirit of an urban or rural population would all be an integral part of the tapestry, and would be accepted as equally important as the need for economic competitiveness.

The core–plus definition of school effectiveness enables schools to meet the requirements of the state in terms of minimal standards in literacy and numeracy (Edmonds 1978), yet make decisions at the school level that would enhance the quality of education for the students of that particular school. Thus the case study schools had a variety of programmes that were designed to meet the needs of a small rural community, a community with a high multicultural population, a community within a housing estate, a community in a satellite town, a newly established community and one that has been in existence for many years. All of them relied upon the school's ability to make judgements about what its community required, and used the resources of the local community, rather than those provided by the state, to ensure that those requirements were fulfilled.

It has been argued that schools may have been seen as effective by those in the current study because they have changed, because they have responded to the changing social circumstances. It could also be argued that schools are better placed now than they were twenty years ago to respond to future changes that will occur in our society. Yet there are those arguing for a return to the educational structures that were in place twenty years ago, such as a concentration on basic academic skills, a standardised curriculum, and formal examinations as a means to standardised testing. It might be argued that the educational structures of twenty years ago were inappropriate then, but even if they were not, it is unlikely that old remedies can satisfactorily resolve totally new problems.

What seems to be needed is not a rearrangement of the toys in the toy box, but a totally new box of toys, as argued by Minzey (1981) and Kerensky (1989). The educational structures of the past will not resolve child abuse, broken homes, the youth drug and alcohol problem, a poor attitude towards continuing education and, in the end, will not resolve unemployment. These current features of our society will only be resolved by a new conception of life-long learning that does not equate schooling and education, but identifies one's time at school as being one aspect of a process that continues from birth to death. It could also be argued that since huge amounts of public funds are utilised on the plant, personnel, facilities and programmes of schools, they should broaden their role from one of being responsible for the

schooling of children, to one of being responsible for the education of communities.

Schools could become the focus for community development
for the whole of the community as well as for the educational
programmes of children. The concept of a core–plus school in the
wider sense, as a learning centre for the whole community, may
well be one outcome of higher levels of community involvement in
school decision-making and management. Given the need for the
conservation and careful utilisation of scarce and expensive
resources, such as the plant and equipment required for a wide
range of school curricula, the core–plus school might be cost-
effective as well as academically effective.

This view indicates support for what Staples (1989) called the
100/100 school. He argued that many schools currently serve
about 20 per cent of the population for about 20 per cent of the
time, and could be labelled 20/20 schools. A school that opened
its doors to the total community, at times that were convenient for
the community as a whole (before school, after school, weekdays,
weekends, holidays) approaches the 100/100 goal. Although no
schools actually get this far, it is a far more cost-effective use of
community resources to have even 50/50 schools than it is to have
20/20 schools.

The core–plus curriculum, which could be considered as maintaining a core of state-mandated requirements for all students,
plus the curriculum determined locally (based on the needs of the
children from particular communities), could be expanded to
become the core–plus school where the core activity, namely, the
education of children, was enhanced by a range of other formal
and informal programmes for the community as a whole. The
school would become a learning facility for all the members of the
community and would be available to them on demand. As Minzey
(1981) indicated, a school can be defined in two ways. Either it is
a community facility that is sometimes used for the education of
children, or it is not a community facility that is sometimes used for
the education of children.

The likelihood of this sort of development is remote, given the
current economic climate and the present attitudes held by the
general community towards school-based learning. The core–plus
building programme, undertaken in Victoria during the late 1970s
and early 1980s, was founded on the basis of the school being a
community facility rather than simply a school. The permanent core

was a group of facilities that could be used by both the school and the community, such as library, canteen and multi-purpose rooms. The plus was a group of portable classrooms that could be added to or subtracted from, depending on the school population. This development foundered in the mid-1980s as the budget allocations for the development of new schools dried up. Perhaps pressure from local communities in the next few years will increase the momentum for the development of schools as education centres by the end of the decade. As the continued advance of adult and community education, which has 'touched the lives of six out of ten adult Australians and . . . is growing faster than any other area of education' (Senate Standing Committee on Employment, Education and Training 1991: 1), demands higher levels of community resources and facilities, the increased use of school buildings for adult learning seems to be a responsible future use of part of the education budget. This would involve further consideration of what the role of an effective school was. Without such a consideration, subsequent activities will be blocked by what Chapman considers to be one of Gaillie's 'essentially contested concepts' (Chapman 1992: 1). There would need to be a better understanding of the relationship between a core–plus curriculum and a core–plus school, with special emphasis on what the core components would be in both cases and how they would mesh together.

Activities in the core–plus school

Current and future predicted employment circumstances suggest that one future part of the core curriculum needs to be an understanding of work, in all its variations, to ensure that every student graduating from secondary school has the basic knowledge and skills required to enter the work force. This would need to include an understanding that the types of work available will change during the course of one's lifetime, and that retraining in a particular job, or even reviewing the type of job one has, is to be expected and planned for. The plus part of the curriculum may provide the specialist training for particular types of work. The core–plus school complement to this curriculum would be the provision of opportunities for people who have left school to upgrade their knowledge in particular jobs, to retrain if necessary and to provide information and the resources to enable people to make decisions about possible future employment. The facilities used for training students during the day could also be used to retrain adults in the evening or at other times when they were not being used. In this way the core–plus curriculum is inextricably linked to future use of the core–plus school's resources by the leaving student.

Other components of this core curriculum would include literacy, numeracy, perhaps computer literacy, but also those activities that foster the development of a positive attitude towards life-long learning, community service, retraining, decision-making, problem-solving and an understanding that schools are community facilities and that school-based learning is appropriate, no matter what one's age might be. The plus components might be specific activities that enable these core understandings to be developed and tested in ways that are appropriate to the local community. Thus the computer literacy development in some areas might include programmes in English as a second language, in other areas using the computer for creative story writing or developing a budget for a small business in the city or for a farm in a rural area.

The core–plus school would assist the development of these activities by providing language programmes for new migrants, by enabling parents to enrol in computer awareness programmes to help them both to assist their children and to learn for themselves, or by offering the facilities of the school for meetings of community members to enable wider community concerns to be resolved. The core–plus school might be able to provide recreational and creative arts facilities, advisory facilities and learning facilities for members of the whole community. Community facilities such as health centres, senior citizens' centres and gymnasia would not need to be duplicated, as the school would be able to provide such facilities within its own plant.

TOWARDS THE CORE–PLUS SCHOOL

A number of steps need to be taken to develop this approach. The development of the core–plus curriculum would need, first, to re-establish what the 'core' should be. Governments would need to be involved in a needs assessment of their communities to establish clearly what they see as the necessary knowledge for the next generation of leaving students. There should be no assumption that what has been the core in the past is still appropriate, although it is highly likely that many aspects of it will be. The criteria to be used for the judgement of the new core might be what Minzey and Townsend (1984: 15) called the new set of '3Rs'. In addition to the current 3Rs, which will, most likely, remain important, Minzey and Townsend argued that new educational programmes should satisfy the need to be 'realistic, relevant and responsive' to defined community needs.

Second, there is a need to improve the quality and effectiveness of the decision-making that occurs at school level to ensure that the plus components of the curriculum fit in with, and extend, those aspects of the core curriculum that can be interpreted differently by different communities. The need for developing a wide-ranging curriculum that incorporates those areas required of all schools, together with other activities that help to develop the knowledge of people on a local basis and which are determined by the local community, was one of the strong outcomes of the current study. Further to improve school-based decision-making, there is a need to continue the development of parental involvement in school activities and to provide professional development programmes for both staff and parents in the areas of decision-making and management, to ensure that the decisions made about the curriculum are the most appropriate to the circumstances of the school.

The development of the core–plus school will take much more time and consideration. Schools of the future will have to direct their attention to a much larger proportion of the community than is currently the case. Consideration of ways in which the re-designing of schools might be able to cope with the future educational needs of the adult population as well as those of the children will have to be undertaken. The use of the school buildings could be increased from the current 10 to 15 per cent of the year (seven hours per day, five days per week, forty weeks per year), through the use of programmes outside normal school hours, year-round schools and holiday activities. If schools could also be utilised by more people, from the current 20 per cent of the population who are between the ages of 5 and 18, to a much higher proportion of the population as a whole, the cost effectiveness of schools could never be questioned.

Issues related to the design, construction and commencement of a core–plus school, together with the development of a concerted programme over a period of years in order to establish how

far a school can go towards resolving the educational and, perhaps, social and other needs of the local community will need to
be considered. The community school movement in the United
States, United Kingdom and Canada provides some background
material on such a study, but even in those countries the development of local community involvement in schools, has not been
fully established. The core–plus school is an exciting possibility for
future generations to consider.

CONCLUSIONS

The Australian study showed that it was not so much what went on
at school that caused the school to be seen as effective or not, but
how things occurred and who was involved. If the level of effectiveness of any particular school is to be judged by the quality of the
people, processes and programmes that exist within it then the
role of educational systems in the future will be different. It will not
be the role of the system to determine specific features or elements
of a school that account for its effectiveness or to make assessments
about the school on the basis of external and standardised testing.
Rather, it will be to provide people at the school level with the
resources and training necessary for schools themselves to make
judgements about their goals and their strategies for achieving
them. It will also be necessary to develop a range of measuring
instruments that will enable people at the school level to check for
themselves the level of effectiveness for a set of criteria identified
by the school itself. This is a far more difficult task than demanding
an external accountability of the school, because elements that
were identified as those that most contribute to a school's effectiveness were the most difficult to measure.

The school of today has more information, more problems and
more people to deal with than at any previous time in history. It
has been constrained by diminishing finances and a poor community attitude to the work that it does. If school is going to
become an institution that will lead the way in dealing with many
of the issues that society has created, as many people in the
community expect, then schools, and the school systems, are going
to need some help. Other groups in the community, such as
business, industry and other government agencies, must work
together with the education system, rather than criticise it for its
shortcomings. Schools must ensure that local communities,

whether or not they have children in the school, are provided with the opportunity to recognise that the school is theirs as well.

The development of the core–plus concept for curriculum is warranted and, indeed, consideration of the design, processes and programmes of what might be considered as the core–plus school may well be the best development for the future of education. The metaphor proposed by Carr best describes the need for change:

> Many schools are like little islands set apart from the mainland of life by a deep moat of convention and tradition. Across the moat there is a drawbridge, which is lowered at certain periods during the day in order that the part-time inhabitants may cross over to the island in the morning and go back to the mainland at night. Why do these young people go out to the island? They go there in order to learn how to live on the mainland.
>
> (Carr 1942: 34)

Managing change relies upon the individual's attitude towards the direction of change and a positive attitude towards change is directly related to the level of the individual's understanding of, and commitment to that change. The core–plus concept suggests that as many people as possible should be involved in decisions that affect their futures, and that schools have a role in providing students with the knowledge and skills necessary to be involved and to have a positive attitude towards that involvement, and being a resource for the community to enable those decisions to be made.

The commitment of the core–plus school is to community improvement and an aspiration towards excellence.

> Those who achieve excellence will be few at best. All too many lack the qualities of mind or spirit which would allow them to conceive excellence as a goal, or to achieve it . . . But many more can achieve it than now do. And the society is bettered by not only those that achieve it but by those who are trying.
>
> (Gardner 1961: 133)

The core–plus school takes school-based decision-making to its next level: community-based decision-making for a range of issues that affect those communities. The empowerment of people, referred to by Rosenholtz (1989), is confirmed. The quality of the programmes offered to students, so critical to the concept of effectiveness, would increase as parents first become aware of what the school is trying to do, and then became more confident in their own ability to help. Because the school would be seen as an educational facility for all of the community, far greater levels of support would be generated both from the parents and other community members. Equity will no longer be seen to be incompatible with quality, as the core–plus school tries to resolve the educational needs of all the community, and in doing so will provide a greater range of options for individual students.

The concept of school effectiveness has been evolving and developing since it was first considered in the early 1970s, and this evolution has not yet finished. Early considerations of the concept were both limited, and limiting, but subsequent refinements have promoted the issue to one that has attained world-wide interest. Although aspects of the research may be used as a basis for the development of educational policy, they cannot be used indiscriminately. What works in one context provides no guarantee that the same set of imperatives will work somewhere else. To discover *what* makes a school effective in practice is a far more difficult and complex task than to identify *whether* a school is effective or not. A business person, an academic, a parent and a student, may all agree that a school is effective, but might have different reasons for saying so. Schools have been under all sorts of pressures in recent years, with some in the community wanting them to change, in a variety of ways, and others wanting them to stay the same as they are, or were. Schools have changed, and continue to change as they try to provide services to a rapidly changing community. It remains a matter of speculation how much further those changes might go.

Chapter 6

Developing the core–plus school: a model for action

Schools work when educators provide education for educatees.
(McKenna 1989)

THE RELATIONSHIP BETWEEN THE CORE–PLUS SCHOOL AND OTHER FORMS OF SCHOOL MANAGEMENT

The core–plus school proposal has a close correspondence with the principles espoused by those who argue for school-based management, although the core–plus concept goes even further, since it considers the whole community of the school rather than just the children of that community. For Marburger (1985: xii) school-based management is a process for change based on democratic principles and trust. It requires that people in the education system outside of the school trust the people at the school level, the principal, teachers, students and parents, in the decision-making process, but it also requires that each of the groups at the school level trusts each other so that they will become fully involved in the decision-making activities. As more control is given to the school and community, public confidence in schools increases, problem identification and solutions are more timely and accurate, and the needs of the students are more likely to be met.

The core–plus school also considers similar issues to those practised by many currently successful businesses. For the core–plus school to operate effectively, it needs to adopt a business-like approach to education. This is not to suggest that the essentially human elements of schools should be made less important, but that a different perspective of those elements should be taken. Just as businesses take care to identify the specific set of people who will be their clients, and then devise ways in which the business can satisfy the needs of those people, so too the core–plus school defines its clients, finds out what they need and then establishes processes and programmes to satisfy those needs. The attention to detail that makes businesses successful will also be present in the plans of the core–plus school. School F, the first school in Britain to achieve the British Standard in Quality Assurance, essentially adopted a business plan that was adapted to both national and local educational needs.

In many respects the issues relating to the core–plus school are fairly clear cut examples of the implementation of a community education philosophy to a particular setting, in this case, the total operations of the school. Community education seems to have emerged almost simultaneously in the UK, the USA and Australia, although it seems to have taken different forms in each country.

In England, the long standing history of provision of adult education activities through mechanics' institutes led to the founding of the Workers' Education Association (WEA) and the development of 'village colleges' in the 1920s. The use of schools as venues for such activities led to the later use of the terms 'community school' or 'community college'.

In Australia, the 1934 General Course of Study of the Victorian Department of Education contained the following statement:

The Teacher and the Community
It is considered that the schools will do their most satisfactory work when they function as community centres and generally share in community life. To aid this it is suggested that the full cooperation of residents and all others interested in education should be sought. School Committees and Mothers Clubs afford the best means of linking school and home in a bond of mutual understanding and sympathetic cooperation. These bodies have rendered excellent service in the past in assisting Head Teachers to make their schools integral parts of the community and generally to improve facilities for boys and girls. A visiting day helps also, parents thus become acquainted with classroom procedure, have opportunities for seeing actual work done by pupils in all subjects and activities, and in addition are able to confer with the Head Teacher and his staff regarding the welfare of their children.

(Education Department of Victoria 1933)

The American version of modern community education has been made more 'professional' and is the subject of more research and literature than in other parts of the world. It probably began in Flint, Michigan in the 1930s with the development of a partnership between Frank Manley, a recreation leader with the city schools and a wealthy, local industrialist, Charles Stewart Mott. They started with the idea 'Give kids something to do and they won't get into trouble' (Minzey and Le Tarte 1979: 7). As time went by the concept developed from a recreation programme for young people to a concern for the educational needs of the whole community. By the late 1960s the concept had expanded so much that people were confused about what the concept now meant. Adult educators saw it as an adult education programme in the school, recreation leaders saw it as school based recreation programmes and other community members saw it as just another repackaging of existing school programmes.

However, one thing was clear. The words 'participation' and 'involvement' took on new significance as 'it was clear that the meaningful involvement of people was crucial to the proper development of community education' (Minzey and Le Tarte 1979: 11). People could *participate* in programmes and activities by attending them, but it soon became a new criterion for community education that it was only when people had extensive and meaningful *involvement* in the identification and the development of these programmes that community education, rather than something else, occurred.

Community education had developed into a process that was more than simply the sum of it's programmes. Minzey and Le Tarte were prepared to identify what community education was *not* (it is not a community school, a community education programme, community control, a programme for the poor or disadvantaged, social work or community development) rather than what it *is*, but it became obvious from the definition they eventually produced, that community education is the *involvement of people in the process* of identification, development, implementation and evaluation of the sorts of activities that have been given the labels listed above.

> Community Education is a process that concerns itself with everything that affects the well-being of all citizens within a given community. This definition extends the role of

community education from one of the traditional concept of teaching children to one of identifying the needs, problems and wants of the community and then assisting in the development (or the identification) of facilities, programs, staff and leadership toward the end of improving the entire community.

(Minzey and Le Tarte 1979: 25)

This argument is developed even further by Minzey and Townsend (1984) when they propose that the two major purposes of a government-funded school (and perhaps private schools as well) are to 'focus on the needs of the individual to become a self-fulfilled, active participant in society' and also 'emphasizes serving the needs of society'. They argue these are no longer mutually exclusive, but in fact complement each other in today's society and will do so even more in the future as society becomes more technologically advanced (Minzey and Townsend 1984: 11). They saw the whole community as the school's client base and saw involvement and empowerment as its major aims.

By empowering the community, the individuals within it get experience at decision-making, at participating, at justifying and all of the other activities that assist the individual to become a participative person.

(Minzey and Townsend 1984: 17)

The major issues relating to the proposal for core–plus schools are those of accountability and self-determination. On the one hand people who have no part to play in the making of decisions can very rarely be held accountable for the activities that follow those decisions and, on the other, if people who are critically involved in the outcomes of the decisions being made are involved in the decisions themselves, then the outcomes of those decisions are more likely to contribute to the development of the community or the individual. Henderson suggested that in

public education as it is now governed, there is no structure at a school that can assure an authoritative discourse on school improvement. The people who must live with the decisions are not the people who make the decisions; if the school community has no power to change the situation, they will not bother to figure out how to improve it.

(Henderson 1988: 7)

Chubb also suggested

> the more control a school has over those aspects of its organ-
> isation that affect its performance – the articulation of its goals,
> the selection and management of its personnel, the specifica-
> tion of its policies – the more likely a school is to exhibit the
> qualities that have been found to promote effectiveness.
>
> (Chubb, in Henderson 1988: 6)

There are two major concerns for any school improvement
activities for schools that accept the core–plus argument in the
future. The first is the development or re-assessment of the school
culture to embrace the core–plus concept, and the second is a
process of redesigning school facilities, organisation and resources
to enable the core–plus concept to be implemented.

School culture

The literature on organisational theory emphasises that each individual institution is unique and schools fall into this category. Each
school has a unique mix of people (staff, students, parents, community), resources, policies, practices, programmes and facilities
(both school and community). These, and the relationships
developed between each of them, help to engender a school
culture that is not duplicated anywhere else in the world.

Much has been written recently on school culture, but in many
respects it still remains a mystery. We know it is there, but we have
difficulty defining or describing it. It is generally agreed that it comprises all of the 'tangible, intangible and symbolic elements of organisational life' (Beare, Caldwell and Millikan 1989: 173) that exist
within the organisation. Some of the tangible features include:

– the school vision or philosophy
– the school goals as the way in which that vision can be
  accomplished
– the policies of the school.

Some of the intangible features include:

– the values held by the people in the school that underpin the
  policies of the school
– the quality of the processes used by the school
– the quality of the relationships brought about by those processes.

Some of the symbolic features include:

- the policy of inclusion
- the way in which the school honours and rewards people for their services
- the way in which the school's experiences are shared.

Each of the elements, the tangible, the intangible and the symbolic, are critical to the development of both the stated and unstated culture of the school. The culture attained by the core–plus school concept will be significantly due to the leadership capabilities of key people within the school and the way in which they go about their tasks.

School restructuring

Until very recently, many developed countries worked on the assumption that what is learned in the compulsory years of school is both a necessary and sufficient condition for the survival of the individual in society for the rest of that person's life. The information taught in school is assumed to be necessary because without it the individual will not be a constructive and productive member of society either socially or economically, and it is assumed to be sufficient because no further learning is needed for the person to survive within society. This is not to assume that people do not go on to higher forms of school, such as universities and college, but only that they do not need to do so in order to survive. The continued acceptance of this set of characteristics is an indication of the power of school to determine certain aspects of the lives of its participants. Yet schooling as an institution is neither universal in time nor in space. The institution that we know as a school, that free, compulsory and secular form of learning, is only about two hundred years old, and in almost all cases is confined to industrialised countries. It is likely that 50 per cent of the world's population have never been to a school, and in many Third World countries what scant school system there is is neither free nor compulsory.

We should not assume that schools will exist forever or, if they do continue, that they will be structured in the same way as at present. Changing demographic conditions in many western countries are putting pressure on education funding. Already there are moves in many countries to cut back on education funding to enable a greater response to the welfare and health needs of the rapidly increasing percentage of older people in the community. Changes in technology, too, have created the possibility that schools themselves may become redundant. As Minzey and Townsend (1984) have indicated:

> Imagine for a moment the possibilities. An interactive television system has access to computer facilities that store in their memory banks educational information. Instead of reading about volcanoes or hearing about them from the teacher, a child can program his computer and see a volcano at work . . . Lessons may be for two or three hours a day broken down into short sessions that account for the child's age, intelligence and attention span . . . A terminal placed in the child's house also does not work set hours. A program may be called at 6:00 a.m. or 7:00 p.m. and consequently could align itself far more easily to the motivational aspects of learning.
>
> (Minzey and Townsend 1984: 15)

At a time when the computer games industry has a higher annual turnover than any other form of entertainment, including motion pictures, and at a time when governments are seeking to curtail the rapidly increasing education budget, it is time for schools to think about their long-term future. If we accept that we are moving from an industrial age to a technological/informational age, then there are some direct implications for schools. It is probably the first time since compulsory schools began that a major need exists to reassess the role of state schools.

It is time to develop a new set of principles for guiding schools in the twenty-first century. If we accept that reading, writing and 'rithmetic were the three Rs for schools in the past, then it could be argued that Relevance, Realism and Responsiveness (Minzey and Townsend: 1984) should be the guiding principles for restructuring schools in the future. The core–plus school would be relevant to both the needs of the state and the needs of the local community because both are involved in determining the programmes of the school; it would be realistic in its response to the current economic constraints by being more cost-effective than current schools through serving a larger proportion of the population; and it could be responsive to the needs of the local community by being readily available to them.

Since teachers, parents and school administrators all have a role to play in decisions related to the development of a school culture and the redesigning of the school itself, it becomes important for these groups to have a good understanding of how the core–plus school might go about this activity. The core–plus school accepts responsibility for school development and uses the model contained in Figure 6.1 as a guide for its implementation.

The model adopts a cyclical approach to school development, one that becomes self-perpetuating once the first implementation has been undertaken. Some of the terms used in the model, like 'vision' (or 'philosophy' or 'mission') and 'goals' are broader in scope and provide a theoretical basis for the development to take place. Other terms such as 'policy', 'process' and 'programme' are used to provide the rationale for subsequent activities. Still others, like 'curriculum', 'classroom activities' or 'community activities' and 'evaluation', are narrower still and are more practical in nature. Each of the stages of the model leads directly to one or more subsequent stages, and the cyclical nature of the model is evident when the evaluation undertaken at the end of the cycle leads directly to a reassessment of community needs and the start of the next cycle.

FEATURES OF THE CORE–PLUS MODEL

In some respects the model can be considered as two separate activities which sometimes have common components. On the one hand, to trace the activities on the left-hand side of the model provides the development of the curriculum component of school activities, which might be called the 'core–plus curriculum'. However, to trace the activities on the right-hand side of the model provides the development of the non-curriculum areas of the school, those that might be considered as aspects of community education, and could be referred to as the development of the 'core–plus school'. However, the linking of each of the two sides through common components of policy, process, programme and evaluation indicates that the two are not to be seen as separate. From this point of view, the curriculum perspective must include regular and meaningful interaction with the community and, in turn, part of the community education perspective would include concern for the regular school curriculum.

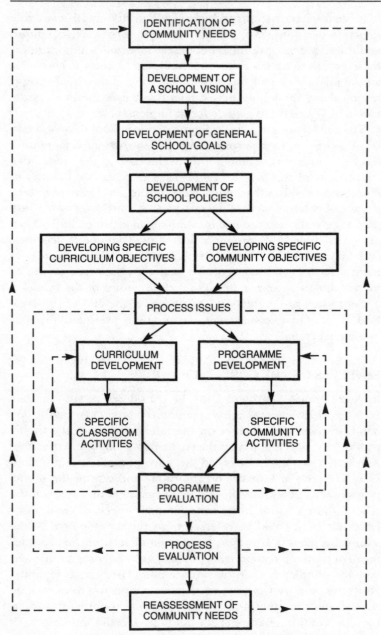

Figure 6.1 A model for the development of the core–plus school

The identification of community needs

Community needs would include the expectations held by the various members of the school community, but also those wider requirements that society expects of all schools. They would include curriculum needs for the students as well as those related to parents and the wider community. The responsibility of the core–plus school is to find out what the specific needs of its local community are. Not all needs might be able to be met by the school, but for those that cannot, the school might act as a broker or an intermediary between community members and the services they require.

Development of a school vision or philosophy

The terms 'vision', 'philosophy' and 'mission' might be seen as interchangeable. They are broad terms that describe perceptions of the world around us. The philosophy of the school identifies what the school community believes about the nature of people and the nature of learning. It will help to identify the orientation of the school as a whole. If the school community accepts that children have a desire to learn and that learning is best accomplished by active involvement with one's environment, the things that happen within that school will be different from a school where the primary belief is that children need to be coerced into learning situations and that these situations should be controlled by adults. The core–plus school would accept the premise that learning never stops, and one aspect of the school's vision would be to provide access for its community to the learning activities and opportunities that they require. The 'vision' or 'mission' of the school reflects its philosophy and guides the school in the direction it wants to go.

Development of general school goals

School goals or aims are a direct reflection of school needs modified by the school's vision of what it hopes to achieve. Minzey and Townsend (1984: 18) argued that 'educational activities should be based on the needs and problems of people for whom they are planned'. It could be argued that the development of educational goals is the natural link between the needs of the community and the activities and structures implemented by the school to fulfil those needs. If the community needs have been properly assessed it is possible to identify a goal that relates specifically to each of the identified needs.

Developing a vision and setting the goals

Sergiovanni (1987) suggested that the development and main-tenance of a school vision is one of the leadership responsibilities in the school, but it is important that as many people within the school community as possible be encouraged to participate in this activity. There are a number of ways in which this exercise might be accomplished but, for any of them, it is critical that the whole school community be involved. This is to ensure that the views expressed are representative of the community and the various groups within it, which is very important, but also to ensure a high level of commitment to following the vision through. Two differ-ent activities are described as examples of how a school mission or a set of school goals might be identified.

Burford, in his paper 'A Vision-Driven Organisation' (1991), used the 'Photo Language Process' to gain maximum involvement of the community. Many photographs, depicting scenes related to nature and human lifestyles, are spread out, and the participants in the exercise spend time looking at them, while reflecting on particular questions to be dealt with, such as 'What would you want this school to be?' or 'What qualities would you want of children who leave this school?' Participants are asked to select up to three of the photographs. People who select the same photograph are asked to work together. In small groups, they are asked to share their thoughts about each of the photographs and how they relate to their vision of the school in the future. A variety of further activities, such as making a collage from the photographs, or discussing the underlying values that emerged, can be undertaken. The results of these experiences are then shared with the other groups, and vision statements, followed by goals and objectives related to those statements, are produced.

A second process considers the needs of the various groups who have a relationship with the school. Each participant is asked, individually, to identify the three most important needs of children, parents, teachers and the wider community that should be addressed by the school. The difference between this activity and that already discussed is that it focuses on real needs (rather than assumptions of what other people need), and it doesn't focus on what the school is or isn't doing, but on what the people associated with the school need from it. Rather than having teachers make assumptions about what students need and building curriculum experiences around those assumptions, students will be able to identify their own needs, and then discuss them with teachers to see if both groups agree. If teachers have been accurate in their judgements, they will have the knowledge that they are addressing real student needs. If there is some discrepancy in the results, then teachers may have to adjust their programmes to suit the needs identified by the students.

The same will be true for the other three groups. Teachers, parents and members of the community will all have the opportunity to discuss their needs with the other groups. The small groups will be asked to repeat the exercise, identifying the three needs that the group feels are most important for students, teachers, parents and community. By having discussion groups that include representatives from the students, the staff, the parents and the local community, it is likely that the discussion will identify and support real needs to be addressed by the school, and that the specific needs of each of the four groups will be seen to be important by the other groups as well. Small groups share with the larger group, and a list of needs that corresponds with the feelings of the whole group is identified. These statements can then be rewritten as goal statements that address each of the identified needs.

Once all this information is available to the school, it has to be sorted and put into some order of priority since schools cannot resolve all community needs. The board of governors, school board or school council needs to be responsible for the activity of developing policy as described above, together with the elaboration of more specific objectives. Parents, staff and other community members might all be involved in the actual exercise of developing the policy goals and objectives, perhaps through the workings of an education committee, but the governing board of the school must take responsibility for the final product.

School policy

The school policy is the 'development and review of a statement of a school's aims, values, general principles and an overview of the arrangements being made to achieve them' (Fordham 1983b: 7). Thus, the needs, translated into goals for the school to achieve, together with the educational philosophy that has been adopted by the school, provide the central core of the school policy. Each of the major goals becomes worthy of a policy statement. The means of achieving the goals and objectives of the school will be guided by the educational philosophy that the school has accepted. As some of the identified needs will relate to curriculum areas and others will relate to wider community concerns, the educational policy of the core–plus school becomes the centre-piece of school development, both in curriculum terms and in terms of community development. The school policy is the mid-point of the continuum between theory and practice, and is the direct link between the vision of what the school hopes to achieve and the reality of what it does.

School objectives

Having identified the major policy statements, which will indicate the goals that the school has accepted and the means by which it intends to achieve them, it is then possible to write more specific objectives which identify target groups, time lines and achievement criteria, that will enable the school to judge how well it is moving towards the fulfilment of those goals. Individual objectives that relate to any specific goal might be coupled with other similar ones that enable the development of a variety of educational programmes within the school, all of which, together, indicate a full recognition of that particular goal. If one objective is achieved, then the school can say that it has moved somewhat towards the achievement of the wider goal, but it cannot say that it has successfully achieved that goal until all the objectives it set itself have been achieved. A consistent monitoring process is a necessary part of the on-going planning to establish whether the failure to achieve all of the objectives was due to poor implementation or because circumstances within the school changed in a very short time. In both cases the ability to identify why the objectives have not been achieved and the flexibility to enable modification of some of the school goals, where necessary, are crucial elements of the core–plus school.

This is the first stage at which the development of the core–plus curriculum and the core–plus school might be considered separately.

Having developed a series of school-wide goals, both curriculum objectives and community development objectives can be identified, sometimes from the same school goal. For instance, a school policy statement that indicates the school's desire for each child to succeed to their maximum potential might generate a curriculum objective for each child to undertake a certain amount of homework per week, based on the child's year level. The same school policy statement could also generate a community development objective for the school to run a parent education programme that explained to parents the value and relevance of homework and provided them with information that would enable their child to enjoy, as well as successfully complete, homework activities.

Another policy statement encouraging parents to be involved in school activities might generate a specific curriculum objective of parents being actively involved in classroom activities and a specific community development objective of parents attending an adult education class at the school. These objectives, although they can be acted on separately and by different people, nevertheless have natural linkings in the core–plus school.

Process issues

The separate considerations for the development of curriculum and community development objectives merge again because both require similar processes to be enacted if they are to be fulfilled to their highest potential. The processes that are undertaken in any school are critical to the overall level of that school's effectiveness, as has been pointed out in Chapter 2. The process issues listed there that have not already been referred to in this chapter include leadership, decision-making, communication, resource allocation and school environment. Each of these is a critical concern to every school, but becomes even more so in the core–plus school. In a core–plus school the base of leadership widens, more people become involved in more decisions, the level of communication rises and becomes more varied, resources need to be allocated over a wider area of activity and the need for raising additional resources emerges. The school needs to have an encouraging environment not only for students, but also for adults, who have different expectations and demands.

To these we might also add professional development to encourage the development of planning skills, and working with other agencies outside the school to establish and develop wider community projects. The latter two are particularly important in the core–plus school. In the first case, more people in the school (teachers and parents) will be involved in planning than has been the case in the past and, in the second case, if the needs of the community spread into the areas of welfare, safety and community development activities, then other community agencies will be involved, and there will be a need for communication at the very least, and collaboration in many activities.

Curriculum development and specific classroom activities

The curriculum development activity would involve turning the specific objectives identified by the school into a comprehensive school-wide programme, broken down into the expectations for each school year. Each aspect of the school curriculum could be related back to the various specific objectives identified for each of the goals. Thus, a specific objective that each child should undertake at least one excursion or camping activity each year (at the primary school level) could be translated into a programme that saw half-day then full-day excursions in the first two years, together with a progression that saw sleep-overs at school, short, and then longer, camping programmes or visits to other schools and perhaps a week-long mobile camping trip in the last year of primary school. The curriculum development activity would see the development of a rationale and aims for the whole programme and a justification for the placement of particular programmes at each of the levels.

The school staff take responsibility for the development of a curriculum that helps to achieve those identified goals. Parents and community members might be involved in the development of curriculum statements through membership of curriculum committees, or by giving their views to those involved, but the principal and staff will take responsibility for the final product, because this is where their background knowledge and experience can be best used.

Classroom activities would be individual day-to-day events, part of the regular school curriculum, that help to achieve those specific objectives. Specific classroom activities are the responsibility of the individual teachers, who plan day-to-day experiences that correspond with the overall goals for each of the subjects being taught. Parents might help in the classroom, or in other ways, to present the specific activities, and groups of teachers may work together to present common experiences to all children of a particular year level, or for particular subject areas, but the final responsibility for these activities lies with the individual teacher. It can be seen from this plan that, as the process moves from the theoretical or philosophical to more specific considerations so, too, the responsibility for the process becomes more specific. Whereas the whole school community needs to take part in, and be responsible for, the development of the school philosophy and goals, when these goals become more focused into objectives and specific activities, the school staff and individual teachers accept higher levels of responsibility and the rest of the school com- munity contributes in a less specific way. Specific activities might change from year to year and might vary from class to class depending on the interests and resources available to individual teachers, but the expectations would remain the same from year to year and from teacher to teacher unless a review of the policy or objectives warranted a change.

From a theoretical viewpoint, each of the specific activities that happen in classrooms should be able to be traced back to one or more of the school policies that exist within the school, and even further back to one of the identified needs expressed by the community. If this linkage cannot be maintained, then either teachers are not using the school policy as a basis for their teaching as well as they might, or the school policies do not reflect accur- ately the needs expressed by the school community.

This process of development from needs through goals, policies, and objectives to curriculum and classroom activities might result in a profile similar to the one indicated in the following example.

EXAMPLE
School X: an inner-city school with more than 50 per cent of its population coming from one of four backgrounds: Greek, Turkish, Vietnamese and Cambodian.
Need   One of the community needs identified by
                the school is 'to recognise the ethnic
                diversity of the local community'.

Vision	The school council adopted the philosophy that the active involvement of the parent group in all activities within the school would lead to higher achievement of the children within the school.
Goal	The school goal agreed upon was to 'establish and maintain a programme that recognises the ethnic diversity of the local community'.
Policy Statement	That the parents of the school would be actively encouraged to participate in school activities and would always be kept fully informed on matters related to their child and general school activities.
Specific objective	To have parents involved in cultural activities within the classroom. (A number of other objectives could be written to help to achieve the same goal.)
School curriculum	A programme incorporating lessons about the language, art and culture of the home countries for each of the students in year four is planned.
Activities	As each country is being studied, parents from that country are invited to participate, in special activities related to food, work, art, language and culture in those countries. Information about the special activities, with an invitation to participate is put into the school newsletter, and the class teacher writes to the parents indicating the aims of the group of lessons, and an outline of the programme to be followed.

Programme development and specific community activities

The programme development activity for the core–plus school would closely mirror that of the curriculum development activity within the core–plus curriculum. However, instead of the school staff being responsible for curriculum development and individual teachers being responsible for day-to-day activities, with parents and other community members playing a supporting role in both, the position would be reversed for community development activities. Here a group of parents and community members (with teachers, if they chose to be involved) might form a committee to oversee the community development programme of the school, and individuals from that committee would take responsibility for overseeing the development of a particular activity. Such a committee might be called a community education committee or a community council, and might have its own rules and budget. It might have a reporting and subordinate role to the school governing board, which would ratify its decisions, or it might simply communicate with the board. These are decisions that would need to be made in the first instance by the school governing board.

The community development programme of the school would need to consider additional issues that are not as critical to the school curriculum areas. Considerations of staffing, both professional and volunteer, and financing, advertising and managing the community development programme will be necessary if the programme is to be successful and on-going. Each of these issues would need to be resolved by the community council to ensure that the community development activities were not a drain on the regular school's activities.

The process of development of a community activity using the model might result in the sequence of planning shown in the following example.

EXAMPLE

School X: an inner-city school with more than 50 per cent of its population coming from one of four backgrounds: Greek, Turkish, Vietnamese and Cambodian.

Need	One of the community needs identified by the school is 'to recognise the ethnic diversity of the local community'.
Vision	The school council adopted the philosophy that the active involvement of the parent group in all activities within the school would lead to higher achievement of the children within the school.
Goal	The school goal agreed upon was to 'establish and maintain a programme that

	recognises the ethnic diversity of the local community'.
Policy statement	That the school would provide a multi-cultural programme for community members that would enable them to learn about others in their community.
Specific objective	To have at least one cultural activity each month, with each culture within the school community being represented at least once during the year.
Community development programme	Each month a different ethnic group will be invited to host an evening which will include a meal, a talk about the country (a travelogue) and folk songs and stories associated with their country. Community members will be given the opportunity to learn a new language. This will culminate in an ethnic festival at the end of the year.
Activities	This is the programme devised by the Italian community for the month of March. Community members are invited to an Italian dinner. They are treated to a brief history and geography of Italy (with slides) by a local historian. Italian members of the community sing folk songs and discuss their memories of home. Italian classes are held two nights a week for the month. Profits from the dinner are used to purchase a set of Italian language tapes and travel books of Italy which can be borrowed by members of the community from the school library.

It can be seen from this that similar needs, goals and policy statements can create both curriculum activities and community development activities, but it is important to realise that different people and different processes might be used to bring each about. Whereas the staff of the school are responsible for the development and implementation of the school curriculum, even though parents and other community members may play a role, the development and implementation of the community development programme is the responsibility of the community itself, even though the principal and other teachers may play a role. In both cases leadership, communication, resource allocation and professional development will be required, but who is involved in the processes and the nature of this involvement will vary from activity to activity.

Programme and process monitoring and evaluation

As has been suggested earlier in this section, it is important to monitor each programme during its implementation as well as to evaluate it once it is completed. The monitoring process can take into account quickly any circumstances that might lead to specific objectives not being achieved and can ensure that the developing needs of the community are still being addressed. The use of debriefing sessions for both participants and organisers keeps the fulfilment of community needs as the central focus during the course of the activity. Information obtained from sessions such as these may see a change to the programme or even a change to the overall goal itself as the community becomes more knowledgeable about its response to the programme. This process shows the differences between the nature of the programmes offered by the core–plus school and those offered by, say, a cinema. The core–plus school modifies its programmes and activities to ensure continued relevance and interest, whereas the cinema gambles on the intrinsic interest of its programmes.

A final evaluation of the success of the activity will assist the school to maintain an ongoing commitment to a quality educational programme. The evaluation can be both summative, that is, look back at what has just happened, or formative, that is, make judgements about what should happen next.

The programme evaluation would concentrate on the activities that have taken place, whether they were part of the school curriculum or part of the community development programme, and questions such as 'How many attended?', 'How valuable did the participants find the activity?', 'Were the specific objectives related to the activity achieved?' and 'What should we do next?' could be asked. The results of the evaluation would help to guide staff, for curriculum activities, or the community council, for community activities, to improve their offerings and to establish whether activities need to be improved, repeated or whether a subsequent activity should be planned.

The process evaluation would concentrate on those aspects related to the planning and implementation of the activity from an organiser's perspective rather than from a participant's perspective. Questions such as 'How many people were involved in the planning?', 'Did they think involvement was worthwhile?', 'How could future planning be improved?' might assist the staff or community council in a reassessment of the way in which the school goes about its business.

Re-assessment of community needs

The formative evaluation discussed above helps to complete the cycle of planning. With planners, organisers and participants all being involved in the evaluation activity, the school can establish whether its programmes are helping to meet the goals it set for itself.

From the programme perspective, if some goals have been met, then others can be addressed. If some goals have been partially met, then a repeat of a current programme or an extension of the current programme can be mounted to move the school closer to its goals. If some goals have not been met at all, then additional efforts need to be made to address those needs specifically. Whichever of these is the case, the school has a new set of achievements to address, and the process of planning and implementing these new achievements can begin.

From the process perspective, if some people who wanted to be involved felt that their involvement was not as good as they would have liked, then the school board of management or community council would have new goals to set. Depending on the results of the evaluation, further training in special areas might be required, the communication lines might need to be improved or those with leadership positions might need to adjust their management style. Further effort might be needed to increase the involvement of community members to ensure that everyone feels represented and that no-one has too much to do.

The implementation of the core–plus development model would enable all schools to move from their current perspective to that of a core–plus school. Further details of how to go about this process are contained in subsequent chapters.

Chapter 7

Leadership in the core–plus school

Outstanding leaders have a vision for their schools – a mental picture of a preferred future – which is shared with all in the school community and which shapes the programme for learning and teaching.

(Beare *et al.* 1989: 99–100)

WHAT IS LEADERSHIP?

There are many texts on leadership, and much of their content is either confusing or contradictory. There has been an evolution over the years in the terms in which leadership has been defined. The early definitions identified the leader as the focus of group processes; the leader was seen as the one who provided direction for the rest of the group. Such a leader was thought to have certain characteristics or traits that non-leaders did not share. But research attempts found that there were very few traits that a range of leaders had in common. Those that emerged were intelligence, dominance, self-confidence, high energy levels and a task-related knowledge (Robbins 1993: 365). But even these had moderate rather than strong correlations.

Later definitions held that the art of leadership was the ability to induce compliance in the rest of the group. The leader possessed the ability to motivate others in the group and was the one capable of generating the highest level of achievement with the least amount of conflict. Leadership was explained in terms of the leader's behaviour providing this motivation. Such an attempt was the Managerial Grid provided by Blake and Mouton (1964). They argued that a team management style was preferable to one that focused on the task to be accomplished with little consideration of the people in the group or one that focused wholly on the group to the detriment of getting the task done, but little evidence was provided to show that this was the case in all management situations.

Since many of the early theories found difficulty in establishing any clear relationship between the leader's behaviour and group performance, it was accepted that leadership theory was more complex than had first been thought. Various contingency theories that tried to fill in the gaps created by the more dogmatic behavioural theories, considered issues such as the quality of leader–group relations, the availability of information, and the relative power available to the leader and members of the group, among others. One such contingency theory of leadership, proposed by Tannenbaum and Schmidt (1958), was called the Leadership–Behaviour Continuum.

Whereas Blake and Mouton confined leadership to a grid constructed from two axes (Blake and Mouton 1964), Tannenbaum and Schmidt characterised leadership as a continuum of behaviours ranging from leader-centred strategies to group-centred strategies. In their model the choice of strategies made by the leader was influenced by three forces:

- Forces within the leader, which include the leader's value system, tolerance and assessment of the group's competence and his or her own ability;
- Forces within the group, which include the group member's need for direction or independence, interest in the project, desire to assume responsibility, knowledge, experience and expectations;
- Forces in the situation, which include organisational structure, predetermined goals, the nature of the task and time constraints.

This model describes the degree of involvement by the leader and the group in the decision-making processes as a continuum. The behaviour of the leader changes from having total authority and making all the decisions through consultation of various kinds, to allowing the group to define the problem and make the decisions themselves. As the group participation increases, the leader authority decreases. Leader behaviour at various points on the continuum, moving from the most leader-centred point to the most group-centred point, would be:

1 leader decides and announces decision to the group. Group plays no part in decision-making at all;
2 leader decides and then 'sells' the decision to the group;
3 leader decides and after announcing the decision, answers questions;
4 leader presents tentative decision, consults with group, then leader decides;
5 leader presents problem, asks for ideas then leader decides;
6 leader presents problem, defines limits and then group decides;
7 leader gives as much freedom as he or she has to the group in order to determine problem and to decide.

(Tannenbaum and Schmidt 1958: 96)

It is possible to judge where on the continuum leaders would be by noting the behaviour that they use when decisions are being made.

Tannenbaum and Schmidt's model demonstrates that leaders are the people in the group who have 'precedence or pre-eminence' and 'a position of authority as commander or director'. It introduces the notions of power differentials and role definitions. There is some structural basis for leadership. The relationship between the leader and the rest of the group is one of commander and follower, the one with precedence and the rest who have none.

We must conclude from this that leadership is interactional; for leadership to occur there must be one who is prepared to lead and others who are prepared to follow. Secondly, we must conclude that leadership involves both an individual, or small group, process and the processes of the whole group. From this we can view leadership as being a combination of two separate but related entities – the behaviour of the leader or leaders and the processes involved in getting the group to act. Leadership seems be a midpoint between other activities such as administration and management where administration involves the implementation and organisation of projects and activities that have established processes and procedures; leadership involves initiating new structures, processes and procedures, rather than implementing current ones; and management is a broad term that contains three parts: planning, leadership and administration. A manager is involved in planning goals for the project, providing leadership to establish the project, and then administering the project itself.

Although the relationship between each of these terms is a fairly loose one, generally speaking as one moves from administration through leadership to management more responsibility for the project is accepted, and there is greater initiating activity on the part of the individual. It can be seen from these definitions that principals of schools could be seen in three ways, as adminstrators, merely implementing decisions made by education authorities or the school management committee; as leaders, moving the school forward to new processes and programmes; or as managers, playing a key role in forward planning and seeing those plans through to fruition.

The processes of leadership

If we view leadership as a group process, we can establish that there are four factors that need to be considered.

1 Leadership is always relative to a situation. Every situation that requires leadership differs because of:
   - the structures of the organisation
   - what has to be done
   - who the leader is
   - who comprises the group.
2 Leadership is directed towards some goal. The leadership may or may not be involved in the construction of the goals but, once they have been identified, leadership is the behaviour of the person whose task is to direct the efforts of the group to ensure that the goals are attained.
3 Leadership involves social interaction. For leadership to occur there must be some group interaction to establish the relationship between the leader and the rest of the group, to define role expectations for the group and to establish relationships between people in the group.
4 Leadership involves a power relationship. Leadership can only exist if there is a legitimate power base. The power of the leader is determined as the ability of the leader to cause others to adjust their behaviour to conform with certain requirements.

In summary, leadership

- cannot be completely explained by referring to personal characteristics of the leader;
- consists of a relationship between an individual and a group according to the needs of a specific situation;

– will involve a demand for a particular leadership style that varies according to each situation and the individuals involved in both the leadership position and the group.

LEADERSHIP IN THE CORE–PLUS SCHOOL

In the past, the principal of the school simply administered, that is, implemented decisions made by remote education systems. But leadership and management skills are becoming increasingly important as each school makes its unique response to the demands made by the state, the education system and the local community. Schools have moved towards greater local control, given different names, such as school-based management, school-site management and the self-managing school, in different parts of the world, but still basically directed towards implementing the curriculum requirements imposed by the state. The introduction of the core–plus philosophy into a school makes the issue of leadership even more critical, since the core–plus concept not only considers demands and structures that are already in place, but moves the school through a process of redesign. As has been discussed in the previous chapter, two major features become the central components of redesigning the school. The first is the development of a new school culture and the second is the restructuring of the school, which will involve the organisation of the school and how resources, including financial, facility and personnel resources, are to be used.

To enable these perspectives to be considered, the core–plus school has to encourage a wide leadership base. As well as the principal and other members of staff exercising leadership in management and the implementation of curriculum areas, the school management committee, whatever it might be called, will need to exercise leadership in its decision-making to ensure that the 'plus' components of the curriculum and the 'plus' components of the whole school programme are relevant to the community in which the school exists.

Because the core–plus school seeks to undertake a continuous development of its community, leadership renewal, for current leaders, and replacement will be part of the school culture. Leadership skills will be enhanced through staff and community development activities and by encouraging people to take responsibility for certain aspects of school activities. In this way, new leaders will emerge to replace those staff or community members who leave the school. From this perspective it is necessary to look at two key components of leadership within the core–plus school. The first is the leadership that comes from the school management committee, which I will refer to here as the core–plus council, and the second considers the chief executive officer of the school, the principal or headteacher.

THE CORE–PLUS COUNCIL

The core–plus council is a representative group of people who live in the community surrounding the school. The council meets to coordinate, plan and implement activities, policies and practices that will enhance the development of community education in that community and especially within the school. The council may consist of members of the school, including staff, students and parents, members of community agencies and groups, and representatives of the community itself. The core–plus council may have any or all of the following purposes:

- to ensure that the regular school programme deals with all of the mandatory curriculum areas determined by the state or government, together with those areas considered by the local community to be of particular relevance for the school's children;
- to ensure the programme is properly developed, presented and evaluated to enable the best chance for student success;
- to enable children to have access to the best resources in terms of personnel and facilities that the community can offer;
- to discover and recognise problems in the community and to work towards the resolution of these problems;
- to provide a means whereby groups or individuals within the community can present ideas or plans that are designed to improve the educational or community services in the community;
- to assist in the coordination of community services and activities, thus giving maximum access for those who require them;
- to assist in the development of a united community to enable support for projects that are too large for individuals or groups to carry out alone;
- to develop, operate and administer, in conjunction with other agencies, programmes that will assist the educational development of the whole community;

- to ensure that the facilities and resources of the school are used to their full potential.

The establishment of a core–plus council

Once the current school management committee has accepted a formal motion of support for the principle of core–plus education, and has established a policy to enable this to occur, it is then time to implement the structures that will allow the development of school-based community education. At this stage there are two options open to the school. The first is to establish a subcommittee of the already existing school management committee that will advise it on matters of implementing the community education philosophy within the school; the second is to expand the membership and role of the school management committee to become the core–plus council.

The second alternative, to expand the school management committee itself and to allow the new core–plus council the opportunity to debate the issues as they are raised, may well be the better option. In this way the whole council would be both school – and community – oriented rather than concentrating more on one viewpoint or the other. It may be difficult to expand the school management committee immediately for constitutional reasons and it may be more useful to establish a core–plus advisory committee with the aim of eventually incorporating it with the school management committee to become the core–plus council.

Why have a core–plus council?

In today's society, education is regarded as a life-long process that can be loosely divided into the pre-school years, the years at school, and those after a person has left school. A core–plus council has the opportunity to make a contribution to each of the three phases.

Pre-school

The core–plus council, by liaising with both pre-school and primary school representatives, can ensure that appropriate formal and informal activities are provided for pre-school children, thus ensuring that they are adequately prepared for their academic career. The provision of appropriate leisure, health and welfare services in the community will help to give the child a happy and supportive home environment which will enable him or her to be healthy and well adjusted on entering school.

School years

Since the child's school achievement is affected by his or her environment, the school, through the core–plus council, can fulfil its obligation to improve the physical, social, economic and psychological environment of the community. Since each community is unique, its members would have the best understanding of the educational needs for that community.

Post-school

In conjunction with other agencies the core–plus council can provide facilities to relieve such problems as adult illiteracy, the need for retraining, unemployment and the need for leisure and recreation facilities. By involving adults in the decision-making processes in the school, the school is assisting them to fulfil their needs for involvement and communication with their fellows.

The following principles are the basis of the argument for participation on the core–plus council:

– People are more likely to accept change when they have participated in the planning for that change.
– People are more likely to change their behaviour if they see that others are changing theirs.
– People are more likely to act upon a request if they feel positive about the request. People, acting as a group, can:
  • stimulate the consideration of new action;
  • analyse the difficulties of implementation;
  • suggest ways of overcoming problems;
  • make decisions about what action should be taken.
– People are more likely to carry out actions if there has been free discussion about them and general support for them has been obtained.
– People, through working with others in group decision-making, may change their attitudes as individuals.

The constitution for a core–plus council

The first major task for the core–plus council is the production of a constitution. If the school is governed by specific regulations laid down by the state or educational authorities, it would be a matter of seeking permission from those authorities to change various parts of those regulations to incorporate new initiatives.

The constitution may be written in such a way as to include all of the current activities of the school management committee, and to simply add new goals and objectives, expand the membership and establish a new range of sub-committees. Once ratified by the parents and any other agencies (such as the education authority) that might be required, the new constitution comes into effect.

Membership of a core–plus council

The membership of the core–plus council should closely represent the community in which it resides. To be really effective the core–plus council needs to reflect its community's diversity in terms of economic background, ethnicity, sex, age and special interest. The broader the base for the membership of the council, the more responsive the council will be to community needs and problems. Generally the list of potential members can be drawn from the following groups:

- School employees: principal, teachers, administrative staff;
- School related groups: students, parents, associations;
- Community representatives: senior citizens, non-parents, youth, young marrieds;
- Agencies: police, health, welfare, churches, local government, recreation;
- Business/industry: Chamber of Commerce, local businesses, industrial representatives;
- Service clubs: Lions, Apex, Rotary;
- Action groups: teachers' union, local union representatives.

In all cases the groups should be allowed to elect or nominate their own representatives. Initially the school management committee can extend an invitation to the groups to attend a preliminary organisation meeting. At this meeting the proposal for a core–plus council should be put forward, together with the philosophy that underlies it and what it hopes to accomplish. Once accepted, the initial membership and specific tasks can be established. It is suggested that the maximum number of members for an effective core–plus council is twenty. If the council becomes too large it will not enable effective discussion and decision-making. Once established, the members of the core–plus council, both collectively and individually, will have roles to play.

The roles of a core–plus council

Collectively, the core–plus council will be seen as the instigator for many areas of activity within the school community. Individually, the members of the core–plus council will need to provide the viewpoint of the group they represent, but also to work for the good of the community as a whole. A number of tasks will need to be undertaken, including:
- assessing the needs of the school and the community through needs assessment and discussion;
- assisting in the evaluation of the most pressing needs and the setting of community priorities;
- providing leadership for school, or community, action campaigns to achieve action on needs assessed as having priority;
- assisting in the uniting of individuals and groups to form a democratic force;
- encouraging community participation in the decision-making process;
- assisting in the coordination of community activities and services;
- developing with the principal and staff, the school philosophy and policy and assisting the principal and staff in providing advice to local, state and federal authorities in matters relating to:
  • building and grounds usage
  • future developments
  • community projects
  • provision of adult education
  • the analysis of social problems in the community;
- initiating support for school or community projects;
- stimulating public awareness of the school;
- acting as a forum for discussion of community issues.

Organisation of the core–plus council

Since the work of the core–plus council will most likely become too much for a single group of people to cope with adequately and since one of the main objectives of the philosophy of community education is to involve as many people in the decision-making as possible, the structure of the council should allow a great deal of flexibility.

In this situation the core–plus council could become the policy-making body and council meetings which need to be held at a regular time each month could become the forum for discussion of wide ranging community issues. An executive committee, consisting of the officers of the council (for example, the principal, president, secretary, treasurer and community education co-ordinator) might implement the policy decisions, after the matters have been discussed by council, and they might also make executive decisions for any matters that need urgent attention.

A sub-committee system allows members of the community who are not interested in policy matters to take part in decision-making in an area of particular interest to them. One member of the council would become the chairman of the sub-committee, and other members would be drawn from the community or co-opted when special skills or information were needed. The sub-committee would engage in research, make decisions, and make recommendations for action to the council. A number of sub-committees could be established bearing in mind the various functions to which the council needs to direct itself. Some of these might include:

– communications and publicity;
– facility maintenance and usage;
– facility planning and renovation;
– youth activities;
– adult education;
– community social, family and welfare concerns;
– community recreation and community affairs;
– social services and health.

The following guidelines may be used in an endeavour to ensure that the work of the core–plus council is effective:

– Ensure that the membership of the council represents as best as possible all of the people in the community.
– Include any group that has an interest in cooperation.

- Hold regular meetings, and regular public meetings, to ensure people have the chance to participate.
- Ensure that the youth of the community is well represented. It is here that future leaders will be trained.
- Ensure that the council structure is simple, accessible, and is developed according to the needs of the community.
- Rotate officers regularly, to give more people leadership training and opportunities.
- Allow public participation at meetings.
- Ensure that any individual or group in the community has access to the council.
- Allow as much discussion as possible before decisions are made.

The core–plus council is the springboard of a healthy community education programme. From the goals, structure and organisation of the council the process elements, so vital to the philosophy as a whole, are developed. At council level the ability to involve the community, the ability to liaise and work with other agencies, and the development of group work skills and planning skills are all crucial. Each of these areas is initiated and controlled at the council level and the presence of them at council indicates a healthy process at all levels. A successfully operating core–plus council might be expected to lead to the following results:

- Improved academic performance by the students in the school.
- Parents showing an interest in school programmes, and assisting in their implementation.
- Parents becoming involved in youth and adult programmes either as participants or leaders.
- More communication between the home and the school.
- Greater community support for the school.
- Open debate and better understanding between community groups.
- Leadership skills developed by members of the community.
- Business, agency and professional support for school issues and programmes.
- A unified community spirit.
- A wider range of educational activities provided for children, youth and adults.
- More access for members of the community to its range of services.
- The development of individual feelings of worth.

THE PRINCIPAL OF THE CORE–PLUS SCHOOL

The role of the principal is critical to the development of the core–plus concept. Despite all attempts to encourage others to accept leadership responsibilities, the principal will still be seen by some people and groups as the person in charge, and in some respects they are right. The principal serves as the administrator in charge of the school and works closely with the core–plus council to implement its policies. The principal is also the chief executive officer of the school with responsibility to manage all its affairs including general financial and curriculum control and the supervision of employees assigned to serve in the school. The principal may be accountable outside the school as well.

But if the principal is to move from being an administrator, implementing the decisions of others, to a leadership role, then a number of possibilities emerge. The principal may behave in any of the following ways. He or she:

- may be a *figurehead*, letting others make the decisions, and simply carrying them out;
- may have a *specific position* in the group with certain set responsibilities;
- may be *charismatic* and induce the group to follow his or her actions;
- may act as a *dictator* who has sufficient power to force the group to do his or her bidding;
- may act as a *facilitator* who enables others within the school to be involved to the levels they feel capable of, and may provide support, training and encouragement to increase those levels of involvement.

There will be various members of the school community who will respond better to the dictatorial principal who makes decisions and is seen as a strong leader, and there will be others who see the principal as a figurehead, simply following through on decisions made by the core–plus council. However, if the leadership role of the principal encompasses the three basic responsibilities namely, to help the school community to get things done, to help the school community work effectively together and to help the school community work effectively with other agencies, then perhaps the role of the principal as facilitator might be the best one for the core–plus school.

In order to fulfil the three main roles of leadership, principals of core–plus schools will need to establish, maintain and regularly consult with the school community and involve the people in decisions which affect them. In order to do this they will need to establish good relationships between each of the various groups within the school and establish processes which will enable each group to work with others in a meaningful and positive way. In this way principals will be able to develop feelings of trust and understanding between the council, community and staff. Core–plus principals will also encourage the core–plus council to exercise its role in the decision-making process and provide its members with necessary support and training to ensure that it is effective.

In carrying out these responsibilities the core–plus principal will need to demonstrate the skills of many different professions, such as those of a teacher, a counsellor, an administrator, a supervisor, a salesperson, a public relations person, a human relations builder and a staff developer. It can be seen from this list that the principal is the centre-point of any development to initiate or maintain the core–plus philosophy. The principal, to a large extent, is able to facilitate (or control) the culture of the school, the means and levels of communication within the school and the tone and direction that the school will take. Much has been written about the principalship and the various activities that describe its task and there is no need for them to be repeated here. The most critical factor for the principal of the core–plus school is that he or she must engender a high level of community support for the school, a high level of participation and activity across a range of curricular and extra-curricular interests, quality communications within the school and the development of good relationships among all those involved. It is unreasonable to expect that individual principals will be able to do this alone, so the essence of leadership in the core–plus school is for it to be an expected responsibility of many, rather than just a few.

Chapter 8

Process issues for core–plus education

> People can be trusted. Those interested in and responsible for the education of children hold the welfare of those children in high regard.
>
> (Hansen and Marburger 1989: 4)

As indicated in the previous chapter the processes used in the development of the core–plus school, starting with the leadership style adopted by the core–plus council and the principal, are critical to the development of the school culture. Three major process issues arise for this development. The first relates to getting parents and the local community involved in the first place; the second relates to the development of the skills required to have them work well together; and the third relates to an on-going evaluation of the success (or otherwise) of these two elements to ensure that people will continue to be involved in the school over time, and that their involvement will be acceptable to them as well as being effective for the school.

GETTING PEOPLE INVOLVED

This is not the place to go into a long discourse on the history of education or on the development of society. Perhaps all that needs to be said is that as populations in most developed countries grew and became more mobile, villages became towns and towns became cities, some of the community spirit that typified, and still typifies, some country areas, dwindled. The natural caring for one's neighbour largely disappeared and people became isolated from one another. People who lived in the same street did not know one another and television provided most of the contact many had with the rest of the world.

In recent years people have tried to recapture the spirit that they once knew, and those who have managed it have felt fulfilled and useful. People who become involved in community activities are usually involved in a number of activities. It is not unusual to see the same faces at the school PTA, the kindergarten, the canteen, at church clubs and children's sport. People are discovering that being involved with others satisfies a real need in themselves.

By actively involving children and adults in decisions about education, about what issues concern them, about aspects of community development, we are providing people with in-service training in democracy. If people become aware of the power of involvement, they may wish to become involved in broader issues. Community involvement in schools might be the first step to a better practice of the democratic ideal.

Rationale for community involvement

In order for appropriate decisions to be made about problems within the community, it must first be established what the needs, desires and problems within a given community might be. The greater the community involvement in the process, the greater the input of different groups within the community, then the more likely that what is generated will be an accurate reflection of that community. The following six areas are the most popular areas of concern and are some arguments for increasing community involvement in the school.

1 Policy making: community participation will contribute to the development of school policies and practices which are most effective and equitable for that community.
2 Service delivery: the capacity of the school to solve educational problems is enhanced if parents and community members are part of the problem-solving.
3 Community development: effective community participation may contribute to the development of a healthy and stable community, where services are adequately and fairly distributed and where people have a sense of community pride, responsibility and power.
4 Individual development: involvement in community activities can contribute to the development of self-confidence, can improve people's abilities and social skills and lead to a feeling of personal contribution.

5 Organisational effectiveness: community participation can contribute both to increased usage of the school and improved
performance by the people in the school. This increases the
cost effectiveness, as well as the organisational effectiveness of
the school.
6 Performance of students: community involvement can contribute to improved academic performance and less problems
within schools.

Improved student performance is a cogent reason for increasing
community involvement in the school, and possibly the best place
to start when attempting to involve greater numbers of parents.
Much research can be cited as evidence that parental aspirations,
interests and involvement have a positive effect on children's
academic ability, self-concept and aspirations. Two books by Anne
Henderson (1981, 1987) from the National Committee for
Citizens in Education on the relationship between parent involvement and school achievement, provide ample evidence of the
research in this area.

Why do people participate?

People may wish to participate in elements of the school programme for one of three reasons:

- they perceive that their input is relevant to the issue and will
  make a difference in the outcome;
- they believe that they will be directly affected by the decision
  being made and wish to have some control over it. The problem
  that is to be discussed is one that concerns the individual;
- they have been asked for their views or involvement. People who
  have been elected or appointed to certain positions want the
  input of individuals and request their involvement.

The core–plus school uses the third of these more frequently than
in the past. Although participation in school affairs might be seen
as the ultimate goal, increased levels of involvement by parents in
their children's education – for instance, by hearing their child
read on a regular basis – will also be seen as success. Increased
involvement, even though the parent may not participate at the
school itself, is worth fostering.

When can we involve the community?

The short answer to this question is 'all the time'. Members of the community can be involved in the identification, and analysis, of community problems, when constructing possible solutions and gathering information about them, when developing and implementing plans of action and for the ongoing review and the final evaluation of the project – both programme and process.

For the involvement to have a long-term chance of success, the involvement activities must be meaningful for those concerned. This can be accomplished by ensuring that those involved have well-defined roles and the size of the group is appropriate to the task. The group must take into account the diversity of community interest and should have well-defined structures and procedures. Those taking leadership responsibilities should be well trained, skilled and experienced in working with others and be able to delegate both power and specific tasks. Open communication is essential. Training must be provided to those who wish to be involved but feel unsure of their capacity and those involved must be given public credit for their work.

Barriers to community involvement

Over the years many excuses have been used to reject the notion of improved community involvement in school decision-making. Some are offered by schools as a means for keeping parents and the community out and some are used by the community as an excuse for not becoming involved. In some cases the excuses given are legitimate and need to be accepted; but in other cases the issue of community involvement is not high enough on the individual's list of priorities to rate serious consideration. People working in the core–plus school, if they really want to increase community involvement in their school, may need to devise some strategies to move this involvement above, say, watching a show on television instead. Some of the barriers that are put in the way of community involvement include:

- lack of administrative support for the concept;
- lack of time;
- apathy;
- difficulty of convincing people of the value of involvement;

- reluctance of professionals to regard the community as potential problem solvers;
- relegation by professionals: participants are given only aide-roles.

If we accept the idea that community involvement is good for all those involved and for the school itself, we must also accept that in the past too little has been done generally to promote the concept. Three issues need to be addressed, once the principle of involvement has been accepted: the ways in which parents can be involved in the school, how to initiate community involvement and how to make that involvement effective.

COMMUNITY INVOLVEMENT IN THE CORE–PLUS SCHOOL

It is possible for parents and members of the community to be involved in the school at the decision-making level, by working in or for the school or by learning or gaining from the school themselves. It is obvious that there are many ways within each of these categories in which community involvement can be manifested in the core–plus school. Activities that might be useful in promoting further involvement in the core–plus school would include:

1 For parents: family programmes, father–child, mother–child programmes, parent education nights, students bringing parents into class, parent acting as tutor, an invitation to all parents to a coffee morning, parent interest nights – nutrition, home budgeting.
2 For the wider community: the invitation of the community to school functions via the local press, the instigation of a senior citizens' volunteer programme, the distribution of community newsletters to local residents, the invitation of local community groups to a coffee morning, the offer of school facilities for club meetings.

Most community involvement attempts fail, not at the initial contact, but because of a lack of adequate follow-up. If people become involved once, there is no guarantee that they will continue, particularly if there is no attempt to discover what they need. It is important, therefore, to involve them fully as soon as possible – to have their input into what is necessary and to maximise the value of the involvement they have offered.

Effective involvement

It is possible to establish five principles which may assist the process of community involvement to become successful. If the core–plus school wishes to establish widespread involvement within its community then the following principles should apply.

Principle of uniqueness Each community has a unique combination of resources, facilities, personnel, needs, attitudes and limitations, and the first principle of community involvement is that the people in the best position to know what these factors are and how they are related are the people in the community.

Principle of ownership As people come to understand that the programme and plans of the school belong to them as members of the community they will come to recognise the legitimacy of their involvement. It is essential that this notion of ownership be maintained at all times.

Principle of skill training It is essential that people who are actively involved in the decision-making processes are given the skills necessary for effective participation in group work. This skill training is most effective when it is done in the context of actual activity. In this way the participation becomes more widespread and effective.

Principle of representation When people from all subgroups in the community are involved in the development of programmes then the programmes and the processes underlying them have a far greater chance of success than if there is little representation. The more representation there is, the greater the possibility of discovering the resources and needs of the community.

Principle of leadership The final principle necessary for effective participation is effective leadership. It is, in fact, this principle that allows the others to exist and determines in what form they will exist.

These five principles of community involvement cover the major process areas of community education. Ownership can only be achieved through the way in which the other principles are put forward. The core–plus council, as the ultimate authority, can maintain its power-base or delegate some or all of it to the community. The extent to which it is prepared to delegate will reflect accurately the ownership that the parents and school community will feel for the programmes.

GROUP WORK SKILLS: BUILDING A TEAM APPROACH

The Australian study discussed in Chapter 3 identified clearly that schools became effective because the teachers, parents and students worked as a team and had common goals. Simply involving people in the core–plus school is not sufficient for a productive school/community relationship. It is also important for those who are responsible for the programme to build the capacity for those involved to work effectively in group situations. Success in this area involves organisation, purpose and training.

One assumption that we make when we meet as a group is that we can accomplish more collectively than as individuals. Some meetings are productive and participants feel that they have accomplished something. Other meetings leave participants feeling frustrated. This section deals with the information necessary to enable productive group sessions to occur. When specific activities designed for team building and improving people's abilities to work with each other are designed, the following areas of skill development need to be considered:

- Getting acquainted
- Effective meetings
- Group deliberations
- Decision-making
- Conflict and conflict resolution
- Communication.

Getting acquainted

Two of the roles of the leader indicated in the previous chapter were to help the group to get things done; and to help the group to work effectively together. Successful groups give their attention equally to both of these dimensions. For maximum efficiency in the first of these roles it is essential that group members get acquainted with each other and have the opportunity to form positive working relationships. It is possible for a person to join a committee where everyone else knows each other and what is going on at the committee. The new member may feel reticent about contributing unless the chair of the committee ensures a welcome.

Ice-breaking activities can be used to break down the reserve of people who do not know each other, and in a short time allow a relationship to be established. The activities can take one of two forms: a whole group or a small group activity. Examples of activities used to 'break the ice' are:

1 Whole group activities: all members write their name and a symbol that describes them on name tags, then circulate around the room, introducing themselves to each of the others in the group and explaining what their symbol represents.
2 Small group activities: people who do not know each other are organised into pairs. Each member of the pair is given up to five minutes to find out as much as possible about the other. Then each person has to introduce the partner to the whole group.

Effective meetings

Meetings are productive and worthwhile if the people involved in them are able to plan them properly as a single occurrence and effectively move from one meeting to the next in an organised fashion. A number of people with designated positions, and consequently the need to make regular reports, may be involved in the meeting. An effective meeting allows time for all those who need to make a contribution, but plans in advance that the contribution should take only a reasonable proportion of the meeting time. It is useful to establish a general rule that the meetings will end at a given time and that a motion from the floor is necessary to extend that time. In this way members who usually have other commitments will know in advance at what time the meeting will finish. It is then the chairperson's job to plan as far as possible to cover the agenda in that time.

One way in which this can be done is through the use of starred items. Many reports at meetings do not make recommendations or are non-controversial. They simply provide information for the members. These items do not need to be discussed at all. Starred items, on the other hand, are those that ought to be discussed. Some items will have already been starred by the chairperson as needing further deliberation. At the start of the meeting members can star other items if they want them discussed. The unstarred items can then be passed without further discussion and a great deal of time is saved. The starred item system relies upon the distribution of the agenda and written reports well in advance of the meeting and the preparedness of members to read all agenda papers.

Not all the activities need be the responsibility of the leader or chair of the group. In fact, distribution of roles improves the working of any committee and makes leadership succession possible. The development of the agenda as the central chart for the meeting is a vital function. Certain items need to be placed on each agenda for the smooth progression from one meeting to the next.

Group deliberations

The strength and leadership within the group will be a reflection of the extent to which individual members' needs are met:

- the need for a sense of belonging;
- the need to feel that the goals are attainable;
- the need to know what is expected of them;
- the need to feel that progress is being made;
- the need to be kept informed;
- the need to have confidence in the group leadership.

It is important that a range of methods are used for the improvement of the discussion processes. By careful planning the process can flow smoothly to appropriate decision-making. Two main discussion methods can be used to generate alternative viewpoints with a view to coming to some resolution. The first, brainstorming, is used to generate ideas. The emphasis is on quantity, not quality. The second, problem-solving, is used to seek to resolve a problem already identified. Here the quality of the solution is paramount. Sometimes, the two techniques can be used in tandem, first to generate possible options and then to consider them.

Brainstorming

This is a group method of providing creative potential solutions to a problem. The point of brainstorming is to generate and collect a large number of ideas within the given topic. Brainstorming is used for gathering ideas that can be used for goal setting, problem-solving, action planning, and so on. The group identifies a problem or issue that calls for ideas and the goal is to generate as many ideas as possible. There are some basic rules:

- ideas should not be criticised or evaluated during the brainstorming;
- each member may say anything that comes to mind;
- brevity is essential;
- no ideas are discussed until the brainstorming is finished;
- all ideas are recorded, usually on a chart so that all group members can see them and the contributor be satisfied as to the accuracy;
- quantity, not quality, is the requirement.

After the brainstorming is completed, generic headings are agreed upon and the ideas are grouped under these headings. This process eliminates repetition, enables contradictions to be resolved, systematises a discrete collection of ideas and leads to greater group cohesion and contribution. The grouped ideas can then be evaluated using the problem-solving technique.

Problem-solving

Successful problem-solving focuses on specific and readily defined tasks, and follows a systematic method of accomplishing those tasks:

- Recognise that there is a problem.
- Assess the problem.
- Clarify the problem and set goals.
- Identify constraints and resources.
- Develop a planning guide.
- Design activity plan to implement guide.
- Check to see if the problem has been resolved.

If the problem has been corrected then the group can start again for the next problem. If it has not been corrected the problem should be re-assessed. Using this method it may be possible to establish an effective and efficient method of decision-making within the group.

Decision-making

One of the most important processes that occurs in a group, decision-making, can reveal much about the way the group itself works. The way in which a decision is made and recognition of those who were involved in the process become important features in the work of any committee. An understanding of the ways by which decisions are reached, and the skill to guide a discussion so that the decision most acceptable to the group is reached, are important to any leader and, indeed, to anyone working with groups. There are three basic methods of decision making:

1   Leader-determined or minority-determined. Here the decision-maker has to seek the support of the group. The leader may make the decision after discussion with the rest of the group, or even without discussion. Alternatively a decision may be made by a minority of those present, with the others abstaining from the discussion or vote either because they are not interested in the issue or because they do not wish to argue against the proposal.

2   Majority-determined. When a group is deadlocked over two opposing propositions and no compromise can be reached a vote may need to be taken. In this situation the minority may feel that they have lost, particularly if they feel strongly about the issue.

3   Consensus. This requires the support of the total group after discussion and debate. Consensus decision-making involves surveying everyone's opinion. Compromises may be made to the original proposition until everyone agrees that they can accept the final decision. Consensus decision-making may be more time-consuming than other methods, but in the long run this form of decision-making has strength in that the implementation of it will get total group support.

Table 8.1 summarises the advantages and disadvantages of each style. Whichever process is used a high level of communication that provides accurate and complete information to those who require it is necessary. Both decision-makers and decision-implementers must share information and feelings so that the end result is that the group's decision-making is followed by effective action.

Conflict and conflict management

When people work in groups, particularly those involved in the process of identifying and solving community problems, conflict is

Table 8.1 The advantages and disadvantages of various styles of decision-making

Style	Appropriate Situations	Advantages	Disadvantages
Leader-determined	Emergencies, where decisions not important, where personal issues are involved, where the group does not have expertise in the area.	Decision can be made quickly.	Personal bias or lack of information may lead to a decision that is unacceptable to the group.
Majority	When there are complex issues and consensus cannot be reached.	Possible input from many people.	Minority may not be satisfied with a decision and have no commitment to its implementation.
Consensus	When support of group members is vital to the decision's implementation.	Feeling of acceptance and commitment to the decision.	Time-consuming, needs a relatively small group.

almost inevitable. Conflict does not mean anger or aggression but simply a difference of opinion. An understanding of the types of conflict reactions and skill in resolving conflict in the group become important components in a leader's store of knowledge. Since members of any group will have different values, beliefs and priorities, conflict must be expected to occur and consequently should be seen as part of the group process. Conflict is not always readily identifiable because people react in different ways to the issue; yet in group decision-making conflict must be managed well to ensure group stability. Generally it is accepted that people will deal with conflict in one of six ways:

1 *Avoidance* is adopted when differences of opinion over issues are not considered to be amenable to influence or change. Conflicts that are avoided may never be completely resolved and may arise again and again.

2   *Accommodation* occurs when a person sees the relationship of the group members as being more important than the issues being discussed. The accommodator sees differences of opinion as detrimental to group functioning and is prepared to accept the other viewpoint rather than to cause conflict.

3   *Coercion* occurs when a group member conceives a conflict as being a win–lose situation and endeavours to coerce others in the group to one point of view. For a coercive person there is only one 'right' solution.

4   *Compromise* occurs when the individual realises that there is no single answer. While everyone should have a say in the decision-making, no one should block the progress of the group. The compromiser expects that after everyone has had the opportunity to contribute, everyone will abide by the majority decision.

5   *Collaboration* is similar to accommodation in that the individual is more concerned about the relationship of the group than the issues involved. In this case, however, the individual encourages other members of the group to deal with conflict when it arises. The collaborator believes in working through conflict which is a symptom of group unease, and in the process of resolving the conflict, a stronger group is developed.

6   *Negotiation* occurs as an endeavour to resolve a conflict when solutions cannot be subject to a compromise. In this form of conflict each party involved in the conflict needs to be aware of self-interest and the compulsion to seek equal power with other parties within the group.

There is no one style of reacting to conflict that is better than others, but there are situations where certain reactions are more appropriate. Nor will individuals use a single style for all issues, but will adopt one that suits the situation in which they find themselves. A group leader must learn how to resolve conflict in a way that allows the group to stay together and to remain productive.

Learning how to manage conflict within a group is difficult and it takes experience to become adept. A number of techniques for the management of conflict can be used, and training sessions within the core–plus council can provide valuable opportunities for potential leaders to explore techniques and to judge which may be appropriate under certain circumstances. The other requisite for competence in conflict management is alertness by the leader to the feelings of the group and the willingness of the leader to practise techniques within the group situation. With training, alertness and practice, group leaders can become competent at recognising and managing conflicts within their groups.

Conflict resolution

Recognising that conflict is a legitimate occurrence within a group activity is the first step in establishing an environment that is conducive to conflict resolution. One method of overcoming conflict is the problem-solving approach. This involves the following steps:

- Focus on the conflict and bring it out in the open. Determine the parameters of the conflict.
- Search for alternative ways of resolving the conflict. Will the group resolve it through a majority vote or will consensus or negotiation occur?
- Plan for action. When it is decided how the conflict is to be resolved, it is then necessary to work out how the decision will be implemented and how it will be determined whether or not that decision has been effective.
- Carry out the plan. Once it has been decided how to resolve the conflict, that procedure is used to break the deadlock.
- Assess the results. The method of conflict resolution is reviewed at a later date. Is it working? What else could have been done?

This is not the only method of resolving conflict but it is a way that concentrates on the problem of conflict and not on the individuals concerned. For a group to remain an effective working body it needs to recognise that:

- Conflicts do occur and are a normal part of proceedings.
- Individuals or sub-groups within the group may differ in their opinions without any one party being entirely right or wrong.
- Conflict does not go away by itself, and by recognising it group members have a better chance of resolving it.
- Conflict can be dealt with.

Communication

Within the core–plus school communication becomes one of the major factors in developing a team approach to school improvement. Communication is a multi-faceted concern because of the

many forms it takes between the school and its various consti-
tuents: home, local community, wider community and education
authority; and between the various groups and individuals within
the school: the principal, the staff, the core–plus councillors, the
parents, the students and visitors to the school.

The critical feature of any form of communication is that it must
be reciprocal, that all parties in the communication activity need
to be able to initiate and receive all messages that are relevant to
them. This is particularly the case in the core–plus school where
the development of teamwork relies on the one hand upon people
being able to contribute to the decisions being made and on the
other, on their always knowing what is expected of them. From
these forms of communication, two major features arise. The first
is public relations, which is the communication between the
school and the various groups it deals with, and the second is the
development of communication skills, which improves the ability
of individuals to work together in a group.

Public relations

Public relations is, quite simply, the establishment and maintenance of a relationship with the public. Essentially there are two
main issues that any school needs to consider in the area of public
relations. The first is the establishment and maintenance of a
general image within the chosen community, and the second is the
communication of particular incidents, activities or issues related
to the school that will both keep the public informed of what the
school is doing and help to maintain or enhance the general
image of the school in the community. Part of this form of public
relations is the willingness of the school to receive input from the
communities it serves.

A public relations programme may be used for a number of
different reasons. It is important at the outset that the goals of the
programme are clearly established. Some possible goals for a
public relations programme in the school are:

– to inform the community of the school's activities;
– to put the school's views on various aspects of education;
– to make the community aware of new programmes;
– to enlist the aid of volunteers;
– to invite the community to come to the school;

– to enlist community support/community involvement in school activities or community activities.

If the school has had little or no involvement in public relations previously, the most logical first step is to attempt to build a positive and acceptable image within the community. Although this may be attempted by running a programme of some sort, it is more likely that the reporting of that programme will become just as important in terms of public relations as the programme itself. The programme is likely to involve those who are currently interested in the school, but the reporting of it may help to generate additional interest.

It is important to keep the public aware of what is happening in the school if the school wants the public to be concerned about it. Once the initial image is established the public relations programme becomes concerned with the maintenance or enhancement of that image. This is best resolved by a consistent interaction with the community, and consistent communication when interaction is not possible.

Publicity for school activities can be provided by the regular forms of interaction, such as a community newsletter, a regular column in the local paper or parents' meetings. These forms of event advertising need to go hand in hand, since one form – the newsletter – will be directed mainly at parents and friends of the school, and the other – newspaper column or advertising – will be directed more at the general community. This will enable the school to have regular communication with its clients, to provide additional publicity for special events, to plan sufficiently in advance to account for any printing or clerical delays and to distribute the publicity at a time when it is most likely to gain maximum exposure and support for a special event.

Most effective public relations are directed to a specific audience. In the case of the school which is trying to involve its local community as a whole, it thus becomes important to collect and maintain information about the local community. The following types of information may prove to be useful when developing a public relations activity: local facilities, characteristics of school families, characteristics of families in the community, community groups and government and non-government agencies.

By knowing the characteristics of the community and the various groups and individuals that are components of it, it is possible to produce a public relations activity that has a good chance of reaching the chosen audience. For instance, in many inner-city suburbs a multi-lingual production will have a greater chance of reaching that audience than one printed only in English. Once the characteristics are identified it is possible to have a number of different activities built into the public relations programme to ensure that in each case the audience receives an appropriate communication and at the same time that no audience which ought to be contacted has been missed.

Within any community a number of different approaches will be necessary for adequate public relations coverage. Because different groups within the community will respond to different forms of communication, the public relations activity must be geared towards a particular audience rather than to the community as a whole. There are basically two major forms of approach. The first form of communication is person-to-person where an individual or group presents the information to the audience. This form of communication includes radio or television interviews, speakers, personal visits, telephone calls, training activities, conferences and seminars.

The second form of communication is where the audience receives the information on paper. This form of communication includes press releases, brochures, letters, newsletters, displays, reports, proposals for funding, publications, new curriculum materials, training materials and advertisements. The benefit of the person-to-person form of public relations is that the people presenting the information can respond to questions from the audience, thus ensuring understanding. The image of the school thus becomes one of 'a people-oriented place'. The benefit of the print-to-person format is that it is relatively inexpensive and can reach many more people.

In order to produce any public relations material in either form of communication, a number of procedures need to be followed. Although the activities that occur in the person-to-person form differ from those in the print-to-person form, the basic procedures are the same. They are: to define the purpose of the public relations activity, to identify the audience, to determine the format of the presentation, to write and edit the material, to develop art work/diagrammatic presentation, to plan the layout/presentation, to produce the material, to implement the activity and to evaluate the success of the activity.

Developing communication skills

Within a group activity we are communicating all the time. Our words, facial expressions, tone of voice and body language all express what we think and feel about issues and other people in the group. Sometimes we are unconscious of the words and messages and sometimes we are not able to interpret adequately what others have said. The reason for focusing on basic communication skills is to increase the group members' awareness and skill for effective communication, since good communication is vital to effective group work. Six basic communication skills are essential to the interaction between the speaker or actor and the listener or viewer. These skills are paraphrasing, checking our perceptions, behaviour description, description of feelings, listening and feedback. Each is necessary to enable any barriers between the meaning of the speaker and the understanding of the listener to be lessened or removed.

Having a working knowledge of communication skills can aid group development and thus improve performance as a group. Paraphrasing, perception checks and descriptions of behaviour or feelings enable all group members to understand each other better. Each of the above may be considered as being part of the feedback that can be available within a group situation and the skills of listening and being heard are essential for any of the other communication skills to be attained.

EVALUATION

Although evaluation is usually considered the final stage of any planning model, it is an on-going activity. Since both programme and process evaluation in Figure 6.1 on page 128 refer back to earlier stages it can be seen that evaluation can occur both before and after an activity has been implemented. Furthermore, the development of specific objectives, the conduct of a needs assessment, monitoring and progress reviews of activities or processes are all forms of evaluation. It would be inappropriate to assume that evaluation only occurs at the end of the activity just because the evaluation is at the end of the model.

Many people are reticent about evaluations. Their reasons include lack of time, feeling that the results will not mean anything, lack of knowledge of how to conduct an evaluation, concern that the results may not be positive and the feeling that evaluation does not produce any changed behaviours. Yet evaluation does occur, even if it is not formal and structured. People involved in an activity ask each other 'Should we run another programme?' 'Should we run this pro- gramme again?' 'Did you enjoy the meeting?' or 'Will you come again?' These and other questions will produce an *ad hoc* evaluation that serves little purpose. It is far better to conduct a proper evalua- tion so that the results have validity and use.

A successful evaluation does not necessarily show that all of the activity's goals have been met, but rather tells how the activity is going, or has gone, and why. An evaluation should enable the group to improve its performance in the future and consequently will always lead to improved public relations. A school that demonstrates that it cares how well it is performing will gain better support than one that does not. Even negative findings, if they are used to improve pro- grammes or processes, are valuable in this context.

The function of evaluation

Evaluation has two major functions. The first is to enable decision-making to be based on acceptable data, and the second is to provide accountability for what has already occurred. The first type of evaluation has been termed formative, proactive or decision-making evaluation because it helps to formulate decisions and thus has to be conducted before the decisions are made. Formative evaluation takes place either before or during an activity and enables decisions – about what action to take, what progress has been made or what alterations need to be carried out – to be based on research data. The second type of evaluation has been termed summative, retroactive or accountability evaluation, because it occurs at the end of the activity and demonstrates whether or not the goals and objectives have been achieved, and if they have not, where they have failed in their purpose. It provides a summary of what has occurred which can be used to account for the success or otherwise of the activity.

Of the two types, most people who have worked in schools have relied on the summative form. This is usually because the results of the evaluation have been tied to reports of what has occurred during the year. However, the need for formative evaluation is demonstrated by the need to use the evaluation for decisions about what to do next – that is, referral back to earlier stages of the model – and although the two types of evaluation can be considered separately they must be related to each other. It will always be the case that future decision-making must be based on what the situation is now, and the situation as it is now can only be determined by some form of summative evaluation.

In this way evaluation can be seen to be the link between what has happened and what will happen. In Figure 6.1 on page 128 different aspects of evaluation are considered: evaluation of programmes and evaluation of processes. In the first aspect the evaluation of programmes can be seen as a needs assessment mechanism for determining new programmes, rerunning successful programmes or changing unsuccessful ones. On the other hand, process evaluation, because it is concerned about the interaction between individuals rather than the knowledge each individual may have gained from a specific programme, needs to be referred back to the core–plus council, the group which controls the mechanisms for the operation of community education in the school. The process evaluation examines areas such as involvement strategies, decision-making efficiency, training activities and the building of relationships between people, all of which are related to how things have occurred rather than what has occurred. As for programmes, the evaluation can be used to account for the success of a current activity or to propose changes to improve activities in the future.

In planning for an evaluation a number of issues need to be considered. Both programme evaluation and process evaluation require consideration of the same issues, but different groups of people may be asked different questions in the gathering of the required information. Some areas of consideration for the conduct of an evaluation would include: what the goals of the evaluation are, who the audience of the report will be, what types of questions need be asked, to whom the questions should be addressed and what sort of data collection devices and data analysis techniques will be used.

There are many texts that provide details of each of these considerations and there is no need for that information to be repeated here. However, as the essence of a core–plus school is its inclusivity, as many people as possible should feel part of the evaluation exercise and the activity itself should be seen as part of the ongoing development of the school.

Evaluating the evaluation

Because an evaluation is an activity that is carried out in the school from time to time it also should be subject to the evaluative exercise. Questions that need to be answered to undertake this activity include:

- Did the evaluation answer the questions that needed to be answered?
- Were the results useful?
- Did the data collected support the evaluation conclusions and recommendations?
- Were the resources involved in the evaluation used efficiently?
- Was it an appropriate time to conduct the evaluation?
- Could the evaluation have been improved? How?

The final stage of the model in Figure 6.1 on page 128 is the completion of the loop that allows both programmes and processes to be more than one-off activities. By using evaluation as the link between past and future activities the school can maintain a continuity of people, goals and activities that will ensure the core–plus education philosophy within the school is maintained and developed.

Chapter 9

From community needs to core–plus policies

> Educational activities should be based on the needs and problems of people for whom they are planned.
>
> (Minzey and Townsend 1984: 18)

The development of a long-term, self-evaluating and self-perpetuating programme in the core–plus school requires a number of issues to be considered. These considerations need to be made for the school curriculum (the core) on the one hand, and the additional programme of activities for the students and parents of the school and the wider community (the plus) on the other. In general the collaborative school management cycle proposed by Caldwell and Spinks (1988) reproduced as Figure 9.1 could be the model used for the overall planning of the two activities, but the people involved in the decision-making and implementation of the programme for the core elements may well be different from those involved for the plus programme.

In this chapter we discuss the three related activities which might be considered from the Caldwell and Spinks model to be the major tasks of the policy group of the school: conducting a needs assessment to establish the needs of the community, setting goals to meet those needs and establishing a core–plus school policy that will move the school towards its goals. In the next chapter consideration will be given to planning and implementing core–plus school programmes.

CONDUCTING A NEEDS ASSESSMENT

Since the success of any school initiative depends on the support of the people it is designed to serve, being able to assess accurately

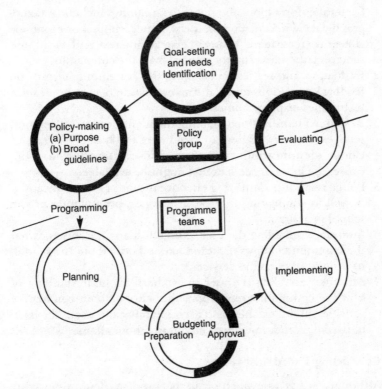

Figure 9.1 The Collaborative School Management Cycle
Source: Caldwell and Spinks 1988

the needs of the people, involving them in the process of determining those needs and being able to respond appropriately to the needs so identified, can be seen as fundamental prerequisites for gaining support for new school activities.

A needs assessment is an inventory or survey instrument that is developed to collect information which will identify the needs of a particular community. It can be employed to accomplish a variety of purposes, such as finding out the needs, wants, concerns or goals of the community. Regardless of its use, the needs assessment is employed to find out what other people think relative to a particular issue or concern. The needs assessment can be used to determine the required information for any of the following areas of interest:

1 General information about the community: including demographic data, information on social, family, cultural or economic
concerns, recreation, leisure, personal interest and facility-use
requirements, ideas and suggestions from the community.

2 Evaluation and feedback: enabling the community to provide
feedback on various topics and an evaluation of communication
techniques or programmes.

3 Resource identification: enabling the identification of facilities,
services, teachers, leaders and volunteer workers.

4 Client identification: identifying those interested in using
classes, facilities or services that might be available.

5 Public relations: identifying effective means of communication,
as well as stimulating interest in services, programmes or the
school in general.

6 Awareness: enabling the user to establish an awareness of what
the community knows or would like to know about the school,
its programmes and its services.

7 Attitudes: enabling the user to establish an understanding of
how the community feels about the school, about community
activities, about teachers and accountability and about the issue
of parent/community involvement in school affairs.

Conducting a needs assessment

Although needs assessments can be used to determine many
different things, the process for conducting them will be the same.
To ensure a useful outcome from the exercise, the following steps
should be considered.

- *Step one*: The core–plus council determines as a group what it
  wants to know.
- *Step two*: The council establishes a needs assessment committee
  and gives it guidelines on what the assessment should include.
  The needs assessment committee should include a range of
  people who may be affected by the study, wish to contribute to
  the survey or use the results.
- *Step three*: The needs assessment committee determines what
  form the assessment will take. Three possible approaches are
  the public meeting, the interview and the questionnaire.
- *Step four*: The needs assessment committee undertakes skill training, if necessary, to enable its members fully to understand the
  procedures associated with the needs assessment method chosen.

- *Step five*: A sample survey instrument is developed using sample questions generated by the committee.
- *Step six*: The sample instrument is tested on a few people in the manner in which the final survey will be used. Thus the procedures for the public meeting, the interview, or the questionnaire will be used for a group of five to ten people representative of the larger sample.
- *Step seven*: The data from the sample survey are tabulated and an appropriate data reduction technique is established by the needs assessment committee.
- *Step eight*: The sample questions are discussed and revised if necessary to remove ambiguities, errors or questions that elicit no useful response. The final survey instrument is constructed.
- *Step nine*: Those who will be carrying out the needs assessment are trained in appropriate techniques for the type of needs assessment being carried out.
- *Step ten*: The needs assessment is carried out, the data are tabulated and an appropriate data reduction is carried out.
- *Step eleven*: The needs assessment committee compiles and presents a report on the findings of the study for the core–plus council.
- *Step twelve*: The council decides whether or not to implement the whole report or merely sections of it.
- *Step thirteen*: The council releases the report or a summary of it to appropriate groups in the community.

The public meeting

This activity can either be conducted formally where a systematic process is followed to identify the needs, wants or concerns of the participants, or informally where those present have an opportunity to talk about any issues of concern. The advantage of this method is that it is a highly personalised and interactive form of communication, and a high level of involvement occurs, with the participants generally accepting and being committed to the results. The disadvantage is that only a limited number of people participate at any single meeting. Larger meetings can lead to the possibility of discussion getting out of hand with a consequent lessening of the feeling of commitment by the participants.

If the purpose of the meeting is to assess group needs and to establish priorities, about an hour to an hour-and-a-half should be allowed for the activity. The organiser will need to provide pencils and paper for each participant and either a chalkboard and chalk, or a large sheet of newsprint and marker pens so that final decisions can be presented to the whole group. The following activities take place:

- All participants write on a piece of paper their own primary concerns about the topic at hand.
- Groups of three or four are formed for discussion. At the end of about ten minutes each group should have developed a priority list of the most important concerns. If a large number of people attend the meeting, four or five of these small groups are amalgamated and the process is repeated. This will produce a prioritised list.
- The entire group is reassembled and the most important item from each group – avoiding duplications – is listed.
- A short time is allowed for the clarification of any items.
- The leader can now point out that a rough priority has been established. There will be a number of items that have been listed as first priority by a number of groups. The final list will contain every alternative from the most to the least popular.
- The leader establishes within the group a general acceptance of the final list.

The interview

This approach involves an interviewer or a team of interviewers asking a predetermined set of questions either of individuals or small groups. The advantage of this method is that it can lead to a thorough understanding by the interviewer of the feelings, perceptions and opinions of the interviewees. The disadvantages are that the process can be time-consuming and labour-intensive, and that the interviewer may give a bias to the response by the way the question is phrased or clarified.

Prior to the interview each interviewer should receive interview materials and be briefed on interviewing procedures. Each interviewer should have a list of names and addresses of interviewees, a letter of introduction and name tag, copies of the questionnaires and questionnaire envelopes. The interviewer should make an appointment to see the interviewee at a time convenient to both parties.

Interviewers will introduce themselves, state who they represent and the purpose of the interview. The letter of introduction, naming the group conducting the survey, what the survey is intended to establish and the name and telephone number of the team leader, should be presented. The interviewer will state that the survey is completely confidential and answer any questions that the interviewee might have about the survey. The interviewee will be given the choice of filling out the survey personally or having the interviewer ask questions and record answers. If respondents object to any specific question the interviewer will proceed to the next question. The interview should be in a quiet place, preferably a room where a television or radio is not turned on. After completion the interviewee will place the questionnaire in the envelope and seal it. The questionnaire should not be left to be mailed or picked up. The interviewee is thanked and the interviewer proceeds to the next name on the list.

The questionnaire

The questionnaire approach is the most common of the three forms of needs assessment because it is easy to administer and generally yields accurate results. The advantages of this method are that the questionnaire is easy to develop and administer and that generally it provides the group with the information that it needs. The disadvantages are that, unless the questionnaires are hand-delivered and collected on a specified day, there is usually a low response rate, and a low level of participation in the processes involved by the person completing the questionnaire. This may lead to a lack of commitment to the results and a distortion between what people say they are prepared to do and what they actually are prepared to do.

Developing a needs assessment instrument

Needs assessment instruments can be constructed in a number of different forms depending what information is being sought. The questions used in the instrument are generally developed from set forms as detailed below.

Data collection questions

These require respondents to indicate one of a number of possible responses to a single question. The objective is to determine potential needs in terms of absolute numbers. Questions such as the following are data collection questions:

(a) How many people live in your household?
(b) How many students are in the age groups listed?
          pre-school (0–4 years)
          primary school (5–11 years)
          secondary school (12–18 years)
(c) What skills/knowledge would you like to learn? (please tick)
          Weaving
          Photography
          World Affairs
          Literature
          Cooking
          Gardening
          Others (please state)

Rating questions

These are used to elicit community attitudes towards various wide-ranging issues. Respondents are asked to rate each question or statement in terms of agreement, value or importance. Generally the responses are on a five-point scale from very important through to unimportant or from strongly agree through to strongly disagree. Examples of such questions or statements are:

(a) How important are the following aspects of education:
          Providing students with skills necessary to enter university?
          Providing students with skills necessary to obtain employment?
          Providing students with a complete programme in music, literature and art?
(b) Do you agree that:
          Parents should be more involved in decision-making in schools?
          Parents should be involved in curriculum development?
          Parents should employ the teachers they want in schools?

Multiple choice questions

These allow for specific responses to each of the questions or statements. The objective is to gain knowledge of attitudes towards a number of possible alternatives. An example of this form of question is:

(a) Do you feel that teachers recognise your children as having special talents, interests or needs? (Tick the response you agree with most.)
>   Teachers are keenly aware.
>   Teachers are usually aware.
>   Some teachers are occasionally aware.
>   Most teachers are rarely aware.

Open-ended questions

These do not require specific answers. They allow the respondents to answer in any way they see fit. The benefit of this sort of question is that it may produce responses of great diversity and some of the responses may be ones that the person constructing the question-naire had previously not considered. Examples of the types of questions that may be placed on an open-ended questionnaire are:

(a) What is your understanding of core–plus education?
(b) How would you like to participate in your child's education?
(c) How would you describe the relationship between the home, the school and the community?

Prioritising questions

A survey using this type of question is carried out when a number of needs or assumed needs have already been identified. Res-pondents are asked to confirm whether the item is seen by them as being a need or not, and also asked to put in order of importance those that are needs. An example of a priority survey is as follows: for each of the items (see Table 9.1) enter either yes or no if you feel the item is important. In the final column indicate with 1 the item which you consider to be most important and with 2 that which you consider to be second most important to you, and so on, for all the items for which 'yes' was your response.

Table 9.1 Examples of priority questions

	Yes/No	Priority
Do you feel adult leisure courses should be held at the school?		
Do you wish to be involved in school activities?		
Do you feel there should be recreational programmes for senior citizens at the school?		
Do you feel there should be parent/teacher information nights?		
Do you feel there should be more social activities at the school?		

Constructing a questionnaire

The following points are intended to provide some yardsticks against which the characteristics of a questionnaire might be measured. Each of these points will be stated as a question. If the answer to most or all of these questions is 'yes' as you appraise your questionnaire, you can be reasonably certain the device you have constructed will obtain legitimate information for you. At the outset it should be realised that meeting all of these standards at their highest level is something which, while attempted in scientific studies, is seldom realised in real life.

The goal is to perform as carefully and thoroughly as possible in constructing questionnaires, yet to be aware that no questionnaire produces completely dependable data. Certainly, the less scientific and thorough the development of the questionnaire the less confidence we can have in the results obtained from it. However, if we are simply gathering the concerns of a given group or documenting their perceptions of educational needs in a rough way, there is not such a crucial need for highly scientific questionnaire-development procedures.

As you develop a questionnaire, ask yourself the following questions:

– Do you really need the information being obtained?
– Do the items really measure what they are intended to measure?

- Is the information obtained reliable? Would we get the same information if we re-administered our questionnaire at a later date?
- Are the items phrased clearly?
- Is the vocabulary level appropriate to the people being asked the questions?
- Does the questionnaire have a consistent format?
- Is the questionnaire easy to answer?
- Are the items specific?
- Do you have appropriate identifying information on the questionnaire?
- Have you allowed for open-ended responses?
- Have you pilot-tested your questionnaire?

Data tabulation and reduction involves counting the number of respondents who have indicated a particular response to a question and then reducing the raw scores into meaningful comparisons or statements to give an accurate indication of what the figures mean to the people who commissioned the survey. For example, a raw score of 50 does not mean much in itself, whereas to know that the 50 is part of a sample of 500 will lead to different conclusions than if the 50 was part of a sample of 60. In the first case only 10 per cent responded, but in the second more than 80 per cent did. Depending on the audience for which the information is being tabulated, there are a wide range of data reduction techniques with varying levels of difficulty. However, the best information is that which is the easiest to understand. Should you require more detail on the collection and use of statistics, any introductory statistics text will provide more information.

Preparing a report

A needs assessment report is intended to inform people who were not actually involved in the process of everything that is necessary for an informed response to the report. The report should contain three sections: the findings, the conclusions and the recommendations.

1 The findings: this section of the report should contain all the information obtained in the needs assessment and should be presented in a simple, clear and accurate format. The information to be included is:

- *The background*: why the needs assessment committee was established and what it was asked to find out.
- *The membership*: who was on the committee, and what group they were representing.
- *The format used*: group meeting, interview or questionnaire.
- *How the survey questions were formulated*: data collection, ratings, multiple-choice, priority or open-ended.
- *A copy of the instrument*: questions asked at the interview or the survey questionnaire.
- *Tabulated results*: number of respondents; number of different groups responding; frequency of responses in each category.
- *Summary of results*: data reduction method used and frequency distribution displayed in terms of percentages or bar-graphs for easy analysis. The use of graphs for each of the questions will enable the reader to see at a glance the general trend in terms of response.

2 The conclusions: the needs assessment committee will extrapolate from the findings certain conclusions about the population, their needs and their attitudes. Each conclusion should be related directly to the findings with reasons indicated.

3 The recommendations: the final step in the writing of the needs assessment report is to make recommendations for future action, each supported by an argument that relates directly to the conclusions and using the findings of the needs assessment as evidence. Recommendations may include the following general issues:

- areas of highest priority for future action;
- topics for future or additional research;
- areas of concern that may need future action;
- possible short-term projects;
- suggestions for resources (people, publications);
- strategies for implementation.

SETTING GOALS IN THE CORE–PLUS SCHOOL

The importance of setting goals for the school cannot be overemphasised. All too frequently we find the situation of a school which exists from day to day or from year to year without any positive direction guiding it. Eventually the school and the people within it become frustrated in their attempts to provide the best possible education for the clients and this frustration manifests itself in apathy, class materials that are out-of-date and a day-to-day existence for teachers, students and community members.

We are entering an age where science, technology and information are increasing the pressure on schools to prepare the adults of tomorrow. We must ask ourselves if we are now providing the sorts of information that young adults will need in the next millenium.

If schools are to set goals that consider the future needs of the students and also include issues of concern to their local communities, the goals:

- should closely relate to the needs of the community.
- should look forward to the final product and not simply be year by year.
- should be attainable by being financially cost-effective yet take into consideration the economic realities of our society.

There are two components to goal setting that need to be considered by the school. The first is the issue of establishing a series of goals based on the needs and the wishes of the school community; the second, since we will not be able to devote our time and money to all goals equally, relates to ordering these goals in a hierarchical list.

Drawing up a list of goals

Processes that could be used to establish a list of goals for the core–plus school were discussed in Chapter 6. Some school goals will have been already determined by educational authorities outside of the school. Other goals, those related to the needs of a specific community, should be determined by the community. Further goals, those that relate to the proper administration of the school and its programmes, will be identified in collaboration with the core–plus council. All goals are likely to fit into one of three categories:

- the programmes of the school;
- the organisation and administration of the school;
- developing school/community relations.

Possible goals for a core–plus school, which go beyond goals accepted at all schools, are:

- to develop a comprehensive educational programme for the students of the school and the community;
- to provide recreation programmes and develop vocational opportunities and leisure skills;
- to develop procedures for community use of school buildings and grounds;
- to encourage community participation in school activities;
- to identify community resources;
- to improve communication channels;
- to establish links with other schools and community agencies.

Ordering a list of goals

It is obvious that not all the goals listed can be implemented immediately. Some will take time, others will take money, most will take both. Some will be more expensive and some will be seen as more urgent than others. It is necessary, then, to undertake an exercise that will produce an order of importance so that our efforts may be concentrated on those goals seen by the school as having greater priority. The following exercise can be used to prioritise any number of goals with any number of people being involved.

Step one

A series of goal statements is identified. These statements may cover the whole range of school operations, or may be more specific in nature, such as those relating to a series of curriculum goals, a range of ways to improve parent involvement in the school or a variety of extra-curricular activities that may be proposed.

Step two

A meeting is held to determine the order of priority for the goals. The membership may include the staff, the core–plus council, parents, students and community members, or some or all of these groups, depending on what is being discussed and how much support is being sought.

Step three

At the meeting, each person is given a list of the identified goal statements. The leader of the session may be asked to clarify what any statement may mean.

Step four

Each person working alone allocates to each goal statement a rating on a five-point scale. Members have at their disposal twice the number of points as there are goals, for example: thirty points for fifteen identified goal statements. The scale ranges from four points to zero, with four representing a goal of the utmost urgency or importance down to one, of least urgency or importance. Zero indicates that the member believes that the goal statement has no relevance to the school. There are certain simple rules in the points allocation:

- no statement may receive more than four points;
- at least one statement must receive four points; more than one can if the member thinks this is appropriate;
- the total number of points allocated must equal twice the number of goal statements: no more, no less.

Step five

When step four is completed, groups of from three to five are now set up, their membership randomly allocated. The score given by each member to each goal statement is recorded. Where there is universal agreement, that score becomes the group's agreed score. Where there are differences, members should explain what has led them to give their points' allocation and a consensus should be sought. It does not follow that if, for example, four of the group have allocated three points and the fifth one point, 'consensus' is achieved by the fifth member conceding. Discussion may lead to a major reconsideration of views by any or all in the group. At the end of this session the group checks that their total matches the required number of points. This session is the most critical, since it is here that the decisions are really made. Parents, teachers and community members have the opportunity to discuss their concerns and hopes for the future. It may take some time to work through this process and it is wise for there to be prior agreement on the length of the session to ensure that any discussion is directed towards the task at hand rather than just becoming a discussion of a more general nature.

Step six

The results are collected from each group and averaged. This list is duplicated or displayed on an OHP or chart. It is rarely productive to seek explanations for a group's significant variation from the average: to do so leads to self-justification, not sound decision-making.

Step seven

It must be remembered that the purpose of this task is to prioritise the goal statements and to gain commitment for action related to those priorities. It is likely that four or five will now stand out as priorities, probably with an average score of about 3.5. It is also likely that all groups involved will have identified as important, and thus be committed to, at least one, and possibly more, of the final list of goals. The meeting is asked whether further discussion would be helpful: there may be a feeling, for example, that three key goals are as many as can be managed. There may be resource implications that some members of the meeting feel should be raised before the decision is finalised. If there is total agreement the meeting has now completed its task.

Step eight

The decisions are now passed to the appropriate groups within the core–plus school to devise action plans.

This exercise is an excellent way to determine the priority of a set of identified goals because:
- everyone feels that they have made a contribution;
- people feel that they have achieved a result;
- everyone is likely to accept the result even though as individuals they may have started with different thoughts;
- by selecting a small group of goals rather than a single first preference it is likely that everyone in the meeting can identify closely with at least one of the goals and is therefore committed to their implementation;
- the group has identified a series of goals to work towards in both the short-term and the long-term and can then move towards ways of satisfying these goals.

POLICY DEVELOPMENT

A school policy might be considered to be 'the major directions of the school programme . . . the determination of curriculum objectives . . . the use of resources available to the school . . . broad organisational policies' (Fordham 1983b). The policy includes aspirations for the students and the community, how it hopes to achieve them, and what types of policies, programmes, procedures and practices will be adopted to bring them to fruition.

Elements of a school policy

A good school policy will contain statements about what the school is doing now (the current situation); what the school hopes to achieve in the future (proposals); how the school intends to achieve its goals (methods); and how the school will tell whether or not it has been successful (monitoring and evaluation). The school policy should contain the following sections:

Introduction

This will contain a statement expressing the purpose of the document to let the reader know what it sets out to do and the way it should be used. It should also contain information about the school community to enable the reader to gain an understanding of the particular characteristics of the school, its students and its community.

Statement of aims and objectives

An aim is a generalised statement of intention which is to be worked towards over a period of time. It is often difficult to know when aims have been fully achieved; and in order to measure our progress towards them we list a series of specific, related objectives which can be tested. The difference can be summed up by referring to aims as 'long-term goals' and objectives as 'short-term goals'. For each aim there will be a number of objectives that bring us closer to it. The statements below indicate the types of aims and objectives that might be given attention within a school policy:

– Identified aim: to encourage parents and the community to participate with staff in the formulation of appropriate curriculum material.

– Related objective: at the beginning of the year staff and parents meet together to determine appropriate strategies for homework activities.

The message is that the thinking behind the formulation of the aims and objectives needs to be consistent to demonstrate how each of the activities within the school contributes to the achievement of the aims and objectives.

How aims and objectives will be achieved

This section of the school policy is concerned with the means that will be adopted by the school to bring about the aims and objectives. It may include statements that describe how the broad guidelines set down by the educational authorities have been adopted and implemented, and specify in general terms how the school intends to achieve what it is setting out to do. This might include statements on:

Programmes   This section will include such things as the broad outline of the content of the curriculum and a brief justification for the sorts of decisions that have been made. It would also include any statement about extra-curricular activities such as before or after school activities or community programmes.

Policies   This section will include a brief description of major school policies in areas such as parent and community involvement in school activities, rules of behaviour or attitude development, and general policies for decision-making by various groups within the school.

Processes   This section will include statements on how the aims and objectives would be implemented. Issues such as class grouping and size, thematic or separated subject areas, teaching strategies and the role that parents can play in the educational progress of their children would all be included.

Procedures   This section will include a brief statement of how the school would enable the student, the parent and the community at large to interact with the school. Lines of communication, accessibility to the school for community members, courtesies to be observed if a parent wishes to communicate with a teacher and information on how the school would respond to various situations that might arise will all be described briefly.

Practices This section will include any statements of activities seen as additional to the regular activities of the school. Statements on the use of excursions, the transition from pre-school to primary or primary to secondary school, the use of community members to provide additional expertise in specialised areas of the curriculum or inter-school exchange programmes for students can all be seen as practices within a particular school that establish a uniqueness within the overall system. It will also identify the range of activities that one can attribute to the core–plus nature of the school. Practices such as retraining opportunities, the delivery of health and welfare information and services and the use of the school as a community meeting place will be included in this section. This element of the school policy is perhaps the most important of all, because it provides the reader with a detailed understanding of what the school is really like in terms of its day-to-day operation. A great deal of attention needs to be paid to the drafting of this section as it is the working part of the document.

School organisation

It is important to outline the way the school is administered and the way in which decisions are made to ensure that there is no conflict between the aims and objectives and the practice of the school. For instance, there is a contradiction if one of the aims states 'to develop in the students and parents the skills and motivation to participate in decisions that affect their lives' but there is an administrative structure that actively precludes any participation from anyone but the school administration. A statement of the way in which the administration sees how it will go about the role of administering the school will enable readers to be clear in their perception of how they can fit into the decision-making processes.

It is also helpful to provide some diagrammatic representation of how the school committee system works. This will help readers, first, to understand the lines of communication and, second, to choose at what level their participation might be of value. Such a diagram would identify the relationship between various committees of the school and also the various people who have responsibility for aspects of the school's activities.

Monitoring and evaluation

Since regular monitoring and a final evaluation of the elements that go to make up a school policy are necessary to ensure that progression towards the aims is being achieved, it is necessary to elaborate within the policy document the means by which the school will judge a successful progression. Details such as how often the school will review its progress, who will be involved in the review and the types of areas the review will cover should all be listed in this section. It is possible to match up specific objective statements with specific questions of evaluation; for instance, the objective 'that all grade six students be successfully placed in a secondary school of their choice by the end of the year' can be evaluated each year by determining the number of students who are placed in the secondary school of their choice.

Other considerations

Since the policy document is a reflection of a particular school in a particular community, steps must be taken to ensure that:

- the resources, needs, interests and problems of the community are adequately addressed within the policy document;
- as far as possible the entire school community be given the opportunity to be involved in the process that results in the production of the final document. In this way there is a greater chance of the document adequately reflecting the attitudes of the community and, secondly and perhaps more importantly, there is a greater chance of its acceptance by the community.

Possible areas of conflict

Since most of the policy document will contain statements that can be directly traced back to certain values held by its authors, it is important that during the process of construction conflicts of opinion should be brought into the open and resolved as much as possible through consensus decision-making and problem-solving. The values will include:

- what the role of schools should be;
- whether schools should 'maintain standards' or 'look after the whole child';

- which teaching methods should be emphasised;
- what the balance of the curriculum should be;
- the relative importance of the 'core' and 'plus' aspects of the school.

The final document should reflect the considered opinions of those involved and, where possible, describe the decision-making processes which took place.

Relevance

For a school policy to have any real meaning it must provide a series of goals and strategies that reflect the nature of school within a large and complex technological society. One can no longer get away with stating a series of empty platitudes with the hope that the programme will make them come true. It can be argued that the whole community should be given the opportunity to have some input into the policy for its local schools. This is not to say that everyone in the community will want to have an input, nor does it suggest that everyone will want to be involved in the entire process, but it does give those who are interested the opportunity. The underlying philosophy of a core–plus school requires that this be the case.

Constructing a school policy

When constructing a policy for the core–plus school, it is critical that everyone in the school community has an opportunity to make a contribution. The following process enables people to contribute at the level of their ability and interest, and helps to make the policy development a joint effort.

- *Step one*: Conduct a needs assessment within the local community. This process can identify: community resources, physical, personnel and financial; perceived community problems; attitudes towards various activities, methods of learning and teaching; people willing to be involved in school activities.
- *Step two*: Conduct a long-term goal-setting exercise. This can provide the core–plus council with an overall perspective of what the school community wants the school to be like in the future.
- *Step three*: A sub-committee of the core–plus council which comprises staff, parents and interested community members draws up a statement of goals and objectives for the school.

- *Step four*: A public meeting discusses, alters and finally confirms the statement of goals and objectives.
- *Step five*: A council sub-committee draws up a draft school policy based on the goals and objectives statement accepted by the public meeting, and submits it to the core–plus council.
- *Step six*: A second public meeting is called to discuss, amend and finally accept the policy statement presented by the council.
- *Step seven*: The council formally adopts the school policy and makes it available for any member of the community who wishes to see or keep a copy.
- *Step eight*: Regular biennial reviews of the policy are needed to ensure that it maintains its relevance to the school and the community at large.

Checklist for school policy formulation

When the school policy has been formulated, each of the following questions should be answered affirmatively. Does your school policy:

- state its purpose?
- provide a profile of the community, its people and the students?
- give general aims for education?
- give specific aims for your school?
- give specific objectives that relate to those aims?
- say how those aims and objectives will be achieved through school programmes? school policies? school processes? school procedures? school practices?
- provide information on how the school is organised, including:
  - channels of communication?
  - staff responsibilities?
  - committee structure?
  - decision-making processes?
  - administrative rules and procedures?
- say how it will evaluate:
  - students' progress?
  - the curriculum?
  - school organisation?
  - the school policy?
  - the core–plus programme?
- say how the school policy was formulated?
- say how it can be changed?

- discuss the relationship of the school with its community?
- say where the school is heading and what actions are being taken to get there?
- say things in simple and easily understood terms?
- make sense?

The policy statement of the core–plus school considers both the curriculum requirements imposed on the school by the educational authorities and processes for determining other curriculum activities of relevance to the students and parents. It also makes clear that the core–plus school has a dual purpose, to educate students and to facilitate and support the self-education of those who have left school. The construction of a core–plus policy will provide specific directions for the day-to-day programme of the school in terms of the classroom activities provided for the students together with the development of a comprehensive programme for the community as a whole.

Chapter 10

Programmes in the core–plus school

> Community education is the over-arching conceptual base, while programs are the activities related to the solution of specific community needs.
>
> (Minzey and Le Tarte 1979: 15)

As the quotation above indicates, good programmes rely upon a solid conceptual base, and the way in which the process issues and the policy development discussed in the previous chapters have been resolved will have a bearing on the long-term success of the core–plus school's programming. It is possible to have:

- poor processes and poor programmes, in which case the school will fail in its attempts to fulfil its goals;
- poor processes but good programmes, in which case the school might have many people attending its activities but the activities themselves may disappear when the organiser leaves the school;
- good processes but poor programmes, in which case the organisers will have a lot of fun but few people will come back to subsequent school activities;
- good processes and good programmes, in which case people will attend the activities because they resolve personal needs, and the programme of the school will continue in the long term because there are many people involved in the organisation of the programme and leadership development is a key component of that involvement.

The previous chapter discussed the first steps in the construction of programmes for the core–plus school, namely, finding out what people in the community want, setting goals that relate to those needs and establishing a school policy that enables those goals to be reached. This chapter considers the 'nitty-gritty' of school activities, the actual programmes that the core–plus school might run and the issues that need to be considered for them to be successful.

PROGRAMME DEVELOPMENT

The material discussed in earlier parts of this book might be considered to be the background preparation for what is the overt manifestation of core–plus education – the running of programmes. Successful programmes can only occur if issues relating to the process, such as the acceptance of a core–plus philosophy and the generation of broad goals by the school management committee, the use of some form of needs assessment to determine the community's perception of its needs and problems, and the development of a mechanism for involving parents and other community members in school activities, are considered before the school starts to run a programme which may be part of its community education activities. If the process elements have been successfully carried out then the programme will have a better basis for success. If a school has considered each of the issues described in previous chapters it will have a fairly accurate indication of what the people in the community want (and therefore are likely to support) and which people are available to assist the school in running the programmes it will offer. Once this information is available a number of steps should be taken to develop the programme itself.

This book will not spend any time discussing the programme decisions related to the curriculum for the core operations of the school, since that will be handled by the principal and staff, with assistance from parents and perhaps community members. Instead, it will concentrate on developing the plus programme of the core–plus school, that part of the programme that considers the role of the school as a community facility. However, many of the procedures considered can be used for both purposes. A number of steps are necessary for a successful programme to be undertaken.

Step one

Establish a core–plus programme committee. Since a number of decisions need to be made about which programmes will run now, which will run later, and which programmes are unlikely to run at all, the establishment of a core–plus programme committee (possibly as a sub-committee of the core–plus council) will enable these decisions to be made without the time of the core–plus council being spent on this facet of the school's activities. The establishment of such a committee also allows for the involvement of people who may not already be involved or who may have a particular interest in developing extra-curricular programmes. In any event the committee will include the principal, a teacher, a parent, one or more community member(s), the community education coordinator, if there is one, and a member of the core–plus council.

In this way issues relating to the availability of rooms, costs, timetabling, staffing and inputs from various groups in the school community can be considered at the time of discussion. The councillor will report back to the core–plus council.

Step two

Using the results of the latest needs assessment, determine what the community perceives to be needs or problems associated with that community. With the information provided by the needs assessment it is possible to gain information such as:

– what problems are seen to be the easiest to resolve;
– what priority those problems are given;
– what the community needs with respect to additional educational opportunities;
– what people are prepared to assist with, rather than simply participate in.

Step three

Analyse each of the problems listed. At this point further information about the problems needs to be found and analysed. Information such as whether other agencies are working on similar problems, how the problem affects the community, what the symptoms of the problem are, what the causes of the problem are, the number of people affected and literature related to the problem, can be used to try to determine what the best course of action will be. It is desirable during this stage to involve additional people who have expertise in the area being discussed. These people can give valuable information in the form of research or case studies that can save the time of the committee.

Step four

Generate and prioritise possible solutions. For each problem a number of solutions may be proposed. However, not all solutions will have the same effect and not all will be appropriate to the school. For instance, if the chosen problem is 'youth unemployment' the following alternative measures might be proposed:

- write to the government expressing the school's concern;
- co-operate with local government to implement a youth work policy;
- provide training sessions entitled 'How to Succeed at Job Interviews' for senior students and other young people in the community;
- establish a volunteer youth scheme in the school;
- provide practical skills programmes with a local college.

It can be seen that a wide range of quite varied solutions may be proposed, some of which will be more effective than others and some of which will be easier to undertake than others.

Step five

Cooperate with other agencies or services to determine the viability of each alternative. At this stage it is necessary to consult with other groups that may also have an interest in the area. If the committee has already established contact then this is of benefit to the planning process. Through discussion it is possible to generate information that will enable the committee to make an informed decision.

Step six

Choose the most appropriate programme, policy or activity for the solution of the problem. It will become obvious that due to factors such as cost, staffing, facility availability, outside assistance and feasibility, some solutions will be more realistic than others. For each of the problems that has been identified, a programme, policy or activity, which may or may not involve groups outside the school, will be considered as the most desirable solution to the problem.

Step seven

Determine which programme or programmes will be organised and operated. Initially it will not be possible to resolve all the identified problems because of cost, lack of facilities, shortage of people who have expressed an interest or lack of staff. Consequently, it is necessary to select those activities that seem most likely to succeed. Factors which need to be taken into account include the number of people likely to attend, whether the school has the facility to run the activity, the availability of appropriate staff and the cost and/or availability of funds. A wide variety of programmes might be considered at this stage. Broad categories will include:

- programmes to be included in the ordinary school programme;
- programmes related to perceived problems within the community;
- out-of-school programmes for children;
- adult education programmes;
- programmes related to re-training;
- joint programmes with other community groups.

It may be decided to concentrate on one category, for example, adult education, and to get those programmes operational before moving to another category. Alternatively, it may be decided to undertake two or more categories of programmes simultaneously. These decisions will depend on the availability of the various components of the programme and how quickly the committee wishes to move.

Step eight

For each chosen programme a set of goals and objectives will be developed. When developing programme goals, two types need to be considered. The first type is directed at the activity as a whole, and the second type is directed at the learning which will take place for each individual. The goals should express broad, wide-ranging expectations which look at the overall contribution of the programme to the learner. For instance, if the core–plus council chooses to run a programme that will provide the adults in the community with the opportunity to study for the year 12 English course, the following goals may be put forward.

Group goals:

- to provide an atmosphere that is conducive to adult learning;
- to provide an avenue for adults to study year 12 English;

Individual goals:

- to enable each participant successfully to complete the examinations for year 12 English;
- to encourage each participant to contribute to the development of the course.

Once the goals for the particular programme are decided, it is possible to write specific objectives that detail the desired results. The goals should be used as a broad guide for writing specific objectives, and these should include details of the criteria to be used to determine whether or not each has been achieved. It is necessary to set down the following details: the group to which the objective refers, the desired result, how that result will be tested and the target date or time. For instance, for the goals referred to above, the following specific objectives may relate to the goals provided.

Group objective:

- that all instructors of adult education classes participate in an in-service course on adult education before they conduct adult classes.

Individual objective:

- that 80 per cent of students who enrol pass their year 12 English examination by the end of the year.

In each case the objective can be related directly to one of the goals. It may be true that many objectives can be written in order to lead the programme successfully towards its goals. In each case the objective can be tested by the programme committee at some stage of the programme. If the planning of the goals and objectives has been thorough and the relationship between the goals and objectives logical then the successful completion of each of the objectives will lead towards the accomplishment of the goals. Equally, if the programme goals have been written with those of the school in mind, then progress towards the programme goals will also lead to progress towards the school's overall goals.

Step nine

Transform specific objectives into specific activities. If the objectives are written with sufficient detail it is an easy matter to transform them into activities that will enable them to be achieved. However, the decisions about what types of activities to run will depend upon a number of criteria including the teacher or activity leader, the facilities, the background of the participants, time and finance available.

It is the programme committee's responsibility to ensure that each of these details is taken into account when the final decisions are made. A wide variety of teaching methods are available for activities that involve some sort of knowledge transmission. Any of the following learning methods might be used within the overall programme: workshops, discussion groups, conferences, case studies, tours, lectures, panels, demonstrations, field trips, games.

Programme development can be viewed as being the selection of the most appropriate activity for the attainment of the goals. This process is appropriate not only to adult education programmes or community activities, but also for the development of the regular school curriculum. The same sort of activity can be used when the school wishes to involve itself in the development of new programmes or the revision of existing ones. At some stage or other the core–plus school will be considering an involvement in many school-based and community programme possibilities. In each case individual activities can be listed that are appropriate to each of those categories.

STAFFING CORE–PLUS PROGRAMMES

When a school considers the implementation of community activities one of the prime areas of concern is that of staffing. Without the assistance of both paid and voluntary staff the core–plus school cannot hope to organise a wide range of school–community activities or to run individual projects. The need for enthusiastic, trained personnel is critical to the success of any endeavours in this field because the process of community education is essentially a people-related rather than programme-related process. The use of volunteers remains one of the most effective ways of developing individual schools. The core–plus school relies on the involvement of its parents and community and additional volunteered contributions by its staff, and the coordination of this volunteer work force becomes one of the responsibilities of the core–plus council and the principal. Some of the issues that need to be considered for the organisation of a volunteer programme are discussed below.

Step one

The core–plus council adopts a volunteer policy. There are a variety of reasons why this ought to be the first step that the council considers, but two are critical. They are: the legal obligations and liabilities of the council in relation to volunteer workers in the school, and the procedures by which volunteers are recruited, trained, recompensed and deployed. The acceptance by the council of a policy for volunteers safeguards both the council and the volunteer and lets both parties know exactly what is expected of them. Any volunteer policy will contain the following sections:

- A rationale for the use of volunteers: arguments might include the lowering of student–adult ratios for school activities, the promotion of the concept that both the school and the community are partners in education and the increase in community support and commitment to the school that volunteer service can bring.
- Activities for which volunteer assistance is desirable: such activities might include serving on school committees, helping the school maintain its facilities, helping the school in its regular programme, and so on.
- Conditions under which volunteers will be used: this section may include a statement of how they will become accredited as 'official school volunteers', the expectations of them and to whom they will be responsible.

The volunteer policy need not be a long or complex document but will cover all the aspects the council sees as being potential issues. The policy will be open to review to enable any issues that were not originally thought of to be incorporated later.

Step two

A teacher-needs assessment is conducted to determine the areas to which a volunteer could contribute during the regular school programme. This step enables teachers to determine the sort of assistance they need. Some teachers may feel they need no assistance and others may have a variety of possible uses for volunteers that can be considered. Some of the areas to be considered as part of the regular school programme might include working with students, assisting the teacher in classroom preparation, coordinating community activities, assisting with public relations for the school or involvement in curriculum design, implementation or evaluation.

The teachers and the council together specify the qualifications and experience or training deemed necessary for the various categories of volunteers. If a volunteer programme is to be successful then the people involved need to know what is to be done and how to do it. It is not always possible to recruit volunteers who know how to go about the activity that they are required to do and so training is necessary. This safeguards the school and the children, and the volunteer, because if they feel that they are not capable of what is asked of them they may not volunteer again. By providing training the school is giving new knowledge to the volunteer, but also, and perhaps more importantly, the volunteer is gaining confidence in interacting with other people.

In some cases no previous experience is necessary and, in others, working with children previously will be an advantage. If volunteers are to be tutors, it will be necessary for them to have knowledge and understanding of the subject matter involved. A short course of training to give an awareness of classroom procedures, specific curriculum details and the recommended methods of teaching should always be undertaken before volunteers work with children. Depending on the background of the volunteer this may take half an hour or half a day.

A volunteer who will act as a coordinator of either a small part of the school's community programme or as the overall coordinator needs to have a variety of attributes to do the job effectively, including commitment, local knowledge, the ability to communicate, coordinating abilities and leadership skills. Other skills and aptitudes will include the ability to initiate programmes, work in a team, assess needs, locate, train and support volunteers and coordinate resources. Training that will enable the volunteer to become skilled in these areas will include the types of skills that are referred to earlier in this book. These skills would include the general skills of participating in the making of decisions, planning, working more productively with others and communicating well, as well as more specific tasks that might relate to individual activities. Depending on the volunteer's background the individual may need to attend a short course designed to impart these skills.

If the school decided to implement a programme of adult education activities, people with previous adult education experience would need to be identified by the school. A thorough knowledge of the subject matter being taught and experience in working with adults would be minimum requirements for these volunteers. Should people not have experience of teaching adults then the school might consider running a course in adult learning.

Step three

The school develops a system for the organisation and management of the volunteer programme. The main reason for the lack of success of many volunteer programmes is the absence of an adequate system for the management, and support, of volunteers in the school. The main purpose of the volunteer programme is to match a suitable person to a given need at a given time. Since it is unlikely that many volunteer systems will get more volunteers than they need, there needs to be an organised way of producing the most effective use of the resources available.

The first step in providing an adequate management system is the appointment of either an individual or a small group to coordinate the programme. If an individual is appointed, it may be necessary for the school to consider paying for this coordination because of the work involved. The coordinator needs planning, timetabling and organising skills. The duties of the coordinator will include:

- to assist, but not be responsible for, recruitment;
- to provide, but not necessarily run, training activities;
- to maintain an index of those who volunteer;
- to respond to teachers' requests by providing the name of a volunteer with appropriate capability and time availability;
- to act as a liaison between the volunteers and the school.

A volunteer information card for each volunteer is kept at the school. The information contained on it will include name, address, telephone number, and the tasks for which, and times at which, the person is willing to serve. Past and required training and experience can also be listed. To facilitate forward planning, teachers are asked periodically to list their requirements, which will include the nature, time and date of the activity, the length of the commitment and whether there is a preference for a particular person or set of skills. The needs assessment conducted in the community will give sufficient information to enable an adult education activity to be coordinated, staffed and run.

Volunteers will be contacted as early as possible to ensure their availability and should any changes to the programme occur the volunteer will be contacted immediately. Should the volunteer not be able to attend he/she will contact the school as soon as possible. The volunteer assistance scheme will be minuted in the core–plus council minutes and volunteers will be asked to sign in and sign out to ensure full insurance coverage in the case of any mishaps. At the end of their involvement volunteers will be asked to provide feedback on their experiences to the volunteer coordinator.

Step four

A recruiting strategy is developed and implemented. Four different types of volunteers are usually available to a school.

- Once-only volunteers: people in this category are usually busy and have limited time, but they may be willing to help a single activity or event.
- Home volunteers: people who are restricted because of a young family, or age or handicap may not be able to attend the school but are willing to help from their home base.
- Short-term volunteers: people who may be able to help for a few hours or a few days either at school or in the community.
- Long-term volunteers: people who are able to work in the school over an extended period of time.

Any strategy for recruiting volunteers will enable and encourage people within any category to offer any service that they see as being relevant. Traditionally schools have been seen as places for young people. In the initial stages of developing an awareness of the school by the community it is necessary for the school to go to the community to publicise its needs. Possible sources of volunteers include local colleges, universities, civic groups, service clubs, churches and senior citizens' groups. By developing and implementing a well planned strategy for recruitment it is possible to obtain a large list of potential volunteers with information about their interests and the times to which they are prepared to commit themselves.

Step five

Relevant training programmes for volunteers are developed and implemented. There are three different areas that might be considered when a programme for training volunteers is devised. The first is that all volunteers should be equipped with the ability to relate to children and adults, motivate students, relate in a multi-cultural situation, promote feelings of self-worth and develop positive school–community relations. A programme developing these skills might consist of mini-lectures, discussion groups, reading, videotapes of case studies or observation. The development of these skills should be seen as an on-going process. The second is that all volunteers should be equipped with the skill to assess student interests and ability levels and develop educational materials. A programme developing these skills might include observations and discussions of student behaviour and practice at developing teaching materials using low-cost materials and media. The third is that all volunteers in the adult education programme should be equipped with skills in the area of adult learning. The assumptions that we make about why and how children learn cannot be made about adults. Over the past few years the science of adult learning has been developed to help fill in the gaps.

It has been shown quite conclusively in the past few years that an adult who wishes to learn has different motivations, techniques and pressures from those of child learners. The science of adult learning has developed because of the acceptance by educators that it is not possible to teach adults in the same way that we teach children. This is not so much because of the knowledge or the techniques of imparting knowledge as because of the people who are seeking to acquire the knowledge. An adult differs from a child in a number of ways that are quite crucial to the processes of learning and of teaching.

Self concept

Whereas child learners regard themselves as dependent on the adult world for most of the major decisions that affect their lives, adults see themselves as as independent of others, and responsible for their own decision-making. Because of the need for self-direction adult learners will object to being placed in situations where their self respect is belittled in some way, by being talked down to, threatened or embarrassed; in other words being treated like a child. If this occurs, very little learning will take place, and the likely result will be the adult's withdrawal from the class.

Learning readiness

It is readily accepted that children become ready to learn things in a naturally ordered sequence. As children mature certain developments of their physical and mental capacities produce a state of readiness for progression through to a new stage of development. However, adults, although they are already fully developed physically, still have states of intellectual readiness where their capacity to learn is at its peak. These states of readiness, however, are more subtle and are more likely to revolve around the social and situational characteristics of the individual rather than physiological processes. The adult educator needs to be aware of these facts to enable optimum learning to take place. The fact that the adult is in the class at all indicates a state of readiness that one cannot assume about a child.

Time perspective

Child learners look at education as being the accumulation of knowledge and skills that will be useful in the future. Their time perspective is one of postponed application. Consequently, children are happy to store up subject matter and are prepared to work with a subject-centred orientation. On the other hand adults think of learning as a method for dealing with the problems they are facing at the time.

Experience as a resource

Child learners look upon the current learning experiences as a resource for future life experiences. What they learn now will be used later to help them deal with situations that arise. Adult learners, on the other hand, have a wealth of life experiences that can be called upon as a resource for current learning experiences.

Background and experience will assist them in dealing with the new knowledge that is placed in front of them. Because of this adult educators must see themselves as facilitators rather than imparters of knowledge.

Two major implications arise from these four basic differences between child and adult learners.

- The teacher must adopt a problem-centred approach with adults, rather than adopting a logical sequence of subject matter.
- The teacher must provide the adult learner with the opportunity to practise the new learning as soon as possible. This may occur in simulated sessions within the class or through adapting the material to real-life situations.

Because many adult education programmes refer to non-credit special interest activities rather than the formal courses associated with schools, colleges or universities, a number of points need to be remembered in order to ensure the best possible chance of success:

- A highly motivated individual learns more rapidly than a less motivated one.
- Learning motivated by success (or reward) is usually preferable to learning motivated by failure (or punishment).
- Learning through the use of intrinsic motivation (a desire to learn) is preferable to learning through extrinsic motivation (a reward for learning).
- Tolerance of failure is best learned by providing a number of successful experiences for every experienced failure.
- Realistic goal setting leads to more satisfactory improvement, and individuals need practice in setting realistic goals.
- The personal background and experiences of individuals can either hinder or enhance their ability to learn.
- Active participation is better than passive reception.
- The more meaningful the task or the materials the more readily they are learned.
- Positive, critical feedback aids learning.

Step six

Implement the programme and thank the volunteers for their contribution. It is important to make volunteers feel part of the team, to belong to the overall programme of the school. It is not necessary that a formal measure of thanks be issued but it is important that they know their contribution is both worthwhile and appreciated.

Step seven

Evaluate the programme. As with any other activity that the school undertakes, the volunteer programme needs to be evaluated to ensure that the people involved in it are happy with the way it is going and that the programme itself is making a contribution to the school.

Chapter 11

Financing and managing the core–plus school

> Parents as managers and partners probably hold out greater
> prospects for school improvement than parents as customers.
>
> (Munn 1993: 177)

The establishment of core–plus education within the school will
involve some increased costs. If the school is going to be open
longer hours, used more, and have staff available for the extra
usage, additional means of funding will have to be found to
support this new approach to education. Since a substantial proportion of the cost will be related to salary items for coordinators,
secretaries, cleaners or teachers of community programmes, the
use of volunteers can make the increased costs minimal. In the
long run, the amount of money spent on financing the new community programmes and the way in which that money is raised will
depend on the importance that the community places on a total
education programme and the unique set of characteristics that go
to make up that community.

With changing demographic patterns in the community occurring all the time, the need for a sense of commitment to the
concept of a core–plus education programme is the first step. As
the general population continues to age, a greater percentage of
people will have little or no direct connection with the educational
programme offered to children. It could be argued that an increasing proportion of the education funds raised through taxation
should be spent alternatively on the people who have left formal
educational programmes but who wish to retrain or provide themselves with further educational opportunities. Schools becoming
involved in these types of activities might be one way in which
additional funds could be raised.

FINANCING THE PLUS IN CORE–PLUS SCHOOLS

Whatever the outcome of the move towards schools as community centres, a number of steps need to be taken to ensure adequate financial capabilities that will allow community activities to occur without jeopardising the regular school programme.

Step one

Draw up a core–plus education budget. The decisions to be made during this process are similar to those identified in the budgeting and approval component of the Caldwell and Spinks (1988) Collaborative School Management Cycle Model shown in Figure 9.1 on page 177. The staff and principal will be involved in advising the council of the budgetary implications of programmes they wish to run for both the core and plus aspects of the regular curriculum. The council and its sub-committees will be involved in identifying the budgetary implications for the additional plus aspects related to community education activities. The decisions about which of these programmes the school can afford to run and the final approval of the budget is the responsibility of the core–plus council.

There are two categories of expenditure that need to be considered when developing a budget for core–plus education within the school: administrative costs and programme costs. This will be the case whether the programme is to be an excursion to a community venue for a group of children, an adult education programme run by the school or a series of meetings related to the discussion of local community issues. The budget for administrative costs may include some or all of the following: salary/wage items for both teaching staff and administration staff, and which may include a community co-ordinator and secretarial services; office expenses, such as telephone, power and heating costs, postage and printing costs, equipment, cleaning and maintenance costs, consumables, advertising costs.

As far as programme costs are concerned the two programme aspects of the school, namely, the regular school curriculum and the community activities, are funded separately. Generally the bulk of the regular curriculum will be covered by normal school grants, although some special programmes may need to be funded by other resources. For community activities, in most situations there is a need for individual programmes to be self-supporting.

Fees charged for the programmes cover the costs of instructors' fees, materials and facility costs. Any fees will be kept to a minimum and successful programmes will assist those that are less popular to survive. As a rule of thumb it is wise to base the budget on a group of fifteen. If fifteen is considered to be the break-even point, then a group of twenty in one programme will help in the survival of another programme with only ten participants.

Budgeting for both the administrative costs and the programme costs before any programme starts enables the council to have some idea of what its commitment will be. Once an appropriate budget has been determined for the core–plus programme it is then necessary to undergo the procedure of raising the money to allow the programmes to proceed. If the programme is to be successful, then it is important that there be a consistent avenue of funding and that the management of these funds is such that the natural resources of the community (people, facilities) are complemented rather than replaced by any finances that are obtained.

Step two

Establish a funding strategy that will allow the project to begin in the short term, and allow it to develop over a period of time.

There are basically four ways of funding the community programme within the school:

- The school may fund the entire activity through fee-charging, fund raising, facility hire or from the ordinary school budget.
- The school may fund the activity partially, and ask one or more funding agencies to provide the rest of the funds.
- A number of funding bodies are approached and each is asked to contribute partially to the cost. The objective is that the project be totally financed by external funds.
- A single funding body is approached and asked to provide total funding.

It could be argued that the second alternative is most appropriate, because it maintains the need for commitment by the community, and rewards them when they show commitment. Since the total budget for the core–plus programme will be out of reach of the resources of most schools in the short term, there is a need to see the financing of the project as an on-going process. It is much better to start the project in a small way and then to apply for support from other bodies than it is to apply for funding. A number of reasons can be given for this:

- If the programme is small, the school may be able to raise the money through the education allowance, local fund raising events, fees, or a combination of these things; but if the project is to be more comprehensive it is likely that some external funding will be necessary.
- By starting in a small way the school will use the interest and enthusiasm that is already present. Waiting for external funding might mean that your community loses its interest or finds another means of satisfying it.
- Already having the project in operation presents evidence of commitment on the part of organisers. It shows that it can be done and funding agencies are swayed by this sort of evidence.

A strategy for raising funds

- Determine the minimum amount of money needed to establish the project in the school.
- Raise the funds needed to establish the project through special fund raising events, a loan or grant from school funds, by asking for donations from local businesses or by charging fees for the activity.
- Maintain liquidity by making activities self-sufficient through the user-pays principle, by hiring out school facilities or by attracting sponsorships.
- Apply for funds for the more comprehensive programmes from appropriate funding agencies.

For many changes towards a core–plus philosophy within the school no money will be required. For instance, involving parents in the decision-making process, letting them come to the school whenever they like and using them as resources for the school's programmes simply requires a positive attitude. However, the core–plus council may wish to embark on other projects for which costs will occur. An adult education programme, a parent and child camp or hosting students from another school will all involve costs of some sort, whether it be transport, food, costs associated with keeping the school open or to pay night-class teachers.

In a situation like this there will be some programme costs and some administrative costs. Many of these costs may be overcome through the use of volunteer help, the school paying the costs of keeping the school open, or by the donation of materials. The establishment of the initial budget will enable those services, materials, personnel or facilities that cannot be received free, to be paid for. It may be that the initial amount could establish quite a substantial programme within the school.

Step three

Draw up a list of agencies or funding bodies that may be potential contributors to the school's programme. Nearly as much time needs to be spent researching the funding bodies as is spent actually preparing the proposal. The school needs to establish:

- whether the agency gives money for projects such as that proposed;
- how much money is granted annually;
- contact points and people.

The final decision on which funding bodies will be approached will not be made before some effort to contact the organisation, either in person or by telephone, is made. The personal contact will provide information such as deadlines for submission, guidelines for writing the proposal, and so on. The final selection will represent both government and non-government agencies or trusts.

Step four

Write a grant proposal to each of the bodies that has been selected. There may be a special format to follow when applying for funds from some funding organisations. If there is not, the following components should be included when writing a proposal for a grant:

Summary statement   This section gives the reader an overview of the application and should include the name of the school, the amount requested, a brief description of the project, whether the school has a tax exempt status and the period of time for which funds are being requested.

Introduction   This section is designed to tell the reader what your school is and does, and to build the feeling in the mind of the reader that any money granted will be well spent. It should include the goals and philosophy of your school, when it was established, past projects or programmes, previous sources of funding, any recognition that has been given and any unique or notable characteristics of the school or school community.

Description of need   This section describes why the project has been created. It requires as much specific data as possible to support the claims being made and should include a description of your community, demographic data, results of surveys, studies or evaluations, the methods used when determining the needs and how the problem has affected the community.

Goals and objectives of the project   This section describes how you want the community to look once your project has been completed successfully. It will include the goals for the project – broad statements of what is hoped will be accomplished and the objectives of the project – specific statements that describe activities the success of which can be measured.

Methodology   This section describes how you will achieve the goals and objectives set out in the previous section. Descriptions need to be graphically portrayed to enable the reader to visualise what will occur. This section should include proposed staffing, information about community usage of the school, the numbers and categories of potential clients and how they will be involved, how the project will be administered and managed, how physical, personnel and monetary resources will be deployed, and possible alternative methods for achieving the goals and objectives.

Evaluation   This section describes how you will measure whether the project has been a success. This is an important section, particularly if funds are being requested to conduct research, and must include a description that links the evaluation of the project to its goals and objectives, who will be responsible for the evaluation, what evaluation instruments will be used, what data will be collected, how it will be collected and how it will be analysed.

Future funding   Since there is no guarantee that funds will be granted from the same funding source in the future, the source will want to know how the project will continue once its funding has been expended, unless it is a one-off project. This section should include evidence of commitments from other funding sources or indications that the project will become self-sustaining, or the school will include it in its regular budget, in the future.

Budget This section will provide a line-item budget that adequately reflects what has been described or implied in previous sections of the proposal. If there are any items that might be considered questionable, then a narrative description justifying them will be included.

Appendices This section allows any supportive evidence to be available without disturbing the narrative flow of the proposal itself and might include a statement of tax-exempt status, job descriptions for proposed staff, letters of endorsement or support, demographic data, any public relations material about the school and any evaluation instruments that will be used.

It must be remembered that it is easier to get money if the project is already in operation than if it is not. Having already established an activity of some sort provides a track record that indicates a need and an ability to satisfy that need. Consequently, if the first application is not granted, it does not mean that future grant proposals will not.

MANAGING CORE–PLUS ACTIVITIES

Once the planning for core–plus activities has proceeded thus far, the next step is to implement the programme itself. Core–plus curriculum components, those that are undertaken for the regular students of the school, have been addressed by much of the educational administration literature and need not be repeated here. However, the management of the community activities of the school, as a new activity for many schools, does need to be addressed. Issues that have not been looked at elsewhere, but are related to the actual running of a community activity include facility usage, time management and programme operation.

In order for the activities to be successfully managed and organised a number of procedures need to be followed.

Step one

The core–plus council determines what facilities will be available for community use. When it is considered that the school facilities are only used for the regular school programme for six to seven hours per day, five days per week, for forty weeks of the year, then it is obvious that the school as a public facility is under-utilised. The school may choose to lengthen the time during which the community can avail itself of the school facilities through a variety of possibilities, including after-school programmes for children, evening adult education programmes, meeting places for community groups, weekend sports and other activities or children's programmes during school holidays.

The core–plus council must determine when and how the school will be made available for use by the community. Decisions about what rooms are available and at what times they will be available for community use should be made in conjunction with decisions about the types of activities the school is prepared to host. It is then possible to place this information on a chart which will indicate to the community that the school is willing to run a substantial community programme with, for example, after-school activities for children, evening activities on some days, specialised programmes for adults during the day and recreational programmes at the weekends. It could also show which classrooms and other facilities are available to the community both during and outside of school hours, and which facilities are not. It will be possible to establish such a chart on a term basis and to have a similar chart for holiday periods. The availability of facilities within a particular school will depend on the security of the buildings, the availability of supervisory staff and the cost involved in keeping the buildings open.

Step two

The core–plus council establishes a policy for the use of the buildings by community groups. It is important to establish a policy on the use of school facilities before actually allowing people to use them in order that no precedents are set through *ad hoc* use of the buildings. When developing the policy and regulations governing the use of school facilities, it is important that some external members of the community, who may be potential users of the facilities, are included in the decision-making process. The final policy will include a statement of the school's philosophy and policy for facility usage, references to any laws that govern facility usage, processes for gaining the use of the facilities, priority allocations where double-booking may occur, any fees required, statements regarding conditions of usage and application forms or permits for facility use.

The information required by the school from members of the community who wish to use school facilities includes the name and address of the organisation or group, the phone number of the person responsible, the title or purpose of the activity, the preferred type of room required, the times and dates the facility is needed and any special equipment or arrangements that might be required.

Priority allocations and fees

Applicants will need to be advised if buildings and ground facilities will be allocated on a priority basis. The priorities will be determined by the core–plus council and may be along the following lines:

- programmes run by the school as part of the ordinary school programme;
- meetings or classes organised by staff or parents within the school;
- community programmes operated by the core–plus council;
- programmes operated by other community groups or agencies on a non-profit basis;
- all other users.

The first three priorities might have no charges allocated for the use of school facilities, although it will be expected that for all community programmes some charge would be built in to cover facility and power costs. For non-profit community groups, fees could be nominal and intended to cover the cost of opening the building. Since groups in the last category are using the facilities for private reasons, which may or may not be profit-making, it is reasonable to charge a fee that is commensurate with the hiring of similar facilities in other parts of the community.

A number of conditions will be placed on groups using school facilities. Deposits will be charged to all groups using the school, regardless of their level of priority and fees, to ensure that the facilities are left in good condition. Conditions for using school facilities will include:

- The activity leader must be present from the time of entry into the facility until the time of departure of the group. The leader must identify himself as the person responsible to the school representative.

- The responsibility and the liability for injury to persons or damage to property must be assumed by the organisation or individual making the application.
- All groups must clean up after use. The rooms and facilities must be returned to the order or arrangement they were in before use.
- The rentee or groups using the buildings or grounds must agree to restore to the original condition any property destroyed or suffering from excessive wear or tear.
- Specific rules for use of special areas such as gymnasia, swimming pools, canteen and library facilities must be adhered to by the users.

Step three

The core–plus council advertises the availability of school facilities within the community. One simple way to let the community know of the availability of school facilities is to develop and distribute a brochure that lets residents know that the facilities are available, what it might cost, and how to go about taking advantage of the service. Components that might be included in such a brochure are the school logo and name, a brief statement of the school's philosophy, general regulations for use of school facilities, the priorities and fee structure and who to contact for further information.

Step four

The school facilities are timetabled on a weekly, monthly and term basis. The more the school is used, the greater the need for coordination and planning. It is important to know quickly whether or not a facility is being used at a given time to enable negotiations to be managed efficiently. It is appropriate for one person to be responsible for the maintenance of the facility usage timetables. The development of a system that enables details to be gathered or checked will save time, and possible embarrassment, when issues related to timetabling programmes occur. It is suggested that the following procedures be followed to enable the timetabling to be efficiently managed:

- Keep a diary: the diary allows for events that have been planned some distance in advance to be timetabled appropriately. It encourages forward planning on the part of applicants and allows efficient management by the school. Rooms, days and times can be listed some time in advance and this allows planning on a term or yearly basis. The diary also provides an accurate record of users for later evaluation procedures.

– Develop a monthly programme: this technique will enable the facilities coordinator to determine at a glance when each room is being used and by whom for the current or following month. It is suggested that this information be updated as soon as it is possible to do so. By planning a month in advance it is possible to overcome any booking problems quickly and efficiently.

EVALUATION OF COMMUNITY ACTIVITIES

The final area of concern for programme development is the evaluation of the success of the activity. Evaluation has been discussed in a previous chapter (see pp. 172–5), and the procedures used there could also be used for an evaluation of programmes. However, from the point of view of the management of community activities it is necessary to have a progress review of the activity as it is in operation. This calls for on-the-spot supervision of all the programmes that are running. This may be undertaken by either a volunteer or a professional who may be on duty for one evening only or attend regularly, but whichever it is, the coordinator needs to know what is happening at the time, what facilities are available and what special requests have been made, and have the ability to make decisions quickly.

Issues that need to be addressed in an evaluation include both minor hiccups and more serious problems, such as the unsuitability of the teacher. The former need to be addressed on the spot; the latter may be resolved only through lengthy and delicate negotiation. What matters is that in both cases the issues need to be resolved in order that the participant is given the best available service. Many people's attitude towards a particular activity may be influenced, either positively or negatively, by their perception of how the programme has run. Constant vigilance during the course of the programme can lead to greater acceptance of it. The on-going review of the activity also enables a more useful evaluation of the programme to take place when it has been completed.

The evaluation activity completes the programme cycle and enables one activity to flow logically on to the next. If the essence of the core–plus school is to address the needs of its community consistently, then the evaluation of its programmes becomes a positive and fruitful way of serving the community.

Afterword: a vision for the next century

The problems in education, we now realise, have no lasting or satisfactory solutions while schools operate out of the framework which has determined their *raison d'être* for the past two hundred years. Education does not need fine-tuning, or more of the same; rather the fundamental assumptions about schools have to be revised.

(Beare and Slaughter 1993: 1)

From the diary of the principal, Newtown Community School, August 2010:

In the late 1980s and early 1990s governments around the world made decisions that changed the face of education. Legislation which governed the operations of schools was altered to create real local control and a true partnership between teachers and parents, between the school and its community. At the time most school management committees consisted of teachers and parents, sometimes with students and sometimes with members of the local community. New legislation required that the membership of school governing bodies included representatives from each of these groups. It became the school community's responsibility to formulate policy for that school, within overall government guidelines that ensured that the policies determined at the local level did not disadvantage any particular groups within the school community, and did not disadvantage that school community compared to any others within the school system. School communities were given new powers to adjust the curriculum offering of their school to suit the needs of that community and their students, provided that the core curriculum, determined by the state, was maintained and respected. Schools needed to generate success for their students in the state controlled examinations, but also needed to fulfil additional goals, determined by the members of their own communities, if they were to be seen as effective.

It took some time for school communities really to take advantage of this new power, and gradually these powers were strengthened even further to include total financial and staffing control as well. For the first time in history, schools were able to respond to the needs of the local community by having decisions made by the local community. Now, fifteen years later, when the children who entered school at that time are on the verge of completing their first use of the school, (the compulsory years of schooling), we have seen a wide range of approaches being applied at local levels, but none better than that in my own local community.

The core–plus council of this school operates on the basis that we must be both realistic about and responsive to changes in our society. At a time when many different agencies and services operate offices and facilities in a community, it was both realistic and responsive to avoid duplication of services. The school became a community complex in 1997, thus providing access to educational, recreational, and human services on one site. The cost to the community of this procedure was to be far less than establishing separate buildings.

At a time when work-related information becomes obsolete at an ever increasing rate, it is realistic and responsive for the school to provide retraining opportunities for the unemployed. At a time when employing authorities call for greater emphasis on literacy and numeracy skills, it is realistic and responsive to provide those in the work force who are functionally illiterate with additional educational opportunities to learn how to read and write. At a time when decision-making is being thrust upon the community and the individual more and more, it is realistic and responsive for the school to let every individual know what the options are through regular communications with our community. At a time when accountability has become a major issue for governments and agencies at all levels, it is both responsive and realistic that this school be accountable, first to its local community and then to society as a whole. At a time when the trend is towards participatory democracy, it is both realistic and responsive for the school to enlarge its decision-making base and to train people in the skills they need to participate effectively.

The best thing of all is that it is all within walking distance of, and is consequently used by, a population of 15,000 people. The first decision that was made related to the balance between the cost-effectiveness of a large-scale educational operation and the need for a warm and receptive environment. Money could be saved if a number of educational, health, welfare and recreational services could be centralised at the school site rather than being duplicated in various parts of the community, sometimes a long way from where people lived. But it was also important that we did not establish something so large and remote that individuals felt overwhelmed by its size.

It was decided that the core–plus community school would contain pre-school, elementary and secondary facilities for nearly 3000 day students, but also should include an adult education centre with a range of personal development, vocational and formal offerings. The latter was provided in conjunction with the local university and could be used by any community member, even students in the K-12 programme.

In order to maintain the friendly atmosphere, the facility was organised into mini-schools with a population of no more than 200, each using its own building, but with shared use of other facilities. Within the complex, two gyms, the indoor/outdoor pool, the auditorium, the library, the cafeteria and the theatre were used on a daily basis by each of the mini-schools. Each mini-school had a total of seven work areas that served as regular classrooms and was their own 'space'. The concept was based on the 'Core–plus' building design, first tried in Victoria, Australia in the early 1980s, but incorporated other human service facilities with the educational ones.

The resultant education complex consisted of a pre-school of 200 in seven separate class groups; five elementary mini-schools of 200, each with children from years 1–6; and eight secondary mini-schools, four of which contained students from years 7–10, one for students of years 11 and 12 who wished to specialise in science and technology, one for students who wished to specialise in humanities, one for students who wished to specialise in commerce or business and one for students who wished to specialise in technical or trade activities. There was continuity right across the school and students who worked together in the kindergarten class could still have the same workmates in year 10. However, requests for changing from one mini-school to another were possible and any needs were always treated fairly and with the student's best interests in mind.

Students from year 6 onwards are able to contract for an increasing amount of their work time. A great deal of discussion between parents, students and staff took place to ensure that the student's choices are based on the best information possible at the time. At year 6, students are able to determine what they will study for one half day per week, and by year 12 the entire curriculum is negotiated to ensure high levels of relevance and interest for every student. There is a regular interaction between students of different ages and the cross-age tutoring programme between the primary and secondary years is working wonders for both groups.

Each of the mini-schools involves parents to the level that they feel able, and every parent interaction that improves the child's ability to succeed is valued. Thus a parent who regularly assists the child with homework is considered to be just as valuable a member of the school community as is the president of the core–plus council. Parents have the opportunity to become involved in the decision-making processes at both classroom, mini-school and school level, and there are never any problems getting people to serve on the various committees. The centre is open thirteen hours, during the day and in the evening, seven days a week for fifty weeks of the year. Recent surveys have indicated that 85 per cent of the community visit the school at least once a year and 60 per cent of the community at least once a month.

The adult education centre, although separate for administration purposes, uses the facilities of the mini-schools both during the day, when adults take classes alongside the younger students, and in the evening as well. Special arrangements are made for students aged 16 and over to enrol in regular classes during the evening while they are encouraged to work part-time during the day. The facilities also includes dental and medical services, where the dentist and the doctor are given use of their specialist facilities free of charge, providing that in return they provide health education programmes within the schools for the equivalent of one day a week across the school. Also provided are counselling services available to both students and community members. The counselling offices contain a wide range of information that helps clients to find appropriate legal, welfare, recreational and family protection services within the local community or act as an agent to bring those services to the community if they were not already provided.

It is now a regular occurrence for me, as the principal of the school, to see parents and children arriving at school together then both heading for their respective classes. The deep recession of the early 1990s spawned a retraining programme that has expanded even though the economy picked up again. Now most people in the community realise that they will never stop their education and this awareness is being passed on to their children. They are staying at school longer and in larger numbers than ever before, and their success rates have continued to move up. The school is not only a learning centre, but a community centre as well.

The core–plus school is more cost-effective than other schools I have been associated with because it is used more often. The core–plus school is used before and after the normal school day, at weekends and vacations. The taxpayer's money is spread over a longer time frame, and the core–plus school is a place that 'wears out rather than rusts out'. Increasing the number of hours that the core–plus school is open decreases the cost per hour that it takes to operate. Increasing the number of people in the community who use the school decreases the cost per person.

Last year when a member of the local government re-commended to the education ministry that it should have more influence over the curriculum of the school and its community activities, he failed to retain his seat in the last election. The federal member for the area suggested that even the national government might lose seats if they tried to take more control of the local decision-making process. The government took the hint and the school continues to be a powerful force in the lives of the local people.

Bibliography

Aglinskas, A., Donaghue, K., Finch, L., Graham, K., Norman, H. and Petrie, G. (1988) 'Perceptions of School Effectiveness.' An unpublished B.Ed. Project, Frankston: Chisholm Institute of Technology.

Ahlawat, K. (1993) 'Role of School Size and Grade Structure for School Effectiveness in Developing Countries: Implications for Education Reform Policy Planning.' Paper presented at the Annual Conference of the International Congress for School Effectiveness and Improvement, Norrköping, Sweden, January.

Aitken, M. and Longford, N. (1986) 'Statistical Modelling Issues in School Effectiveness Studies', *Journal of the Royal Statistical Society, Series A*, 144, 419–61.

Aitken, M., Bennett, N. and Hesketh, J. (1981) 'Teaching Styles and Pupil Progress: A Re-analysis', *British Journal of Educational Psychology*, 51 (2), 170–86.

Angus, L. B. (1986a) *Schooling, The School Effectiveness Movement and Educational Reform*, Geelong: Deakin University Press.

Angus, L.B. (1986b) 'The Risk of School Effectiveness: A Comment on Recent Education Reports', *The Australian Administrator*, 7 (3), 1–4.

Ashenden, D. (1987) 'An Odd Couple? Social Justice. Performance Indicators.' A public lecture sponsored by the Victorian State Board of Education, Melbourne, Australia.

Aurin, K. and Lenz, J. (1989) 'Country Report: Federal Republic of Germany.' Paper presented at the Annual Conference of the International Congress for School Effectiveness, Rotterdam, the Netherlands, January.

Austin, G.R. (1979) 'Exemplary Schools and the Search for Effectiveness', *Educational Leadership*, 37 (1), 10–14.

Australian Education Council (1990) *The Hobart Declaration on Schooling*, Hobart: AEC.

Banks, D. (1988) 'Effective Schools Research and Educational Policy Making in Australia.' Paper presented at the Annual Conference of the International Congress for School Effectiveness, London, January.

Bartolotta, A. and Finn, P. (1980) 'Community Expectations of Education.'

An unpublished B.Ed. Project, Frankston: State College of Victoria at Frankston.

Bashi, J. and Gordon, D. (1989) 'Country Report – Israel.' Paper presented at the Annual Conference of the International Congress for School Effectiveness, Rotterdam, the Netherlands, January.

Beare, H. and Slaughter, R. (1993) *Education for the Twenty-First Century*, London: Routledge.

Beare, H., Caldwell, B.J. and Millikan, R.H. (1989) *Creating an Excellent School: Some New Management Techniques*, London: Routledge.

Berman, P., Izu, J.A., McClelland, R. and Stone, P. (1988) *The Hawaii Plan: Educational Excellence for the Pacific Era*, Los Angeles: Berman, Weiler Associates.

Blake, R.R. and Mouton, J.S. (1964) *The Managerial Grid*, Houston: Gulf.

Boyson, R. (1975) *The Crisis in Education*, London: Woburn.

British Columbia Ministry of Education (1989) *Enabling Learners: Highlights: Year 2000: A Framework for Learning*, Victoria: Province of British Columbia.

Burford, C. (1991) 'A Vision-driven Organisation.' A paper presented at the Annual Conference of the Australian Council for Educational Administration, Gold Coast, Australia, October.

Caldwell, B. and Misko, J. (1984) 'School-Based Budgeting: A Financial Strategy for Meeting the Needs of Students', *Educational Administration Review*, 2 (1), 29–59.

Caldwell, B. and Misko, J. (1986) *The Report of the Effective Resource Allocation in Schools Project*, Hobart: Centre for Education, University of Tasmania.

Caldwell, B. and Spinks, J. (1986) *Policy Making and Planning for School Effectiveness*, Hobart: Department of Education.

Caldwell, B. and Spinks, J. (1988) *The Self Managing School*, Lewes, Sussex: Falmer Press.

Caldwell, B., Misko, J. and Spinks, J. (1988) 'Australian Research on School Effectiveness: National and International Adaptations.' A paper presented at the Annual Conference of the Australian Asso- ciation for Research in Education, Armidale, Australia, July.

California State Department of Education (1977) *School Effectiveness Study: The First Year*, Sacramento: Office of Program Evaluation and Research.

Carmichael Report (1992) *The Australian Vocational Certificate Training System*, Canberra: National Board of Employment, Education and Training.

Carnegie Corporation (1983) *Education and Economic Progress: Towards a National Economic Policy*, New York: Carnegie Corporation.

Carnegie Task Force on Teaching as a Profession (1987) *A Nation Prepared: Teachers for the 21st Century*, New York: Carnegie Forum on Education and the Economy.

Carr, W.G. (1942) *Community Life in a Democracy*, Washington, DC: National Congress of Parents and Teachers.

Chapman, J. D. (1988) 'School Improvement and School Effectiveness in Australia.' Paper presented at the Annual Conference of the International Congress for School Effectiveness, London, January.

Chapman, J.D. (1991) 'The Effectiveness of Schooling and of Educational Resource Management.' Paper presented to the OECD, Paris.

Chapman, J.D. (1992) 'Leadership, School Based Decision Making and School Effectiveness' in Dimmock, C. (ed.) *Leadership, School Based Decision Making and School Effectiveness*, London: Routledge.

Cheng, Y.C. (1992) 'School Improvement and School Effectiveness in Hong Kong', *Network News International*, 2 (3), 6–7.

Chubb, J. (1988) in Henderson, A.T. 'Introduction' to The Information Clearinghouse about Public Schools, *ACCESS Printout on School Based Improvement and Effective Schools: A Perfect Match for Bottom-Up Reform*, Columbia, Maryland: National Committee for Citizens in Education.

Cirone, W.(1990) 'School Woes Begin at Large.' *Goleta Sun*, December 6, 14.

Cohn, E. and Rossmiller, R.A. (1987) 'Research on Effective Schools: Implications for Less Developed Countries', in *Comparative Education Review*, 3 (3), 377–99.

Coleman, J.S., Campbell, E., Hobson, C., McPartland, J., Mood, A., Weinfield, F. and York, R. (1966) *Equality of Educational Opportunity*, Washington, DC: US Govt Printing Office.

Coleman, P. (1987) 'Implementing School Based Decision Making', *The Canadian Administrator*, 26 (7), 1–11.

Committee on Economic Development (1985) *Investing in Our Children: Business and the Public Schools*, New York: Committee on Economic Development.

Commons, D.L. (Chair) (1985) *Who Will Teach our Children? A Strategy for Improving California's Schools*, Sacramento: California Commission on the Teaching Profession.

Cotter, M. (1981) 'An Evaluation of Parents' and Teachers' Expectations of Primary School Education: A Case Study of a Semi-Rural Environment.' An unpublished B.Ed. Project, Frankston, Australia: State College of Victoria at Frankston.

Cox, C.B. and Boyson, R. (1977) (eds) *The Black Paper 1977*, London: Temple Smith.

Creemers, B. and Knuver, A. (1989) 'Country Report: School Effectiveness in the Netherlands.' A paper presented at the Annual Conference of the International Congress for School Effectiveness, Rotterdam, the Netherlands, January.

Creemers, B. and Scheerens, J. (1989) 'Developments in School Effectiveness Research', *International Journal of Educational Research*, 13, 691–707.

Creemers, B., Peters, T. and Reynolds, D. (eds) (1989) *School Effectiveness and School Improvement*, Amsterdam: Swets & Zeitlinger.

Cuttance, P. (1986) *Effective Schooling: A Report to the Scottish Education Department*, Edinburgh: Centre for Educational Sociology.

Cuttance, P. (1987) 'Curriculum, the Frog Prince of School Effectiveness Research', *Journal of Curriculum Studies*, 19 (1), 77–85.

Cuttance, P. (1988a) 'Intra-System Variation in the Effectiveness of Schooling', Edinburgh: University of Edinburgh (mimeograph).

Cuttance, P. (1988b) 'The Effectiveness of Catholic Schooling in Scotland', Edinburgh: University of Edinburgh (mimeograph).

Cuttance, P. (1988c) 'The Effects of Institutional Differentiation in a

School System: The Legacy of Victorian and Edwardian Educational Developments', Edinburgh: University of Edinburgh (mimeograph).

Dickson, G.S. and Lim, S. (1991) 'The Development and Use of Indicators of Performance in Educational Leadership.' Paper presented at the Annual Conference of the International Congress for School Effectiveness and Improvement, Cardiff, Wales, January.

Dimmock, C. (1993) 'Reorganising Schools for Effective Learning: An Australian Perspective.' Paper presented at the Annual Conference of the International Congress for School Effectiveness and Improvement, Norrköping, Sweden, January.

Douglas, J.W.B. (1964) *The Home and the School*, London: Panther Books.

Dunmall, E.M. (1980) 'Parental Opinions on Curriculum Relevancy – A Case Study Conducted at Mentone Primary School.' An unpublished B.Ed Project, Frankston, Australia: State College of Victoria at Frankston.

Eager, H.J. (1992) 'Overview of the School Effectiveness and School Improvement Program for the Seventh-Day Adventist Educational System of the Far East', *Network News International*, 2 (2), 4–5.

Edmonds, R. (1978) 'A Discussion of the Literature and Issues Related to Effective Schooling.' A paper presented to National Conference on Urban Education, CEMREL, St Louis, USA.

Edmonds, R. (1979) 'Effective Schools for the Urban Poor', *Educational Leadership*, 37 (1), 15–27.

Educare News (1991) '"New Age" Parents Re-think the Basics', *Educare News*, 24, 6.

Education Department of Victoria (1933) 'General Course of Study for Elementary Schools, 1934', *Victorian Education Gazette and Teachers Aid*, 33, October, 434–531.

Education Department of Victoria (1976) 'School Councils Act and Regulations, 1975', *Victorian Education Gazette and Teachers Aid*, 76 (8a), 403–10.

Education Department of Victoria (1984) 'School Councils Act and Regulations, 1984', *Victorian Education Gazette and Teachers Aid*, 84 (8), 361–8.

Education Reform Act, 1988 (1988) London: HMSO.

Effective Schools Project (1991) *Effective Schools* (videotape), Melbourne, Australia: ACER.

Einsiedler, W. (1992) 'Effective School Research and School Improvement Activities in Germany', *Network News International*, 2 (4), 2–3.

Fantini, M. (1986) *Regaining Excellence in Education*, Columbus, Ohio: Merrill.

Fink, D. and Stoll, L. (1993) 'School Effectiveness and School Improvement: Voices from the Field.' Paper presented at the Annual Conference of the International Congress for School Effectiveness and Improvement, Norrköping, Sweden, January.

Finn, C.E. (1984) 'Towards Strategic Independence: Nine Commandments for Enhancing School Effectiveness', *Phi Delta Kappan*, 65 (8), 518–24.

Finn Review (1991) *Young People's Participation in Post-compulsory Education and Training – Report of the Australian Education Council Review Committee*, Canberra: Australian Government Publishing Service.

Fordham, R. (1983a) *Ministerial Paper No. 1: Decision Making in Victorian Education*, Melbourne, Australia: Victorian Education Department.

Fordham, R. (1983b) *Ministerial Paper No. 4: School Councils*, Melbourne, Australia: Victorian Education Department.

Fordham, R. (1985) 'A New Government's Organisational Review' in Frazer, M., Dunstan, J. and Creed, P. (eds) *Perspectives on Organisational Change: Lessons from Education*, Melbourne: Longman Cheshire.

Freedman, S. (1988) 'Carnegie School Program', memo to the Community Education National Network, Quincy, Massachusetts: Massachusetts Department of Education (mimeograph).

Gaillie, W.B. (1964) 'Essentially Contested Concepts' in Gaillie, W.B. *Philosophy and Historical Understanding*, London: Chatto & Windus.

Galton, M. and Simon, B. (1980) *Progress and Performance in the Primary School*, London: Routledge and Kegan Paul.

Galton, M., Simon, B. and Croll, P. (1980) *Inside the Primary School*, London: Routledge and Kegan Paul.

Gardner, J.W. (1961) *Excellence*, New York: Harper & Row.

Goldstein, H. (1980) 'Fifteen Thousand Hours: A Review of the Statistical Procedures', *Journal of Child Psychology and Psychiatry*, 21 (4), 363–6.

Goldstein, H. (1984) 'The Methodology of School Comparisons', *Oxford Review of Education*, 10 (1), 69–74.

Goldstein, H. and Cuttance, P. (1988) 'National Assessment and School Comparisons' (mimeograph).

Gray, J. (1981) 'From Policy to Practice – Some Problems and Paradoxes of Egalitarian Reform' in Simon, B. and Taylor, W. (eds) *Education in the 80's: The Central Issues*, London: Batsford.

Gray, J., Jesson, D. and Jones, B. (1986) 'The Search for a Fairer Way of Comparing Schools' Examination Results', *Research Papers in Education*, 1, 91–119.

Green, L.J. (1968) *Parents and Teachers: Partners or Rivals?*, London: Allen and Unwin.

Guthrie, I.W., Pierce, L.C. and Koppich, J.E. (1990) 'High Politics, Policy and Change: A Theory of Educational Reform.' Paper presented at the American Educational Research Association, Boston, USA, March.

Halasz, G. (1989) 'The Efficiency Problem and the Policy of School Autonomy in Hungary.' Paper presented at the Annual Conference of the International Congress for School Effectiveness, Rotterdam, the Netherlands, January.

Hansen, B.J. (1983) 'School Transformation: A Trust Process.' An unpublished thesis, Maryland: International College.

Hansen, B.J. and Marburger, C.L. (1988) *School Based Improvement: A Manual for District Leaders*, Columbia, Maryland: National Committee for Citizens in Education.

Hansen, B.J. and Marburger, C.L. (1989) *School Based Improvement: A Manual for Training School Councils*, Columbia, Maryland: National Committee for Citizens in Education.

Hanushek, E. (1986) 'The Economics of Schooling: Production and Efficiency in Public Schools', *Journal of Economic Literature*, 24, 1141–77.

Henderson, A.T. (1981) *Parent Participation–Student Achievement: The Evidence Grows*, Columbia, Maryland: National Committee for Citizens in Education.

Henderson, A.T. (1987) *The Evidence Continues to Grow: Parent Involvement Improves School Achievement. An Annotated Bibliography*, Columbia, Maryland: National Committee for Citizens in Education.

Henderson, A.T. (1988) 'Introduction' to The Information Clearinghouse about Public Schools, *Access Printout on School Based Improvement and Effective Schools: A Perfect Match for Bottom-Up Reform*, Columbia, Maryland: National Committee for Citizens in Education.

Henderson, A.T. and Lezotte, L. (1988) 'School-Based Improvement and Effective Schools: A Perfect Match', *Community Education Today*, 15 (3), 4–5.

Henderson, A.T. and Marburger, C.L. (1986) *Beyond the Bake Sale: An Educator's Guide to Working with Parents*, Columbia, Maryland: National Committee for Citizens in Education.

Herzberg, F. (1987) 'One More Time: How do you Motivate Employees? *Harvard Business Review*, September–October.

Hixson, J. (1991) 'The Ecology of School Restructuring and Renewal: Designing the Schools we Need.' Paper presented at the Annual Conference of the International Congress for School Effectiveness and Improvement, Cardiff, Wales, January.

Hodgkinson, H.L. (1990) 'The Same Client: The Demographics of Education and Service Delivery Systems.' Paper presented at the Annual Conference of the National Community Education Association Convention, San Antonio, December.

Holcomb, E. (1991) *A Handbook for Implementing School Improvement*, Madison: National Center for Effective Schools Research and Development.

Holdaway, E.A. (1990) 'Recent Developments in Education in Britain: Issues and Implications', *The Canadian Administrator*, 29 (7), 1–9.

Hoyle, J.R., English, F. and Steffey, B. (1985) *Skills for Successful School Leadership*, Arlington, Virginia: American Association of School Administrators.

Imsen, G. (1992) 'School Effectiveness and School Improvement: A Brief report from Norway', *Network News International*, 2 (4), 4–8.

Jencks, C., Smith, M., Ackland, H., Bane, M., Cohen, D., Gintis, H., Heyns, B. and Micholson, S. (1972) *Inequality: A Reassessment of the Effect of Family and Schooling in America*, New York: Basic Books.

Karmel, P. (1973) *Schools in Australia: Report of the Interim Committee for the Australian Schools Commission*, Canberra, ACT: Australian Government Publishing Service.

Kerensky, V. M. (1989) *The Sovereign: New Perspectives on People, Power and Public Education*, Dubuque, Iowa: Kendall/Hunt.

Kirner, J. (1989) 'Improving the Quality of Australian Schools', *Network News*, 1 (3 and 4), 4–6.

Klintestam, L., Grosin, L. and Holmberg, P. (1989) 'Sweden Report.' Paper presented at the Annual Conference of the International Congress for School Effectiveness and Improvement, Rotterdam, the Netherlands, January.

Kyro, M. and Pirttiniemi, J. (1992) 'The State of School Effectiveness and Improvement in Norway', *Network News International*, 2 (4), 5–6.

La Roque, L. (1983) *Policy Implementation in a School District: A Matter of Change?*, Burnaby, BC: Simon Fraser University.

Leithwood, K. (1987) 'A Review of Research Concerning Characteristics of Exemplary Secondary Schools.' A working paper prepared for the Student Retention and Transition Project, Toronto: OISE.

Lewin, K. and Lippitt, R. (1938) 'An Experimental Approach to the Study of Autocracy and Democracy: A Preliminary Note', in *Sociometry*, 1, 292–380.

Little, J. (1987) 'Teachers as Colleagues' in Richardson-Koehler, V. (ed.) *Educators' Handbook: A Research Perspective*, New York: Longman.

Longo, A. (1992) 'State of Effectiveness of Chile's Educational System', *Network News International*, 2 (2), 2–4.

McGaw, B., Banks, D. and Piper, K. (1991) *Effective Schools: Schools That Make a Difference*, Hawthorn, Australia: ACER.

McGaw, B., Banks, D., Piper, K. and Evans, B. (1992) *Making Schools More Effective*, Hawthorn, Australia: ACER.

McGregor, D. (1960) *The Human Side of Enterprise*, New York: McGraw–Hill.

McKenna, G. (1989) 'Building Stable Communities.' Paper presented at the Annual Conference of the National Community Education Association Convention, Seattle, December.

McPherson, A.F. and Willms, J.D. (1986) 'Certification, Class Conflict, Religion and Community: A Socio-historical Explanation of the Effectiveness of Contemporary Schools', *Research in Sociology of Education and Socialisation*, 6, 227–302.

Madaus, G., Airasian, P. and Kellaghan, T. (1980) *School Effectiveness: A Reassessment of the Evidence*, New York: McGraw–Hill.

Mann, D. (1984) 'The National Council for Effective Schools', *Social Policy*, 15 (2), 49–51.

Marburger, C. (1985) *One School at a Time: School Based Management, A Process for Change*, Columbia, Maryland: National Committee for Citizens in Education.

Marcelo, C. (1992) 'School Effectiveness and School Improvement in Spain', *Network News International*, 2 (2), 7.

Maslow, A. (1954) *Motivation and Personality*, New York: Harper & Row.

Mayer Committee (1992) *Employment-related Key Competencies for Post-compulsory Education and Training: A Discussion Paper: Executive Summary*, Melbourne (Interim Report).

Mellor, W. and Chapman, J. (1984) 'Organizational Effectiveness in Schools', *Educational Administration Review*, 2 (2), 25–36.

Michigan State Board of Education (1985) *Using Michigan K-12 Program Standards of Quality for School Improvement Planning*, East Lansing: Michigan State Board of Education.

Minister of Education (1988) *Tomorrow's Schools: The Reform of Educational Administration in New Zealand*, Wellington: NZ Government Printer.

Minzey, J.D. (1981) 'Community Education and Community Schools.' An address at the State College of Victoria, Frankston, Australia.

Minzey, J.D. and Le Tarte, C. (1979) *Community Education: From Program to Process to Practice*, Midland, Michigan: Pendell.

Minzey, J.D. and Townsend, A.C. (1984) *Core–plus Education: A Model for Schools of the Future*, Ypsilanti, Michigan: Eastern Michigan University.

Mortimore, P. and Sammons, P. (1987) 'New Evidence on Effective Elementary Schools', *Educational Leadership,* 45 (6), 4–8.

Mortimore, P., Sammons, P., Stoll, L., Lewis, D. and Ecob, R. (1986) *The Junior School Project: A Summary of the Main Report,* London: ILEA Research and Statistics Branch.

Mortimore, P., Sammons, P., Stoll, L., Lewis, D. and Ecob, R. (1988) *School Matters,* Shepton Mallet, Somerset: Open Books.

Munn, P. (ed.) (1993) *Parents and Schools: Customers, Managers or Partners?,* London: Routledge.

Murphy, J., Hallinger, P. and Mesa, P. (1985) 'School Effectiveness: Checking Progress and Assumptions and Developing a Role for State and Federal Government', *Teachers College Record,* 86, 615–42.

National Commission on Excellence in Education (1983) *A Nation At Risk: the Imperative for Educational Reform,* Washington, DC: US Government Printing Office.

National Education Association (1986) *The Role of the Principal in Effective Schools,* Washington, DC: NEA.

Noruwana, J.M. (1988) 'Report on the Activities of the ICSE in Some Black School Systems in the Southern African Region.' Paper presented at the Annual Conference of the International Congress for School Effectiveness and Improvement, Rotterdam, the Netherlands, January.

Nyagura, L.M. (1992) School Effectiveness and Improvement in Zimbabwe', *Network News International,* 2 (3), 1–4.

OECD (1983) 'Educational Development and Problems in Resource Deployment', Paris: OECD (mimeograph).

OECD (1989a) 'Schools and Quality: An International Report', Paris: OECD (mimeograph).

OECD (1989b) 'Decentralization and School Improvement: New Perspectives and Conditions for Change', Paris: OECD (mimeograph).

OECD (1991) 'The Effectiveness of Schooling and of Educational Resource Management', Paris: OECD (mimeograph)

Ouchi, W. (1982) *Theory Z: How American Business Can Meet the Japanese Challenge,* New York: Avon Publishing.

Pipes, M. (1993) 'Moving Towards Full-Cost Services in Education.' Paper presented at the Annual Conference of the International Congress for School Effectiveness and Improvement, Norrköping, Sweden, January.

Plowden Report (1967) *Children and Their Primary Schools,* London: HMSO.

Raaen, F. D. (1990) *Evaluation of pupils in a new perspective. Final Report from the project 'Evaluation and Guidance'.* Oslo: Grunnskoleradet (The Council for Grunnskolen).

Renihan, F. (1992) 'School Effectiveness and School Improvement: Issues in Policy Articulation.' Paper presented at the Annual Conference of the International Congress for School Effectiveness and Improvement, Victoria, British Columbia, January.

Renihan, F. and Renihan, P. (1984) 'Effective Schools, Effective Administration and Institutional Image', *The Canadian Administrator,* 3, 1–6.

Renihan, F. and Renihan, P. (1989) 'School Improvement: Second Generation Issues and Strategies' in Creemers, B., Peters, T. and Reynolds, D. *School Effectiveness and School Improvement,* Amsterdam: Swets & Zeitlinger.

Renihan, F. and Renihan, P. (1991) 'Pastoral, Cosmetic and Participative Considerations in Institutional Image: Implications for School Improvement.' Paper presented at the Annual Conference of the International Congress for School Effectiveness and Improvement, Cardiff, Wales, January.

Reynolds, D. (1976) 'The Delinquent School' in Woods, P. (ed.), *The Process of Schooling*, London: Routledge.

Reynolds, D. (1982) 'The Search for Effective Schools', *School Organisation*, 2 (3), 215–37.

Reynolds, D. (1988) 'Research on School and Organisational Effectiveness: The End of the Beginning?' A paper presented to the BEMAS Third Research Conference on Educational Management and Administration, Cardiff, Wales.

Reynolds, D. (1990) 'School Effectiveness and School Improvement in the 1990s', *Network News*, 2 (1 and 2), 3–9.

Reynolds, D. and Pack, C. (1989) 'School Effectiveness in England and Wales.' Paper presented at the Annual Conference of the International Congress for School Effectiveness and Improvement, Rotterdam, the Netherlands, January.

Reynolds, D., Sullivan, M. and Murgatroyd, S. (1987) *The Comprehensive Experiment*, Lewes, Sussex: Falmer.

Reynolds, D., Creemers, B.P.M. and Peters, T. (1989) (eds), *School Effectiveness and Improvement: Proceedings of the First International Congress*, Groningen: Rion.

Robbins, S.R. (1993) *Organizational Behavior* (6th edn), Englewood Cliffs, New Jersey: Prentice–Hall.

Robinson, V. (1984) 'School Review: A New Zealand Experience' in Hopkins, D. and Wideen, M. *Alternative Perspectives on School Improvement*, Lewes, Sussex: Falmer.

Rosenholtz, S.J. (1989) *Teachers Workplace: The Social Organization of Schools*, New York: Longman.

Rutter, M., Maughan, B., Mortimore, P. and Ouston, J. (1979) *Fifteen Thousand Hours: Secondary Schools and Effects on Children*, Boston: Harvard University Press.

Sackney, L.E. (1989a) 'School Effectiveness: The Canadian Scene: Report No. 2.' Paper presented at the Annual Conference of the International Congress for School Effectiveness and Improvement, Rotterdam, the Netherlands, January.

Sackney, L.E. (1989b) 'School Effectiveness and Improvement in Canada' in Reynolds, D., Creemers, B.P.M. and Peters, T. (eds) *School Effectiveness and Improvement: Proceedings of the First International Congress*, Groningen: Rion.

Sammons, P., Nuttall, D. and Mortimore, P. (1993) 'Continuity of School Effects: A Longitudinal Analysis of Primary and Secondary Effects on GSCE Performance.' Paper presented at the Annual Conference of the International Congress for School Effectiveness and Improvement, Norrköping, Sweden, January.

Santa Clara County Office of Education (1984) 'School Factors Which

Promote Student Achievement', San Jose, California: Santa Clara School Effectiveness Program (mimeograph).

Scheerens, J. (1990) 'Process Indicators of School Functioning', *School Effectiveness and Improvement: An International Journal of Research, Policy and Practice*, 1 (1), 61–79.

Scheerens, J. and Creemers, B. (1989) 'Towards a More Comprehensive Conceptualization of School Effectiveness' in Creemers, B., Peters, T. and Reynolds, D. *School Effectiveness and School Improvement*, Amsterdam: Swets & Zeitlinger.

Senate Committee on Employment, Education & Training (1991) *Come In Cinderella: The Emergence of Adult and Community Education (Overview)*, Canberra, ACT: Senate Printing Unit.

Sergiovanni, T. (1987) *The Principalship: A Reflective Practice Perspective*, (4th edn) New York: McGraw–Hill.

Sewell, S.W. (1975) 'Discovering and Improving Store Image', *Journal of Retailing*, 50, 3–7.

Silver, P. and Moyle, C. (1985) 'The Impact of School Leadership on School Effectiveness', *Educational Magazine*, 42 (2), 42–5.

Smink, G. (1991) 'The Cardiff Conference, ICSEI 1991', *Network News International*, 1 (3), 2–6.

Staples, B. (1989) 'Ten Years Ago, and Ten Years Ahead.' An address to the Annual Conference of the Alberta Community Education Association, Banff Springs, Canada, November.

Stoll, L. and Fink, D. (1989) 'An Effective Schools Project: The Halton Approach' in Reynolds, D., Creemers, B.P.M. and Peters, T. (eds) *School Effectiveness and Improvement: Proceedings of the First International Congress*, Groningen: Rion.

Stoll, L. and Fink, D. (1990) 'Reorganization for Effectiveness: The Halton Approach.' Paper presented at the Annual Conference of the International Congress for School Effectiveness and Improvement, Jerusalem, Israel, January.

Stoll, L. and Fink, D. (1992) 'Assessing the Change Process: The Halton Approach.' Paper presented at the Annual Conference of the International Congress for School Effectiveness and Improvement, Victoria, Canada, January.

Tannenbaum, R. and Schmidt, W.H. (1958) 'How to Choose a Leadership Pattern', *Harvard Business Review*, March–April, 96.

Thorndike, R.L. (1973) *Reading Comprehension; Education in Fifteen Countries*, Stockholm: Alonqvist & Wiskell.

Tiller, T. (1990) *The Kangaroo School: The Big Leap. Evaluation based on Faith*, Oslo: Gyldendal.

Torrance, H. (1985) 'Current Prospects for School-Based Examining', *Educational Review*, 37 (1), 39–51.

Tyler, R. (1987) 'Education Reforms', in *Phi Delta Kappan*, 69 (4), 277–80.

Weber, G. (1971) *Inner City Children Can Be Taught to Read: Four Successful Schools*, Washington, DC: Council for Basic Education.

Wildy, H. and Dimmock, C. (1992) 'Instructional Leadership in Western Australian Primary and Secondary Schools', Nedlands: University of Western Australia (mimeograph).

Index